reader's digest
baking bible

Carrot and Brazil Nut Cake (page 135)

reader's digest
baking bible

More than 200 recipes for cakes, pies, tarts,
cookies, muffins, breads and pizzas

Published by The Reader's Digest Association, Inc.
London • New York • Sydney • Montreal

Reader's Digest Baking Bible

Published in 2010 in the United Kingdom by Vivat Direct Limited
(t/a Reader's Digest), 157 Edgware Road, London W2 2HR

Reader's Digest Baking Bible is owned and under licence from
the Reader's Digest Association, Inc. All rights reserved.

Copyright © 2010 The Reader's Digest Association, Inc.
Copyright © 2010 Reader's Digest Association Far East Limited.
Philippines Copyright © 2010 Reader's Digest Association Far East Limited
Copyright © 2010 Reader's Digest (Australia) Pty Limited
Copyright © 2010 Reader's Digest India Pvt Limited
Copyright © 2010 Reader's Digest Asia Pvt Limited

Adapted from *Baking with Love* published by Reader's Digest
(Australia) Pty Limited in 2006

For Vivat Direct

Editorial Director Julian Browne

Art Director Anne-Marie Bulat

Managing Editor Nina Hathway

Picture Resource Manager Sarah Stewart-Richardson

Prepress Technical Manager Dean Russell

Production Controller Jan Bucil

Product Production Manager Claudette Bramble

We are committed both to the quality of our products and the
service we provide to our customers. We value your comments so
please do contact us on **08705 113366** or via our website at
www.readersdigest.co.uk

If you have any comments or suggestions about the content of our
books you can contact us at **gbeditorial@readersdigest.co.uk**

Printed and bound in China

Front cover: *main image,* Gingerbread
Cupcakes (page 44).

Spine: Yeast Party Rolls (page 187).

Back cover: *top left,* Pizza alla Napoletana
(page 269); *top centre,* Pumpkin Pie (page
139); *top right,* Crunchy Date Bars, (page 58).

Cranberry and Almond Biscotti (page 73)

contents

introduction

More and more people are realising that baking can be one of life's pleasures, rewarding for both the cook and those lucky enough to sample the results. And making light-as-air cakes, biscuits with plenty of crunch and pie crusts that melt in the mouth isn't difficult when you've got the *Reader's Digest Baking Bible* by your side.

In this essential cookbook, you will find everything you need to know to master the craft of baking. There are 200 foolproof recipes for making cakes, biscuits, muffins, tarts, breads, pizzas, sweet and savoury pies, festive specialities and much more. You'll discover favourite treats such as chocolate muffins and lemon meringue pie together with exciting new dishes such as galettes, the little round pastries from France, and the savoury Mexican turnovers known as empanadas.

More than just a recipe book, *Reader's Digest Baking Bible* is a master class in the skills that are the bedrock of successful baking. A clear step-by-step techniques section shows you how to make all the doughs, batters and cake mixtures that you'll ever need. If you aren't sure when your cake is perfectly risen or think your cookies have become too hard, turn to the question-and-answer section for solutions to common baking problems. And if you don't understand a baking term, the glossary will explain it clearly and simply. This is a baking book that you will turn to again and again.

The Editors

Quiche Lorraine (page 250)

classic
cakes

Marble Cake

Cocoa powder gives this cake a rich chocolate flavour, but for an extra chocolate boost, try adding a little chopped chocolate to the batter.

250 g (1 cup/9 oz) butter

230 g (1 cup/8 oz) white (granulated) sugar

Few drops of vanilla essence (extract)

4 eggs

500 g (4 cups/1 lb 2 oz) plain (all-purpose) flour

1 ½ tablespoons baking powder

150 ml (⅔ cup/5 fl oz) milk

3 tablespoons cocoa powder

SERVES 8–12

PREPARATION TIME 20 minutes

COOKING TIME 60–70 minutes

1 Use a 30- x 11-cm (12- x 4¼-in) loaf tin. Lightly grease and flour tin, tapping out any excess. Preheat oven to 180°C (350°F, gas mark 4).

2 Place butter in a large mixing bowl; beat until creamy. Add sugar (reserve 1 tbsp) and essence and beat until well combined and pale and fluffy. Add eggs one at a time, stirring until well combined. Sift flour and baking powder onto a plate. Reserve 2 tbsp milk and stir the rest into the batter, alternating it with the flour. Spoon two-thirds of the batter into the prepared tin.

3 Stir sifted cocoa powder, 1 tbsp sugar and the last of the milk into the remaining cake batter and spread over the batter in the tin.

4 Twist a fork through the layers of batter to produce a marbled effect. Smooth the top and bake for 60–70 minutes until a skewer comes out clean. Turn cake out onto a wire rack to cool.

Try this, too...

For an extra treat spread melted chocolate over cooled cake and scatter with chocolate sprinkles.

Gugelhupf

To achieve the right look and texture, this cake needs to be cooked in a special tin.
A gugelhupf tin has a chimney in the middle to allow the mixture to cook evenly throughout.

40 g (¼ cup/1½ oz) almonds

250 g (1 cup/9 oz) butter

125 g (1 cup/4½ oz) icing
(confectioners') sugar

4 egg yolks

1 tablespoon rum

Grated zest of 1 lemon

60 g (½ cup/2 oz) sultanas
(golden raisins)

220 g (1¾ cups/7½ oz) plain
(all-purpose) flour

40 g (⅓ cup/1½ oz) cornflour
(cornstarch)

1 tablespoon baking powder

125 ml (½ cup/4 fl oz) milk

3 egg whites

1 Use a 2-litre (8-cup) gugelhupf
tin. Lightly grease and flour the
tin, tapping out any excess. Preheat
oven to 180°C (350°F, gas mark 4).
Soak almonds in a bowl of boiling
water. Peel and chop into slivers.

2 Cream butter and icing sugar
until light and fluffy. Gradually
incorporate the egg yolks. Add the
rum, lemon zest, slivered almonds
and sultanas.

3 Sieve the flour, cornflour and
baking powder. Stir into batter,
a little at a time, alternating with
the milk. Beat egg whites until stiff
and fold into the mixture using a
metal spoon.

4 Pour batter into prepared tin;
bake for 55–60 minutes. Remove
from the oven; cool in tin for a few
minutes. Turn out onto a wire rack
to cool. Dust with icing sugar.

SERVES 12

PREPARATION TIME 25 minutes

COOKING TIME 1 hour

Black Forest Cherry Cake

This all-time favourite is worth the effort it takes to make. If you're in a hurry, but still crave that combination of chocolate, cherries and cream, make the cake without the shortcrust pastry base. It will still taste delicious.

FOR THE PASTRY

125 g (1 cup/4½ oz) plain (all-purpose) flour

½ teaspoon baking powder

60 g (4 tbsp/2 oz) butter

2 tablespoons sugar

2 egg yolks, lightly beaten

FOR THE CAKE

7 eggs

250 g (1 cup/8 oz) sugar

60 g (¼ cup/2 oz) butter

155 g (1¼ cups/5½ oz) plain (all-purpose) flour

40 g (⅓ cup/1½ oz) cornflour (cornstarch)

40 g (⅓ cup/1½ oz) cocoa powder

FOR THE FILLING

1 jar pitted sour (morello) cherries (about 800 g/4 cups/1 lb 12 oz)

5 g (1½ teaspoons) powdered clear gelatine

Pinch of ground cloves

1 cinnamon stick

100 g (⅓ cup/3½ oz) sour cherry jam

60 ml (¼ cup/2 fl oz) Kirsch

750 ml (3 cups/26 fl oz) cream, for whipping

Few drops of vanilla essence (extract)

FOR DECORATION

Good-quality chocolate, for grating

SERVES 14

PREPARATION TIME 1½ hours

COOKING TIME 30 minutes plus 10–12 minutes

1 Use a 25-cm (10-in) springform tin. Line base and side with baking (parchment) paper. To make the pastry, place all the ingredients in the bowl of a food processor and process until the mixture forms a ball. Wrap pastry in cling wrap and chill for 30 minutes.

2 To make the cake, place a bowl over a pan of gently simmering water. Add eggs and sugar; whisk until mixture is hand-hot, pale and creamy. Remove bowl from pan. Stir mixture until it is cold.

3 Melt butter and allow to cool. Preheat oven to 180°C (350°F, gas mark 4). Sift the flour, cornflour and cocoa powder and fold into the egg mixture, using a metal spoon. Fold in the melted butter.

4 Pour mixture into tin, smooth top and bake for 30 minutes. Remove from oven and leave for a few minutes. Turn out onto a wire rack and leave to cool. Reduce the oven temperature to 160°C (315°F, gas mark 2–3). Slice the cake into 3 horizontal layers.

5 Roll out chilled pastry; cut out a circle of dough 25 cm (10 in) in diameter. Place pastry base on a baking tray lined with baking paper and prick several times with a fork. Bake for 10–12 minutes until golden brown. Remove from oven; cool.

6 To make the filling, drain the jar of cherries, saving the juice. Sprinkle gelatine over a little cold water; soak for about 10 minutes. Heat 250 ml (1 cup/9 fl oz) juice in a pan with the ground cloves and cinnamon stick. Remove cinnamon after a few minutes. Stir gelatine into the hot juice to dissolve; cool.

7 Spread jam over the pastry base. Place a cake layer on top. Drizzle with a little Kirsch; spread with half of the thickened cherry juice. Place half the cherries on top. Beat the cream and vanilla essence until thick and spreadable. Spread a quarter of the cream over cherries.

8 Place second cake layer on top. Drizzle with a little Kirsch and cover with the remaining thickened juice. Place cherries on top, keeping 14 for decoration. Spread another quarter of the cream over cherries. Place third cake layer on top; drizzle with Kirsch. Spread cream around the side of the cake. Spoon the rest into a piping bag.

9 Coarsely grate chocolate over the top and side of the cake. Pipe cream rosettes on top; place a reserved cherry on each one.

Dundee Cake

Candied peel, dried fruit, ground almonds and sherry result in a cake that improves with keeping. The topping of blanched almonds is traditional.

375 g (3 cups/13 oz) plain (all-purpose) flour

1 teaspoon baking powder

250 g (1 cup/9 oz) butter, softened

285 g (1¼ cups/10 oz) caster (superfine) sugar

4 eggs, lightly beaten

About 80 ml (⅓ cup/2½ fl oz) sweet sherry or milk

225 g (1½ cups/8 oz) currants

185 g (1½ cups/6½ oz) sultanas (golden raisins)

180 g (¾ cup/6 oz) glacé (candied) cherries

3 tablespoons each candied orange, lemon and lime peel, chopped

80 g (¾ cup/2¾ oz) ground almonds

Grated zest of 1 orange and 1 lemon

155 g (1 cup/5½ oz) whole

1 Use a 20-cm (8-in) tin. Grease lightly; line base and side with baking (parchment) paper. Preheat oven to 160°C (315°F, gas mark 2–3).

2 Sift flour and baking powder onto a plate. Place the butter and sugar in a bowl and beat until light and fluffy. Gradually beat in the eggs, a little at a time, beating well after each addition. If mixture begins to curdle, add a little of the flour. Add remaining flour and fold in gently. Stir in sufficient sherry or milk to mix to a soft, dropping consistency. Fold in the fruit, peel, ground almonds and grated zest.

3 Spoon batter into prepared tin and smooth the top. Arrange the almonds in concentric circles on top of the cake, dropping, not pressing them lightly into place.

4 Bake in the centre of the oven for 2¼–2½ hours or until firm to the touch; a skewer inserted in the centre should come out clean. Cover top with a sheet of foil after 1 hour to prevent almonds overbrowning. Remove from oven and leave in the tin to cool completely. Turn out and store in an airtight container. Keep for 2–3 days before serving to allow the cake to mature and the flavours to develop.

SERVES 12

PREPARATION TIME 30 minutes

COOKING TIME 2¼–2½ hours

Frosted Carrot Cake

A cake that tastes great and is good for you is handy to have in your repertoire.

450 g (3¾ cups/1 lb) self-raising (self-rising) flour

1½ tablespoons ground mixed spice (allspice)

1½ teaspoons bicarbonate of soda (baking soda)

500 ml (2 cups/17 fl oz) buttermilk

125 ml (½ cup/4 fl oz) vegetable oil

330 g (1½ cups/11½ oz) white (granulated) sugar

3 large eggs

1 tablespoon vanilla essence (extract)

Finely grated carrot to make about 450 g (3 cups/1 lb); you will need 8 or 9 medium carrots, peeled

225 g (1 cup/8 oz) reduced-fat cream cheese, at room temperature

1 tablespoon buttermilk, extra

250 g (2 cups/9 oz) icing (confectioners') sugar, sifted

1 Use a 25-cm (10-in) fluted ring tin. Coat lightly with non-stick cooking spray and dust with flour, tapping out any excess. Preheat the oven to 180°C (350°F, gas mark 4).

2 Sift the flour, mixed spice and bicarbonate of soda into a large bowl and make a well in the centre. Whisk buttermilk, oil, sugar, eggs and 2 tsp essence in another bowl until frothy. Pour into flour mixture and whisk until just combined. Fold in the grated carrots.

3 Pour batter into tin; smooth the top. Tap the tin lightly on a flat surface a few times to break up air bubbles. Bake for about 50 minutes, or until a skewer inserted in centre comes out clean. Cool in the tin for 10 minutes; turn onto a wire rack; flip top-side up; cool completely.

4 In a medium bowl, beat cream cheese with remaining vanilla essence and extra buttermilk until softened. Gradually stir in the icing sugar just until frosting is smooth. Place cake on a serving plate and coat with the frosting, letting some run down the side. Refrigerate cake until ready to serve.

SERVES 12

PREPARATION TIME 20 minutes

COOKING TIME 50 minutes

Lemon and Poppyseed Loaf

This simple classic not only tastes good, it's a good source of B vitamins.

1½ tablespoons poppyseeds

60 ml (¼ cup/2 fl oz) vegetable oil

1½ tablespoons unsalted butter

250 g (1 cup/9 oz) white (granulated) sugar

2 eggs

1 egg white

3 teaspoons grated lemon zest

1 teaspoon bicarbonate of soda (baking soda)

250 g (1 cup/9 oz) low-fat natural (plain) yogurt

150 g (1 cup/5½ oz) fine yellow cornmeal

155 g (1¼ cups/5½ oz) plain (all-purpose) flour

1 Use a 20- x 13-cm (8- x 5-in) loaf tin. Grease the tin. Preheat oven to 180°C (350°F, gas mark 4). Place poppyseeds in a baking dish; bake for 5 minutes or until lightly toasted and crunchy.

2 Place oil, butter and sugar in a medium bowl and beat with electric beaters to combine. Add the whole eggs and the egg white one at a time, beating well after each addition. Beat in the lemon zest.

3 Combine bicarbonate of soda and yogurt in a small bowl. Combine cornmeal and flour on a plate. Fold cornmeal mixture and yogurt mixture alternately into egg mixture, beginning and ending with cornmeal. Fold in poppyseeds.

4 Spoon into loaf tin. Bake for 55 minutes or until a skewer inserted in centre comes out clean. Cool for 10 minutes in the tin, then turn out onto a wire rack to cool completely.

SERVES 12

PREPARATION TIME 10 minutes

COOKING TIME 55 minutes

Butter Cake

This rich little cake is soaked with butter when cooked and eaten while hot.
Should there be any leftovers, it also tastes wonderful cold.

160 g (2/3 cup/5 1/2 oz) butter, softened

115 g (1/2 cup/4 oz) caster (superfine) sugar

3 large eggs

210 g (1 2/3 cups/7 1/2 oz) plain (all-purpose) flour

2 teaspoons baking powder

60 g (1/2 cup/2 oz) sultanas (golden raisins)

1 tablespoon milk

2 tablespoons light brown sugar

1/2 teaspoon ground cinnamon

SERVES 8

PREPARATION TIME 30 minutes

COOKING TIME 15–20 minutes

1 Use an 18-cm (7-in) springform tin. Grease with butter and line the base with baking (parchment) paper. Preheat oven to 170°C (325°F, gas mark 3).

2 Place approximately two-thirds of the butter and all the sugar in a bowl and beat until mixture is light and fluffy.

3 Add eggs one at a time; stir to combine. Sift flour and baking powder onto a plate and fold into the egg mixture. Stir sultanas and milk into the batter.

4 Pour batter into tin and smooth the top. Bake for 15–20 minutes or until cake has risen well, is firm to the touch and is golden brown.

5 Mix the remaining butter with the brown sugar and ground cinnamon.

6 Remove cake from oven. Leave it in the tin and immediately spread the butter mixture over it, letting it soak in for a few minutes. Turn cake out onto a serving plate; eat while still hot or very warm.

Apricot Pound Cake

Dried fruit adds an intense flavour to this cake and the cooked apples make it beautifully moist. Serve with whipped cream for an extra treat.

300 g (1²⁄₃ cups/10 oz) dried apricots, chopped

200 g (³⁄₄ cup/7 oz) unsweetened puréed cooked apple

1½ tablespoons unsalted butter

1½ tablespoons light olive oil

60 ml (¼ cup/2 fl oz) buttermilk

3 eggs

2 teaspoons vanilla essence (extract)

2 teaspoons grated orange zest

350 g (1½ cups/12 oz) caster (superfine) sugar

425 g (3½ cups/15 oz) plain (all-purpose) flour

1 teaspoon baking powder

½ teaspoon bicarbonate of soda (baking soda)

SERVES 12

PREPARATION TIME 20 minutes

COOKING TIME 1½ hours

1 Use a 23-cm (9-in) round tin. Lightly grease tin and line with baking (parchment) paper. Preheat oven to 180°C (350°F, gas mark 4).

2 Place 60 g (⅓ cup/2 oz) dried apricots, all the apple purée and 120 ml (½ cup/4 fl oz) water in a saucepan. Simmer for 5 minutes or until the apricots have softened. Transfer mixture to a blender or food processor. Add the butter, oil and buttermilk and process until smooth. Leave the mixture to cool slightly, then add the eggs, vanilla essence and orange zest, blending just until smooth. Transfer to a large bowl and stir in the sugar.

3 Sieve the flour, baking powder and bicarbonate of soda into a bowl. Fold the flour mixture into the apricot mixture in 3 batches. Fold in remaining apricots; place mixture in prepared tin.

4 Bake for 1½ hours or until a skewer inserted in the centre comes out clean. Remove from the oven and leave to cool in the tin for 10 minutes. Turn out onto a wire rack to cool completely.

Top Tip

To make chopping or dicing dried apricots easy, use kitchen scissors, first spraying the blades with non-stick cooking spray. Cut the fruit into strips and then cut into dice.

Lemon Cake

For a stronger lemon taste, pierce the cake with a skewer several times immediately after baking, and pour over a mixture of 4 tablespoons each of lemon juice and icing sugar.

200 g (1 2/3 cups/7 oz) plain (all-purpose) flour

40 g (1/3 cup/1 1/2 oz) cornflour (cornstarch)

2 teaspoons baking powder

140 g (2/3 cup/5 oz) white (granulated) sugar

2 eggs

125 g (1/2 cup/4 1/2 oz) butter, softened

Juice and grated zest of 1 lemon

4 tablespoons icing (confectioners') sugar

1 Use a 24- x 15-cm (9½- x 6-in) loaf tin. Grease and flour tin. Preheat oven to 180°C (350°F, gas mark 4). To make the batter, mix flour, cornflour and baking powder in a bowl.

2 Add sugar, eggs, butter, lemon zest and juice (retaining 2 tbsp for the icing) to flour mixture. Using electric beaters, beat until smooth and pale.

3 Place mixture in the tin; smooth the top. Bake for 45 minutes or until a skewer inserted in the centre comes out clean. Remove cake from oven and leave to cool slightly; turn out onto a wire rack.

4 Mix the remaining 2 tbsp juice with the icing sugar. Pour over the cake while still warm. Leave cake to cool completely.

SERVES 12

PREPARATION TIME 25 minutes

COOKING TIME 45 minutes

Fruity Loaf

Tart blackcurrants make an excellent summer cake that is fruity without being too sweet. Mint adds a fresh, herbal note. When blackcurrants are cheap, buy enough to make a few loaves. The loaves will keep in the freezer for up to two months.

340 g (2³⁄₄ cups/12 oz) self-raising (self-rising) flour

45 g (3 tbsp/1 ¹⁄₂ oz) unsalted butter, cut into small pieces

115 g (¹⁄₂ cup/4 oz) brown sugar

125 g (1 cup/4 oz) fresh blackcurrants

3 tablespoons chopped fresh mint

125 ml (¹⁄₂ cup/4 fl oz) orange juice, or as needed

SERVES 12

PREPARATION TIME 20 minutes

COOKING TIME 1 ¹⁄₄ hours

1 Use a 30- x 11-cm (12- x 4¹⁄₄-in) loaf tin; grease and line tin with baking (parchment) paper. Preheat oven to 180°C (350°F, gas mark 4). Sift flour into a large bowl; rub in butter until mixture resembles fine breadcrumbs. Stir in sugar; make a well in the centre.

2 Place blackcurrants and mint in the well and pour in the orange juice. Gradually stir dry ingredients into juice mixture until thoroughly combined; the mixture should be soft. Add a little more orange juice, if necessary.

3 Turn mixture into the prepared tin and smooth the top. Bake for about 1¹⁄₄ hours or until cake has risen, has browned and is firm to the touch. If the surface looks as if it is browning too much after about 50 minutes, loosely place a piece of over the top.

4 Leave the cake to cool in the tin for 5 minutes, then turn it out onto a wire rack to cool completely. For the best flavour, leave overnight before serving. Cake can be kept in an airtight tin for up to 3 days.

Try this, too...

To make a Cranberry Pecan Loaf, which is delicious for breakfast or for a mid-morning snack, use chopped fresh cranberries in place of blackcurrants. Add 1 tsp ground cinnamon instead of the mint, sifting it in with the flour. Add 125 g (1 cup/4 oz) chopped pecan nuts with the sugar.

Top Tip

If you have berries left over, freeze them for another time. Place in a shallow baking tray and spread them out in a single layer without crushing. Freeze until rock-hard, then pour fruit into freezer bags. For many recipes it is unnecessary to thaw the fruit before using.

Viennese Sachertorte

Use the best-quality dark chocolate you can afford for this cake. Store the cake for a day, if possible, to allow the full depth of the flavour to develop.

150 g (1 cup/5½ oz) dark (semisweet) chocolate

150 g (⅔ cup/5½ oz) butter

150 g (1¼ cups/5½ oz) icing (confectioners') sugar

Few drops of vanilla essence (extract)

6 eggs, separated

125 g (1 cup/4½ oz) plain (all-purpose) flour

¼ teaspoon baking powder

3–4 tablespoons apricot jam

200 g (1⅓ cups/7 oz) dark (semisweet) chocolate

SERVES 8

PREPARATION TIME 30 minutes

COOKING TIME 60–70 minutes

1 Use a 23-cm (9-in) springform tin. Line base of tin with baking (parchment) paper. Preheat oven to 150°C (300°F, gas mark 2).

2 Break up chocolate. Melt in a bowl placed over simmering water. Using an electric mixer, beat the chocolate, butter, icing sugar, vanilla essence and egg yolks in a medium bowl until well combined. Sift flour and baking powder; stir into the batter. Beat egg whites in a separate bowl until stiff and fold into batter with a metal spoon.

3 Place batter in tin and smooth the top, building the mixture up a little higher towards the edge. Bake for 60–70 minutes. Remove from oven; let stand for 5 minutes. Remove the outer ring of the tin.

4 Cover cake with baking paper. Weigh down with a small board and leave to cool completely. Turn onto wire rack and remove tin base.

5 Sieve jam into pan, add a little water and heat gently. Spread evenly over cake and allow to set. Melt the chocolate in a bowl placed over simmering water and spread over the cake. To prevent cracking, lift the cake onto a serving platter before the chocolate hardens.

Middle Eastern Orange Cake

The combination of orange juice and ground almonds makes this cake very moist.
Yogurt is a good accompaniment because its slight acidity offsets the richness of the cake.

5 large oranges

6 eggs, lightly beaten

225 g (2¼ cups/8 oz) ground almonds

285 g (1¼ cups/10 oz) caster (superfine) sugar

1 teaspoon baking powder

Natural (plain) yogurt, to serve

SERVES 12

PREPARATION TIME 2½ hours

COOKING TIME 1 hour

1 Use a 23-cm (9-in) springform tin. Place 2 oranges in a pan with water to cover. Bring to the boil, cover and simmer for 2 hours. Allow oranges to cool, cut them open and remove pips, membrane and peel. Roughly chop the flesh.

2 Preheat oven to 180°C (350°F, gas mark 4). Grease and flour the tin. Process chopped oranges, eggs, ground almonds, sugar and baking powder in a food processor.

3 Pour batter into the prepared tin. Bake for 1 hour or until the centre is firm. Cool in the tin. Turn cake out onto a serving plate; it is very moist and needs to be handled carefully to prevent it breaking.

4 Peel the remaining oranges with a small paring knife. Cut along both sides of each dividing membrane to separate the orange segments. Serve cake with orange segments and yogurt.

Vanilla Angel Cake

Almost fat-free, this very light cake is made using egg whites only, no yolks. During baking it develops a delicious golden crust that hides the pure white interior.

115 g (1 cup/4 oz) plain
  (all-purpose) flour

85 g (⅔ cup/3 oz) icing
  (confectioners') sugar

8 large egg whites, at room
  temperature

150 g (⅔ cup/5½ oz) caster
  (superfine) sugar

Pinch of salt

1 teaspoon cream of tartar

1 teaspoon vanilla essence (extract)

225 g (1½ cups/8 oz) each of
  strawberries, raspberries and
  blueberries

Low-fat natural (plain) yogurt,
  to serve

SERVES 12

PREPARATION TIME 15 minutes

COOKING TIME 35 minutes

1 Use a 25-cm (10-in) non-stick ring tin. Preheat the oven to 180°C (350°F, gas mark 4). Sift the flour and icing sugar onto a plate and set aside.

2 Put the egg whites in a large bowl and whisk until frothy. Add the sugar, salt, cream of tartar and vanilla essence, and continue whisking until the mixture forms stiff peaks.

3 Add the flour mixture to the egg whites and, using a large metal spoon, fold in gently until well blended.

4 Spoon mixture into the ring tin. Tap the tin on a level surface to break up any air bubbles. Bake for 35 minutes or until the cake is well risen, golden brown and springy to the touch.

5 Invert the cake, still in the tin, onto a wire rack; leave upside down to cool completely. Slide a knife around the side of the tin to loosen the cake, then invert onto a serving plate.

6 Just before serving, combine the strawberries, raspberries and blueberries and spoon into the hollow in the centre of the cake. Serve with the yogurt. This cake is best when eaten the day it is made. However, if it is stored in an airtight tin or wrapped in cling wrap, it will keep for 1–2 days.

Swiss Roll with Peaches

Let the sponge roll stand for 30 minutes before serving to allow the flavours to develop.

FOR THE BATTER

4 egg whites

75 g (⅓ cup/2½ oz) caster (superfine) sugar

4 egg yolks

90 g (¾ cup/3¼ oz) plain (all-purpose) flour

FOR THE FILLING

1 lemon

500 g (1 lb 2 oz) ripe peaches

250 ml (1 cup/9 fl oz) cream, for whipping

½ teaspoon vanilla essence (extract)

2 tablespoons honey

SERVES 8

PREPARATION TIME 40 minutes

COOKING TIME 12–15 minutes

1 Use a 33- x 23-cm (13- x 9-in) Swiss roll tin. Line with baking (parchment) paper. Preheat oven to 180°C (350°F, gas mark 4). Beat egg whites with 1 tbsp water until soft peaks form. Add sugar. Beat the egg whites until stiff peaks form. Use a large metal spoon to gently stir the egg yolks into the egg whites. Sift flour over the mixture and fold in with a whisk.

2 Spread mixture in tin; bake for 12–15 minutes. Turn out onto a damp cloth kitchen towel and cover with a second damp towel; leave to cool completely.

3 Grate 1 tsp lemon zest; squeeze 1 tbsp juice. Place peaches in a bowl and pour boiling water over them. Remove fruit with care; peel, halve and stone. Cut the flesh into small pieces; mix with lemon juice.

4 Whip cream with the vanilla and lemon zest until stiff. Stir 1 tbsp honey into the cream; gently mix in the fruit. Remove the towel and baking paper from the sponge. Spread two-thirds of peach cream over the sponge. Starting at a short end, roll up the sponge. Spread the rest of the cream over the roll and drizzle with the remaining honey.

Frosted Chocolate Ring Cake

Chocolate cake is always popular. This interesting version is enriched with
a sweet prune purée and topped with creamy frosting. Serve it as a morning snack
or for dessert. It's perfect with some fresh berries on the side.

140 g (²/₃ cup/5 oz) pitted,
   ready-to-eat prunes

150 ml (¹/₂ cup/5 fl oz) boiling water

60 g (¹/₄ cup/2 oz) unsalted butter,
   at room temperature

140 g (³/₄ cup/5 oz) light brown
   sugar

¹/₂ teaspoon vanilla essence (extract)

2 eggs, lightly beaten

100 g (³/₄ cup/3 ¹/₂ oz) self-raising
   (self-rising) flour

100 g (³/₄ cup/3 ¹/₂ oz) self-raising
   wholemeal (self-rising whole-
   wheat) flour

1 teaspoon baking powder

4 tablespoons cocoa powder

250 g (1 cup/9 oz) ricotta cheese

¹/₂ teaspoon vanilla essence (extract)

1 tablespoon icing (confectioners')
   sugar, or to taste, sifted

SERVES 10

PREPARATION TIME 25 minutes
   plus 30 minutes soaking

COOKING TIME 25 minutes

1 Use a 20-cm (8-in) deep ring tin. Grease the tin. Place prunes in a bowl and pour boiling water over them. Cover and leave to soak for 30 minutes. Preheat oven to 180°C (350°F, gas mark 4).

2 Beat butter until soft and pale. Gradually beat in sugar. Purée prunes with the soaking liquid in a blender until smooth, then add to the butter and sugar mixture with vanilla essence and beat until well mixed. Gradually beat in the eggs.

3 Sift the white flour, wholemeal flour, baking powder and cocoa powder over the mixture, tipping in any bran left in the sieve. Fold in dry ingredients until thoroughly combined. The mixture should be of a soft dropping consistency; add a little water if necessary. Spoon the mixture into the ring tin and level the top.

4 Bake for about 25 minutes or until well risen, slightly cracked on top and firm to the touch. Leave in the tin for 10 minutes, then run a knife around the inside to loosen the cake. Turn it out onto a wire rack to cool. This cake can be kept in an airtight container for 3 days before topping is added.

5 Sieve ricotta into a bowl. Add vanilla essence and icing sugar; beat until smooth.

6 Place cake on a serving plate and spoon the ricotta frosting evenly over the top. Using a knife, swirl the frosting slightly, taking it a short way down the side of the cake. Place a little cocoa powder in a small sieve and dust it over the frosting. Serve as soon as possible.

Try this, too...

For a nutty taste and texture, add 90 g (³/₄ cup/3¼ oz) finely chopped walnuts after sifting in the flour. Decorate the frosting with a few walnut halves.

For a fruit-filled ring cake, slice the ring horizontally into two layers and sandwich them together with half the ricotta frosting and some sliced strawberries or whole blueberries. Top the cake with the remaining frosting and decorate with strawberries or blueberries.

Fallen Chocolate Soufflé Cake

A fallen cake is usually bad news, but this rich-tasting one is a spectacular success.

170 g (¾ cup/6 oz) caster (superfine) sugar

60 g (½ cup/2¼ oz) unsweetened cocoa powder

60 ml (¼ cup/2 fl oz) cold water

3 tablespoons dark (semisweet) chocolate chips

1½ teaspoons vanilla essence (extract)

1 large egg, separated, plus 4 large egg whites

30 g (¼ cup/1 oz) plain (all-purpose) flour

25 g (¼ cup/1 oz) toasted wheat germ

¼ teaspoon cream of tartar

About 550 g (3⅔ cups/1 lb 4 oz) fresh or thawed frozen strawberries

80 ml (⅓ cup/2½ fl oz) orange juice

750 g (3 cups/1 lb 10 oz) vanilla frozen yogurt

SERVES 12

PREPARATION TIME 15 minutes

COOKING TIME 25 minutes

1 Use a 23-cm (9-in) springform tin; line it with baking (parchment) paper and coat lightly with non-stick cooking spray. Preheat oven to 190°C (375°F, gas mark 5).

2 Combine 115 g (½ cup/4 oz) sugar, the cocoa and cold water in a pan and stir until smooth. Add the chocolate chips and cook over low heat, stirring until chips have melted. Stir in 1 tsp vanilla essence. Cool to room temperature. Stir in the egg yolk, flour and wheat germ.

3 Beat the 5 egg whites in a bowl until frothy. Add the cream of tartar; continue beating until soft peaks form. Add remaining sugar, a tablespoon at a time; beat until stiff peaks form.

4 Using a metal spoon, fold a quarter of the egg whites into the chocolate mixture to lighten its texture. Fold the chocolate mixture into remaining egg whites just until combined. Pour batter into tin. Bake cake for about 25 minutes or until a skewer inserted in centre comes out clean. Place tin on a wire rack, leaving cake to cool in the tin.

5 Meanwhile, purée strawberries, orange juice and remaining vanilla essence in food processor.

6 Remove side of tin. Slice cake and serve with the strawberry sauce and frozen yogurt.

Top Tip

Need an excuse to indulge in this cake? Here are several to consider. This recipe uses dark chocolate and cocoa powder to give the cake a rich flavour. Dark chocolate is a good source of copper and it also provides useful amounts of iron, while cocoa powder contains five times as much iron as chocolate.

Chocolate, in particular the dark variety, contains valuable amounts of phenols, substances which work as an antioxidant and which help prevent harmful LDL cholesterol—the cholesterol that clogs arteries.

Genoise Sponge Cake

This sponge is perfect for afternoon tea. Use a good-quality jam or preserve that has a full, fruity flavour.

4 eggs

110 g (½ cup/3¾ oz) caster (superfine) sugar, plus extra for sprinkling

½ teaspoon vanilla essence (extract)

100 g (⅔ cup/3½ oz) plain (all-purpose) flour

1 teaspoon baking powder

60 g (¼ cup/2¼ oz) butter, melted

115 g (⅓ cup/4 oz) strawberry jam

325 ml (1¼ cups/11 fl oz) cream, for whipping

SERVES 8

PREPARATION TIME 25 minutes

COOKING TIME 20 minutes

1 Use 2 x 20-cm (8-in) straight-sided sandwich tins. Grease and line the bases with baking (parchment) paper. Preheat oven to 190°C (375°F, gas mark 5).

2 Beat eggs and sugar in a large heatproof bowl over a saucepan of simmering water until thick and creamy. Sift flour and baking powder into the bowl and, using a metal spoon, carefully fold it into the creamed mixture. Gently fold in the cooled melted butter.

3 Divide mixture equally between the 2 tins and spread evenly. Bake for 20 minutes or until cakes are well risen, springy to the touch and have shrunk slightly from the side of the tins. Cool for 5 minutes. Turn out on a wire rack and leave to cool completely.

4 Place one cake upside-down on a serving plate and spread evenly with the jam. Whisk cream until it is just thick enough to hold its shape and spread evenly over the jam, just up to the edge of the sponge. Place second cake on top of the filling and sift caster sugar evenly over the top.

Try this, too...

For a Passionfruit Cream Sponge, omit the jam for the filling and the caster sugar for sprinkling. Whip cream with 1 tbsp icing (confectioners') sugar until it holds its shape. Fold through 2 tbsp fresh passionfruit pulp and use to fill and top sponge sandwich. Coat top with 2 tbsp passionfruit pulp.

Cappuccino Chiffon Cake

Very easy to make, this sweet treat is lower in fat than most.

280 g (2¼ cups/10 oz) plain (all-purpose) flour

345 g (1½ cups/12 oz) caster (superfine) sugar

1 tablespoon baking powder

1 teaspoon cinnamon

2 large eggs, plus 4 large egg whites

125 ml (½ cup/4 fl oz) walnut oil

185 ml (¾ cup/6 fl oz) brewed espresso coffee (at room temperature)

2 tablespoons unsweetened cocoa powder

1 teaspoon vanilla essence (extract)

½ teaspoon cream of tartar

2 tablespoons icing (confectioners') sugar

SERVES 16

PREPARATION TIME 15 minutes

COOKING TIME 45 minutes

1 Use a 25-cm (10-in) ring tin. Do not grease the tin. Preheat oven to 160°C (315°F, gas mark 2–3). Place the flour, sugar, baking powder and cinnamon in a medium bowl and stir to combine. Separate the whole eggs. Whisk walnut oil, egg yolks, espresso coffee, cocoa powder and vanilla together in large bowl until smooth. Fold flour mixture into egg mixture until well combined.

2 Beat 6 egg whites in a medium bowl until frothy. Beat in cream of tartar and continue beating until stiff peaks form. Gently fold the egg whites into the batter.

3 Place batter in the tin and bake for about 45 minutes or until a skewer inserted in the centre comes out clean.

4 Leave the cake in the tin and invert onto a wire rack to cool. (Cooling this cake the right way up will cause it to sink.) Run a knife around the side and turn the cake onto a serving plate. Dust with the icing sugar.

Top Tip

Walnut oil is a valuable source of heart-friendly monounsaturated and polyunsaturated fats as well as the antioxidant vitamin E. It may help lower the risk of heart disease by increasing HDL or the 'good' cholesterol. Use extra-light olive oil instead, if preferred.

Summer Fruit Cheesecake

This dessert has the creamy consistency a cheesecake should have but uses a soft cheese with a lower fat content than normal. Add an amaretti biscuit base without butter and vitamin C-rich strawberries and kiwi fruit for a healthy result that's big on flavour.

125 g (1 cup/4½ oz) amaretti cookies, crushed

450 g (1¾ cups/1 lb) ricotta or cream cheese

3 eggs, separated

120 g (½ cup/4 oz) caster (superfine) sugar

Finely grated zest of 1 small orange

125 ml (½ cup/4 fl oz) cream, for whipping

2 tablespoons plain (all-purpose) flour

FOR THE TOPPING

About 300 g (2 cups/10½ oz) strawberries, halved or sliced

2 kiwi fruit, peeled and sliced

1 tablespoon icing (confectioners') sugar, sifted

SERVES 8

PREPARATION TIME 30 minutes

COOKING TIME 1¼ hours

1 Use a 20-cm (8-in) springform tin. Grease tin; line base with baking (parchment) paper. Sprinkle amaretti crumbs evenly over paper lining and set aside. Preheat oven to 160°C (315°F/gas mark 2–3).

2 Place ricotta, egg yolks, sugar, orange zest and cream in a blender or food processor. Blend until smooth and mixed well. Pour mixture into a bowl. (Alternatively, beat ingredients using an electric mixer.) Sift flour over the surface and fold it in.

3 In a separate bowl, whisk the egg whites until stiff. Using a metal spoon, gently fold them into the cheese mixture. Pour into the tin, taking care not to disturb the crumbs; smooth the surface.

4 Bake for 1 hour or until slightly risen, lightly set and golden brown. Turn off oven and leave the cake for 15 minutes. Remove from oven; set aside to cool. Chill before serving, if desired.

5 Remove cheesecake from tin and place on a serving plate. Pile strawberries and kiwi fruit on top and dust with the icing sugar.

Try this, too...

Instead of amaretti, use the same amount of crushed digestive or oat cookies for the base.

Use the finely grated zest of 1 small pink grapefruit or 1 lime in place of the orange zest.

Top the cheesecake tart with a mixture of sliced fresh peaches or nectarines and blueberries.

For a Raspberry Cheesecake, sprinkle crushed gingernuts on the base of the tin in place of amaretti. For the cheesecake mixture, use light brown sugar instead of caster sugar. Lemon zest can be used in place of the orange zest. Top the cheesecake with about 250 g (2 cups/9 oz) raspberries, then sift icing sugar over the fruit.

Upside-down Pear Cake

Everyone will love this ginger-flavoured, flipped-over, fruit-topped cake.

2 tablespoons dark brown sugar

3 firm, ripe pears

155 g (1 1/4 cups/5 1/2 oz) plain (all-purpose) flour

1 teaspoon ground ginger

3/4 teaspoon baking powder

1/4 teaspoon bicarbonate of soda (baking soda)

60 ml (1/4 cup/2 fl oz) extra-light olive oil

165 g (3/4 cup/5 3/4 oz) white (granulated) sugar

1 1/2 teaspoons grated lime zest

1 large egg, plus 1 large egg white

185 ml (3/4 cup/6 fl oz) buttermilk

SERVES 10

PREPARATION TIME 15 minutes

COOKING TIME 35 minutes

1 Use a 23-cm (9-in) round non-stick cake tin. Coat base with non-stick cooking spray. Sprinkle brown sugar over it; shake tin to coat evenly. Preheat oven to 180°C (350°F/gas mark 4).

2 Peel, core and halve the pears. Slice crosswise into 5 mm (1/4 in) slices. Spread slices in tin, making sure the base is completely covered.

3 Sift flour, ginger, baking powder and bicarbonate of soda on a plate. Using an electric mixer, beat the olive oil, white sugar and lime zest in a mixing bowl. Beat in the whole egg and the egg white until the mixture is thick.

4 Using a rubber spatula or large metal spoon, alternately fold the flour mixture and buttermilk into the egg mixture, starting and ending with flour mixture, until just blended.

5 Pour batter over the pears and smooth the top, making sure pears are completely covered. Bake for 35 minutes or until a skewer inserted in the centre comes out clean. Transfer to a wire rack and leave in the tin for 10 minutes to cool. Invert onto a plate and allow to cool a little longer before slicing.

Glazed Gingerbread

Hints of molasses and mixed spice give extra layers of flavour to this moreish cake.

165 g (1 ⅓ cups/6 oz) plain (all-purpose) flour

1 ½ teaspoons ground mixed spice (allspice)

¾ teaspoon bicarbonate of soda (baking soda)

½ teaspoon salt

135 g (½ cup/4 ¾ oz) unsweetened apple sauce

90 g (½ cup/3 ¼ oz) light molasses

1 large egg, lightly beaten

4 tablespoons butter

115 g (½ cup/4 oz) dark brown sugar

2 teaspoons grated, peeled fresh ginger

3 tablespoons finely chopped crystallised ginger

90 g (¾ cup/3 ¼ oz) icing (confectioners') sugar, sifted

SERVES 8–10

PREPARATION TIME 30 minutes

COOKING TIME 45 minutes

1 Use a 20-cm (8-in) square cake tin; coat generously with non-stick cooking spray. Preheat oven to 180°C (350°F, gas mark 4). Mix flour, mixed spice, bicarbonate of soda and salt in a medium bowl. Mix the apple sauce, molasses and egg in a separate bowl.

2 Using electric beaters at high speed, cream butter and brown sugar in a medium bowl until light, for about 4 minutes. Reduce speed to low and beat in the apple sauce mixture. Stir in flour mixture with a wooden spoon, just until combined. Stir in fresh ginger.

3 Place batter in the tin and bake for about 45 minutes or until a skewer inserted in the centre comes out with moist crumbs clinging to it. Cool in the pan on a wire rack for 10 minutes. Remove from pan and set right-side up on the rack. Leave to cool completely.

4 Scatter crystallised ginger on top of gingerbread. Mix icing sugar with a little water to make a spreadable glaze. Drizzle glaze over the crystallised ginger, letting some glaze run down the sides.

Top Tip

The combination of fresh and crystallised ginger gives this cake an intense flavour. When buying fresh ginger, make sure it is very firm and smooth. The skin should be glossy and a pinkish-tan colour. Fresh ginger should not look dry or shrivelled.

muffins
& cookies

Chocolate Muffins

Use chocolate with at least a 60 percent cocoa content. You can ice the baked muffins and decorate them with chocolate sprinkles for an extra treat.

100 g (⅔ cup/3½ oz) bitter (unsweetened) chocolate

125 g (½ cup/4½ oz) butter

150 g (⅔ cup/5½ oz) caster (superfine) sugar

2 eggs, lightly beaten

175 g (¾ cup/6 oz) sour cream

60 ml (¼ cup/2 fl oz) brandy

¼ teaspoon ground cinnamon

Pinch of ground cardamom

210 g (1⅔ cups/7½ oz) plain (all-purpose) flour

1 teaspoon baking powder

3 tablespoons cocoa powder

MAKES 12

PREPARATION TIME 25 minutes

COOKING TIME 20–25 minutes

1 Use a 12-hole (80 ml/⅓ cup/ 2½ fl oz) muffin pan and line with paper cases. Preheat oven to 180°C (350°F, gas mark 4). Melt the chocolate and butter in a bowl set over simmering water. Cool. Stir in the sugar, eggs, sour cream, brandy and spices.

2 Sift remaining ingredients into a bowl. Add chocolate mixture to dry ingredients and stir until just combined.

3 Fill paper cases two-thirds full. Bake muffins for 20–25 minutes. Place pan on a wire rack; let muffins cool briefly before serving.

Try this, too...

For Chocolate Muffins with Cherries, prepare the mixture as for the main recipe, adding 4 tbsp Kirsch instead of brandy. Remove the stones from 200 g (1 cup/7 oz) cherries. Pour the chocolate batter into paper cases. Spread cherries over the batter and press down gently. Sprinkle 50 g (⅓ cup/2 oz) chopped almonds on top. Bake as for the main recipe.

Top Tip

To make sure that the muffins are featherlight, do not mix the batter too vigorously. To achieve the best result, mix the liquid and the dry ingredients with a wooden spoon, not with electric beaters. Mixing should be brief and the ingredients only just blended.

Blueberry Muffins

A variety or combination of fruits such as fresh cranberries, redcurrants,
raspberries or blackberries can be used in this classic recipe.

About 410 g (2½ cups/14½ oz)
   blueberries

125 g (½ cup/4½ oz) butter

3 eggs

140 g (¾ cup/5 oz) brown sugar

1 teaspoon vanilla essence (extract)

150 g (⅔ cup/5½ oz) sour cream

350 g (2¾ cups/12 oz) plain
   (all-purpose) flour

1 tablespoon baking powder

Icing (confectioners') sugar, for
   dusting

MAKES 24

PREPARATION TIME 25 minutes

COOKING TIME 20 minutes per pan

1 Use 2 x 12-hole (80 ml/⅓ cup/
2½ fl oz) muffin pans; line with
paper cases. Preheat oven to 180°C
(350°F, gas mark 4).

2 Wash blueberries; leave to dry
on paper towels.

3 Place butter, eggs, sugar, vanilla
essence and sour cream in a
bowl; stir to combine. Sift the flour
and baking powder in another bowl.
Add butter mixture; stir until just
combined. Gently fold blueberries
into the batter.

4 Fill the paper cases two-thirds
full with batter. Bake for about
20 minutes. Place pans on a wire
rack and leave muffins to cool. Dust
with icing sugar just before serving.

Top Tip

You can bake the muffins without
the paper cases. Grease the holes
in the pan carefully and dust with
flour, shaking out any excess.

41

Banana Maple Muffins

Here's the perfect way to use very ripe bananas. The softness of the fruit contributes to the moist texture of the muffins.

300 g (2⅓ cups/10½ oz) self-raising (self-rising) flour

40 g (⅓ cup/1½ oz) plain (all-purpose) flour

½ teaspoon bicarbonate of soda (baking soda)

115 g (½ cup/4 oz) light brown sugar

60 ml (¼ cup/2 fl oz) maple syrup

250 g (⅔ cup/9 oz) mashed banana (2 small bananas)

2 eggs, lightly beaten

250 ml (1 cup/9 fl oz) buttermilk

80 ml (⅓ cup/2½ fl oz) vegetable oil

1 Use 1 x 12-hole (80 ml/⅓ cup/ 2½ fl oz) muffin pan. Grease pan. Preheat oven to 200°C (400°F, gas mark 6).

2 Sift flours, bicarbonate of soda and sugar into a large bowl; stir in syrup, banana, eggs, buttermilk and oil just until combined.

3 Spoon mixture into muffin pan. Bake for about 20 minutes. Turn onto wire racks to cool.

Try this too...

Add a nutty texture by including 55 g (½ cup/2 oz) chopped pecan nuts or walnuts to the mixture.

Use a different sweetener and try honey or light corn syrup instead of maple syrup.

MAKES 12

PREPARATION TIME 10 minutes

COOKING TIME 25 minutes

Marzipan Orange Muffins

The triple combination of almond-flavoured ingredients—marzipan, almond liqueur and flaked almonds—gives these muffins a delicious taste and texture.

175 g (6 oz) marzipan paste, chopped

2 eggs, lightly beaten

80 g (⅓ cup/3 oz) butter, softened

200 ml (¾ cup/7 fl oz) buttermilk

80 g (⅓ cup/2¾ oz) caster (superfine) sugar

2 teaspoons grated orange zest

2 tablespoons almond liqueur

210 g (1⅔ cups/7½ oz) plain (all-purpose) flour

1 teaspoon baking powder

1 large orange

Flaked almonds, for decoration

MAKES 24

PREPARATION TIME 30 minutes

COOKING TIME 20 minutes per pan

1 Use 2 x 12-hole (80 ml/⅓ cup/2½ fl oz) muffin pans; line with paper cases. Preheat oven to 180°C (350°F, gas mark 4).

2 Beat the marzipan, eggs and butter with a wooden spoon until smooth. Gradually mix in the buttermilk, sugar, orange zest and liqueur with a wooden spoon until light and fluffy.

3 Sift flour and baking powder into a large bowl. Add marzipan mixture; stir until just combined.

4 Peel orange very thickly so that white pith is removed. Segment the orange and halve the segments.

5 Place 1 tsp of mixture in each paper case and place a halved orange segment on top. Add more mixture until cases are two-thirds full. Sprinkle with flaked almonds.

6 Bake for about 20 minutes until golden brown. Place pans on a wire rack; leave muffins to cool.

Try this, too...

To make Chocolate Apple Muffins, replace orange zest and liqueur with ½ tsp ground cinnamon, 2 tbsp hazelnut spread and ½ tbsp cocoa powder. Peel, halve and core 2 tart apples. Cut into small cubes and stir into the mixture after Step 3. Continue as for the main recipe.

Gingerbread Cupcakes

The combination of ground, fresh and crystallised ginger gives these delicious cupcakes a multi-layered flavour that lovers of ginger will find irresistible.

165 g (1⅓ cups/5¾ oz) plain (all-purpose) flour

1 tablespoon ground ginger

1 teaspoon mustard powder

1 teaspoon bicarbonate of soda (baking soda)

½ teaspoon ground cinnamon

Pinch of ground cloves

95 g (½ cup/3¼ oz) dark brown sugar

90 g (¼ cup/3¼ oz) molasses

2 tablespoons vegetable oil

2 egg whites

125 ml (½ cup/4 fl oz) buttermilk

5-cm (2-in) piece of fresh ginger

60 g (½ cup/2¼ oz) icing (confectioners') sugar

2 tablespoons chopped crystallised ginger

MAKES 12

PREPARATION TIME 15 minutes

COOKING TIME 20 minutes

1 Use 1 x 12-hole (80 ml/⅓ cup/ 2½ fl oz) muffin pan and line with paper cases. Preheat oven to 180°C (350°F, gas mark 4). Sift flour, ginger, mustard, bicarbonate of soda, cinnamon and cloves into a bowl.

2 Place sugar, molasses and oil in a large bowl and beat until well combined. Beat in egg whites one at a time until incorporated and the mixture has a light texture. Fold the flour mixture and buttermilk into the sugar mixture alternately: start and end with flour mixture. Spoon into cases. Bake 20 minutes or until a skewer inserted in the centre of a cake comes out clean. Place pan on a wire rack and leave cupcakes to cool completely.

3 Peel the fresh ginger and grate finely. Squeeze to extract the juice and measure 2 tsp. Combine icing sugar and ginger juice in a bowl to make a glaze. Add a little water if necessary. Spread glaze over the tops of the cupcakes and sprinkle with crystallised ginger.

Top Tip

To extract the maximum amount of juice from grated fresh ginger, press it with your fingertips, press it into a tea strainer or place in a square of muslin and wring tightly. Ginger can be helpful in alleviating motion sickness and heartburn.

Apricot Pecan Muffins

Muffins are very versatile and are popular for breakfast and brunch
as well as being the perfect snack food at any time. This delicately spiced version
is packed with flavoursome fresh fruit and nuts.

335 g (2⅔ cups/12 oz) plain
  (all-purpose) flour

3 teaspoon baking powder

100 g (½ cup/3½ oz) brown sugar

1 teaspoon ground cinnamon

3 tablespoons wheat bran

1 teaspoon grated lemon zest

240 ml (1 cup/8 fl oz) milk

2 eggs, lightly beaten

60 g (¼ cup/2 oz) butter, melted

About 225 g (8 oz) ripe but firm
  apricots, stoned and diced

55 g (½ cup/2 oz) pecans chopped

MAKES 12

PREPARATION TIME 25 minutes

COOKING TIME 20–25 minutes

1 Use 1 x 12-hole (80 ml/⅓ cup/
2½ fl oz) muffin pan. Grease
lightly. Preheat oven to 200°C (400°F,
gas mark 6).

2 Sift flour, baking powder, sugar
and cinnamon into a bowl. Stir
in the wheat bran and lemon zest.
Combine milk, eggs and butter in a
jug, mixing well. Pour onto the dry
ingredients; add the apricots and
pecans. Stir until just combined.

3 Spoon into muffin pan, filling
cups two-thirds full. Bake for
20–25 minutes or until risen and
golden and a skewer inserted in the
centre of a muffin comes out clean.
Leave in the pan for 2–3 minutes,
then turn out onto a wire rack to
cool completely. Eat the same day.

Try this, too...

For Raspberry Muffins, use 220 g
(1⅔ cups/8 oz) fresh raspberries
instead of apricots. Use orange
zest in place of the lemon zest
and omit the pecan nuts.

45

Dried Cranberry Scones

These fruity scones will quickly melt in your mouth.

375 g (3 cups/13 oz) self-raising (self-rising) flour

55 g (¼ cup/2 oz) caster (superfine) sugar

310 g (1¼ cups/11 oz) sour cream

30 g (1 oz) butter, melted

1 large egg, lightly beaten

150 g (1 cup/5½ oz) sweetened dried cranberries

60 g (½ cup/2 oz) icing (confectioners') sugar

1 teaspoon freshly grated orange zest

1 tablespoon fresh orange juice

SERVES 18

PREPARATION TIME 15 minutes

COOKING TIME 15 minutes

1 Use 2 large baking trays and line with baking (parchment) paper. Preheat oven to 200°C (400°F, gas mark 6). Combine the flour and sugar in a large bowl; make a well in the centre. Combine sour cream, butter and egg in a small bowl and pour into well. Stir with a fork until moistened; stir in cranberries. With floured hands, gently knead dough in the bowl just until combined.

2 Turn dough onto lightly floured work surface and shape into a 23-cm (9-in) square, about 2.5 cm (1 in) thick. Cut into 9 pieces 7.5 cm (3 in) square. Cut each square into 2 triangles. Place scones on baking trays 2.5 cm (1 in) apart. Bake until golden, about 15 minutes.

3 Place wire rack on a sheet of baking paper. Combine icing sugar, orange zest and juice for a glaze. Place the scones on the rack and, while still hot, drizzle glaze over them.

Try this, too...

If dried cranberries are not available, use currants or dried cherries and substitute lemon zest for orange.

Breakfast Muffins

These muffins are perfect for breakfast, providing the energy the body needs in the morning.
They offer plenty of dietary fibre from the wholemeal flour, wheat germ and raisins.

85 g (½ cup/3 oz) plain wholemeal (all-purpose whole-wheat) flour

150 g (1¼ cups/5½ oz) plain (all-purpose) flour

2 teaspoons bicarbonate of soda (baking soda)

Pinch of ground cinnamon

45 g (¼ cup/1½ oz) dark brown sugar

30 g (⅓ cup/1 oz) wheat germ

165 g (1⅓ cups/6 oz) raisins

220 g (1 cup/9 oz) plain low-fat yogurt

80 ml (⅓ cup/2½ fl oz) sunflower oil

1 egg

Grated zest of ½ orange

60 ml (¼ cup/2 fl oz) orange juice

MAKES 12

PREPARATION TIME 15 minutes

COOKING TIME 15–20 minutes

1 Use 1 x 12-hole (80 ml/⅓ cup/ 2½ fl oz) muffin pan. Grease pan. Preheat oven to 200°C (400°F, gas mark 6).

2 Sift flours, bicarbonate of soda and cinnamon into a bowl; tip in any bran left in the sieve. Stir in the sugar, wheat germ and raisins; make a well in the centre.

3 Put yogurt, oil, egg, orange zest and juice in a bowl and whisk lightly. Pour into the well in the dry ingredients; stir until just combined

4 Spoon mixture into the muffin cups. Bake for 15–20 minutes or until the muffins are well risen and just firm to the touch. Leave them to cool in the tray for 2–3 minutes.

5 These muffins are best eaten freshly baked and preferably still slightly warm from the oven. They can, however, be left to cool completely. Store in an airtight container for up to 2 days.

Try this, too...

Substitute chopped prunes or dried dates for the raisins.

For Carrot and Spice Muffins, use 1 tsp ground mixed spice (allspice) in place of cinnamon. Stir 100 g (⅔ cup/3½ oz) grated carrot into the flour mixture with the wheat germ and reduce the amount of raisins to 125 g (1 cup/4½ oz).

Top Tip

Wheat germ is the embryo of the wheat grain and as such contains a high concentration of nutrients, which are intended to nourish the growing plant. For the human diet, 1 tbsp wheat germ provides about 25 percent of the average daily requirement of vitamin B_6.

Sunken Cherry Cupcakes

Bake these cupcakes outside the cherry season, too. Have a supply of cherries
on standby in the freezer with the stems and pits removed. First freeze cherries by spreading
them on a tray in a single layer. Then place in bags and store in the freezer.

500 g (1 lb 2 oz) sweet or sour
   cherries

185 g (³/₄ cup/6¹/₂ oz) butter

165 g (³/₄ cup/5³/₄ oz) caster
   (superfine) sugar

1 teaspoon grated lemon zest

1 tablespoon Kirsch

4 eggs

280 g (2¹/₄ cups/10 oz) self-raising
   (self-rising) flour

MAKES 24

PREPARATION TIME 35 minutes

COOKING TIME 20–25 minutes
   per pan

1 Use 2 x 12-hole (80 ml/⅓ cup/
2½ fl oz) muffin pans and line
with paper cases. Remove cherry
stems and stones. Preheat oven to
180°C (350°F, gas mark 4).

2 Using electric beaters, beat the
butter, sugar, grated lemon zest
and Kirsch in a bowl until mixture
is pale and creamy.

3 Gradually stir in the eggs. Sift
in 250 g (1 cup/9 oz) flour. Stir
until combined. Place remaining
flour on a deep plate. Make sure
cherries are dry, then toss them in
the flour.

4 Carefully stir the cherries into
the cake mixture. Fill the paper
cases two-thirds full with mixture.

5 Bake for about 20–25 minutes
until golden brown. Place pans
on a wire rack and leave muffins to
cool. Serve with whipped cream, if
liked, on the day of baking.

Try this, too...

For Cherry Chocolate Cupcakes,
melt 150 g (⅔ cup/5½ oz) butter
and 75 g (½ cup/2½ oz) bitter
(unsweetened) chocolate (about
70 percent cocoa) in a bowl set
over simmering water. Let cool.
Place 100 g (½ cup/3½ oz) sugar,
a few drops of vanilla essence
(extract) and 2 tbsp red wine in a
large bowl. Add melted chocolate
mixture and stir well. Mix in the
eggs and flour as for main recipe.
Add 1 tbsp cocoa powder; fold in
the cherries. Transfer mixture to
paper cases; bake as for the main
recipe. Cool; drizzle lightly with
melted white chocolate.

Top Tip

Buy loose cherries in preference to
pre-packaged ones. Fresh cherries
should be plump, firm and shiny,
with their flexible green stems still
attached. Avoid sticky fruit; it has
been damaged and is leaking juice.
You can use a paper clip to remove
cherry stones. Or, some cookware
shops stock a specially made tool.

Blueberry Popovers

Popovers are a much-loved American classic, and this sweet version is perfect
for breakfast or brunch. The batter is baked, with blueberries added, in deep muffin or Yorkshire
pudding tins. The popovers are served with sweet, fresh berries to add extra vitamin C.

FOR THE BATTER

125 g (1 cup/4½ oz) plain
   (all-purpose) flour

1 teaspoon caster (superfine) sugar

2 eggs

250 ml (1 cup/9 fl oz) milk

80 g (½ cup/2½ oz) blueberries

1 tablespoon icing (confectioners')
   sugar

FOR THE BERRY SALAD

160 g (⅔ cup/5½ oz) raspberries

100 g (⅔ cup/3½ oz) blueberries

200 g (1⅓ cups/7 oz) strawberries,
   thickly sliced

1 tablespoon icing (confectioners')
   sugar, or to taste

MAKES 8

PREPARATION TIME 20 minutes

COOKING TIME 20–35 minutes

1 Use 1 x 12-hole (80 ml/⅓ cup/ 2½ fl oz) deep muffin pan and grease 8 cups. Preheat the oven to 220°C (425°F, gas mark 7).

2 To make batter, sift flour and sugar into a bowl and make a well in the centre. Break eggs into the well, add milk and combine with a fork.

3 Using a wire whisk, gradually work the flour into the liquid to make a smooth batter with the consistency of pouring cream. Pour into a large jug.

4 Pour batter into muffin cups; they should be two-thirds full. Drop blueberries into the batter in each cup, dividing them equally.

5 Bake on the centre rung of the oven for 25–30 minutes or until popovers are golden brown, well risen and crisp around the edges.

6 Meanwhile, make the berry salad. Press 90 g (⅓ cup/3½ oz) raspberries through a nylon sieve into a bowl to make a purée. Add remaining raspberries to the bowl with blueberries and strawberries. Sift icing sugar over the fruit and gently mix to combine.

7 Unmould the popovers with the help of a round-bladed knife and dust with icing sugar. Serve hot, with the berry salad.

Try this, too...

Use frozen blueberries, thawed and well drained. You can use thawed frozen raspberries and blueberries for the berry salad, too.

For a Baked Sweet Batter Pudding, make batter as for main recipe, adding 4 tbsp sparkling mineral water or cold water. Pour into a 1.5-litre (6-cup/52-fl oz) shallow baking dish lightly greased with butter. Omit blueberries. Bake for 30–35 minutes or until crisp and well risen. Spoon the berry salad into the centre of the pudding while still hot and scatter 2 tbsp toasted flaked almonds over the top. Sift icing sugar over the top; serve immediately.

Top Tip

Over-ripe fruit need not be thrown away. Purée it with a little caster (superfine) sugar and lemon juice. This can be served as a sauce over hot baked or frozen desserts. Also, it can be folded into natural (plain) yogurt, thickly whipped cream or a soft cheese such as ricotta to make an easy, delicious dessert.

Fruity Cookies

You can vary the spices in this recipe. A teaspoon of ground coriander works well.

125 g (½ cup/4½ oz) butter, softened

80 g (⅓ cup/2¾ oz) brown sugar

1 egg

200 g (1⅓ cups/7 oz) plain wholemeal (all-purpose whole-wheat) flour

½ teaspoon grated lemon zest

4 drops bitter almond essence (extract)

½ teaspoon ground mixed spice (allspice)

60 g (½ cup/2 oz) sultanas (golden raisins)

Icing (confectioners') sugar

MAKES 30

PREPARATION TIME 35 minutes

COOKING TIME 15 minutes per baking tray

1 Use 2 large baking trays; line with baking (parchment) paper. Preheat oven to 180°C (350°F, gas mark 4). Place the butter and sugar in a bowl; beat until fluffy. Separate the egg; add the egg yolk to butter mixture. Whisk the egg white with a few drops of cold water; set aside.

2 Add flour, zest, essence, spice and sultanas to butter mixture. Knead into a smooth dough. On a floured work surface, shape dough into a cylinder about 1 cm (½ in) in diameter. Cut into 30 slices 5 mm (¼ in) thick, then flatten a little.

3 Place slices on baking trays and prick several times with a fork. Bake for 10 minutes; cookies should be a pale yellow.

4 Remove from oven. Brush with egg white; sprinkle with icing sugar. Return to oven and bake for a further 5 minutes. Remove from oven. Cool cookies on the tray for 5 minutes; then transfer to a wire rack to cool completely.

Shortbread

This lovely crisp, rich buttery treat, which originated in Scotland, will keep
in an airtight container for about 4 weeks.

210 g (1²/₃ cups/7¹/₂ oz) plain
(all-purpose) flour

50 g (¹/₂ cup/1³/₄ oz) cornflour
(cornstarch)

110 g (¹/₂ cup/3³/₄ oz) caster
(superfine) sugar

55 g (¹/₂ cup/2 oz) ground
blanched almonds

100 g (³/₄ cup/3¹/₂ oz) icing
(confectioners') sugar

190 g (³/₄ cup/7¹/₂ oz) butter,
softened

MAKES 24

PREPARATION TIME 25 minutes plus
1¹/₂ hours cooling

COOKING TIME 30 minutes

1 Use a large baking tray and line
with baking (parchment) paper.
Place all the ingredients in a bowl;
mix with a fork until very crumbly.
On a floured work surface, knead to
form a smooth dough. Shape into a
ball and wrap in cling wrap; chill for
at least 30 minutes.

2 Cut dough in half; shape each
half into a ball. Place on baking
tray and press with the balls of the
hands into rounds about a finger-
width thick.

3 With a knife, lightly score each
round into 12 equal triangles.
Prick lightly with a fork at regular
intervals; press edges with the tines
of a fork. Chill rounds in refrigerator
for about 1 hour.

4 Place baking tray in cold oven.
Set oven to 180°C (350°F, gas
mark 4); bake shortbread for about
30 minutes until lightly browned.
Remove from oven. Cool on tray for
15 minutes, then transfer to a wire
rack to cool completely.

Peanut Bites

These crunchy, flavoursome bites are also good if the orange zest is omitted and a few squares of chocolate, roughly chopped, are added to the mixture.

125 g (1 cup/4½ oz) plain (all-purpose) flour

1 teaspoon baking powder

75 g (⅓ cup/2½ oz) brown sugar

70 g (¼ cup/2½ oz) butter

60 g (¼ cup/2¼ oz) crunchy peanut butter

1 egg

½ teaspoon ground mixed spice (allspice)

1 teaspoon grated orange zest

MAKES 12

PREPARATION TIME 25 minutes

COOKING TIME 15 minutes

1 Use a large baking tray and line with baking (parchment) paper. Preheat oven to 190°C (375°F, gas mark 5).

2 Sift flour and baking powder into a large bowl. Add all the remaining ingredients and mix to a smooth dough using the dough hooks of an electric hand mixer, or by hand.

3 Use 2 teaspoons to scoop 12 equal mounds of the mixture onto the baking tray, placing them about 2.5 cm (1 in) apart.

4 Bake for 12–15 minutes. Remove from oven. Leave on baking tray for 2–3 minutes to cool a little and harden slightly. Transfer cookies to a wire rack to cool completely.

Top Tip

To make peanut butter, place about 80 g (½ cup/3 oz) unsalted roasted peanuts in a food processor. Blend until chunky pieces form. Remove half; process the remainder finely. Mix all the processed nuts with 1 tbsp sunflower seed oil.

Almond Cookies

These simple cookies require few ingredients and are quickly made.

40 g (¼ cup/1½ oz) blanched almonds

1 egg

110 g (½ cup/4 oz) caster (superfine) sugar

½ teaspoon baking powder

55 g (½ cup/2 oz) ground almonds

120 g (1 cup/4½ oz) semolina

½ teaspoon grated lemon zest

4 drops almond essence (extract)

MAKES 16

PREPARATION TIME 25 minutes

COOKING TIME 10 minutes

1 Use a large baking tray and line with baking (parchment) paper. Preheat the oven to 200°C (400°F, gas mark 6). Chop almonds finely. Spread on a plate and set aside.

2 Place egg and sugar in a bowl and beat until pale and fluffy. Add remaining ingredients; stir well.

3 With moistened hands, shape the dough into 16 walnut-sized balls. Dip one side of each one into the reserved almonds. Place balls 2 cm (¾ in) apart, almond-side-up, on the baking tray.

4 Bake for 8–10 minutes until well risen and golden brown. Leave to cool on tray for 1 minute, then transfer to a wire rack to cool completely. Dust with a little icing (confectioners') sugar just before serving, if desired. Store in an airtight jar or tin.

Apple and Muesli Rock Cakes

A little diced apple makes these rock cakes moist and fruity. This is a very good recipe for younger members of the family to make. Not only will they easily master the basic cooking skills, they'll enjoy eating the results of their labours.

225 g (1¾ cups/8 oz) self-raising (self-rising) flour

100 g (⅓ cup/3½ oz) butter, cut into small pieces

45 g (¼ cup/2 oz) brown sugar, plus extra for sprinkling

1 teaspoon ground cinnamon

2 dessert apples, peeled and diced

75 g (¾ cup/2½ oz) sugar-free muesli

1 egg, lightly beaten

4–5 tablespoons low-fat milk

MAKES 24

PREPARATION TIME 20 minutes

COOKING TIME 15 minutes per tray

1 Use 2 large baking trays and grease lightly. Preheat oven to 190°C (375°F, gas mark 5). Place the flour in a bowl, add butter and rub in with fingertips until the mixture resembles fine breadcrumbs.

2 Stir in the sugar, cinnamon, diced apples and muesli. Stir in the egg and enough milk to roughly bind the mixture.

3 Drop 24 spoonfuls of mixture onto the baking trays, leaving space between each cake to allow for spreading. Sprinkle tops with extra sugar. Bake for 15 minutes or until golden and firm to the touch.

4 Transfer to a wire rack to cool. Serve warm or cold. The cakes can be kept in an airtight container for up to 2 days.

Try this, too...

Replace the muesli with a mixture of 3 tbsp original rolled (porridge) oats, 2 tbsp sunflower or sesame seeds and 55 g (⅓ cup/2 oz) finely chopped almonds, hazelnuts (filberts) or nuts of your choice.

To make Tropical Fruit Rock Cakes, replace the apples, muesli and cinnamon with 55 g (⅔ cup/2 oz) desiccated (shredded) coconut and 170 g (2⅓ cups/6 oz) ready-to-eat dried fruits such as mango, pineapple and papaya, chopped.

Meringue Nut Cookies

A batch of these pretty little cookies makes an attractive gift.

60 g (½ cup/2¼ oz) walnuts

60 g (½ cup/2¼ oz) icing (confectioners') sugar, plus extra for dusting

4 teaspoons unsweetened cocoa powder

½ teaspoon cinnamon

2 large egg whites

MAKES 36

PREPARATION TIME 10 minutes

COOKING TIME 30 minutes per tray

1 Use 2 large baking trays and line with baking (parchment) paper. Preheat oven to 150°C (300°F, gas mark 2). Toast the walnuts in a small pan, stirring them frequently until crisp, about 7 minutes. Cool briefly, then chop roughly.

2 Sift icing sugar, cocoa powder and the cinnamon onto a plate.

3 Using an electric mixer, beat the egg whites in a large bowl until stiff peaks form. Gently fold cocoa mixture into the egg whites with a metal spoon. Fold in nuts.

4 Drop the batter in generous teaspoonfuls onto the baking trays, spacing them 2.5 cm (1 in) apart. Bake for about 20 minutes, or until set. Turn onto a wire rack to cool. Dust with the extra icing sugar just before serving.

Top Tip

Meringues are very sensitive to humidity (they absorb moisture and become sticky), so it's best to bake them on a dry day. Store in an airtight container once they are completely cool. Should you live in a humid climate, seal the cookies in a freezer bag and freeze them.

Crunchy Date Bars

These bars are a welcome addition to the lunchbox, as well as coffee or teatime.
This recipe contains dates for natural sweetness and nuts and sunflower seeds for extra crunch.

100 g (1/3 cup/3 1/3 oz) unsalted
butter

3 tablespoons sunflower oil

55 g (1/4 cup/2 oz) light brown
sugar

60 ml (1/4 cup/2 fl oz) clear honey

Grated zest of 1 orange

2 tablespoons orange juice

110 g (2/3 cup/3 1/2 oz) dried dates,
pitted and chopped

75 g (3/4 cup/2 1/2 oz) walnuts,
chopped

250 g (2 1/2 cups/9 oz) original
rolled (porridge) oats

30 g (1/4 cup/1 oz) sunflower seeds

MAKES 16

PREPARATION TIME 15 minutes

COOKING TIME 20 minutes

1 Use a shallow, non-stick baking tin measuring 28 x 18 x 2.5 cm (11 x 7 x 1 in) or use a 20-cm (8-in) square tin. Grease lightly. Preheat oven to 180°C (350°F, gas mark 4).

2 Place butter, oil, sugar, honey and orange zest and juice in a heavy-based saucepan. Heat gently, stirring until the butter has melted. Remove the pan from the heat and stir in the dates and walnuts. Add oats, stirring until they are evenly coated with the butter mixture.

3 Spoon mixture into the baking tin, pressing it down firmly and evenly. Sprinkle sunflower seeds on the top and press down so they are lightly embedded in the surface.

4 Bake for 20 minutes or until deep golden around the edges. Remove from the oven; leave in tin to cool slightly. Using a sharp knife, score the top into 16 equal pieces.

5 Leave to cool completely, still in the tin, before cutting into bars along the marked lines. Bars can be kept in an airtight container for up to 1 week.

Try this, too...

For a coconut flavour and texture, add 30 g (1/3 cup/1 oz) sweetened desiccated (shredded) coconut, reducing the sugar by the same amount.

Sprinkle top with pumpkin seeds instead of sunflower seeds.

For Apricot and Hazelnut Bars, use 110 g (2 1/3 cup/3 1/2 oz) ready-to-eat dried apricots, finely chopped, in place of the dates. Instead of the walnuts, use 75 g (3/4 cup/2 1/2 oz) chopped hazelnuts (filberts).

For Muesli and Ginger Bars, make the butter mixture as in the main recipe but use just 2 tbsp honey and replace orange zest and juice with 2 tbsp apple juice, 2 pieces of finely chopped preserved stem ginger and 1 tbsp ginger syrup from the jar. Add 340 g (2 1/3 cups/ 12 oz) muesli with the dried fruit and nuts. Before baking, sprinkle top with flaked almonds.

Top Tip

Oats are an excellent source of soluble fibre, which can help to reduce high blood cholesterol levels. Sunflower seeds are a rich source of vitamin E and provide vitamin B_1, niacin and zinc.

Chocolate Pretzels

If you'd like the shapes of the pretzels to be as uniform as possible, make a template and trace shapes onto sheets of baking (parchment) paper. Then pipe the dough onto the outlines.

250 g (1 cup/9 oz) butter, softened

400 g (3½ cups/14 oz) icing (confectioners') sugar

1 whole egg and 1 egg yolk

350 g (2¾ cups/12 oz) plain (all-purpose) flour

2–3 tablespoons unsweetened cocoa powder

10 g (1 tbsp) butter

Chocolate sprinkles (optional)

MAKES 100

PREPARATION TIME 35 minutes

COOKING TIME 10–15 minutes per baking tray

1 Use 4 large baking trays. Beat the butter in a large bowl until fluffy. Add 100 g (¾ cup/3½ oz) icing sugar and the combined egg and egg yolk, stirring to combine. Sift flour over the dough and stir in.

2 Preheat oven to 200°C (400°F, gas mark 3–4). Cut 4 pieces of baking (parchment) paper to fit the trays. Using a template or a cookie cutter, draw pretzel shapes onto the paper. Place the baking paper onto the trays. Spoon dough into a piping bag; the nozzle should have a small, round, plain hole.

3 Following the drawn outlines, pipe dough onto each baking tray. Bake pretzels, a tray at a time, for 10–15 minutes or until golden. Remove from the oven and transfer to a wire rack; leave to cool.

4 To make a glaze, combine the remaining icing sugar with the cocoa and about 2 tbsp boiling hot water. Dip pretzels in the glaze and dry on a wire rack covered with foil. Before the glaze is completely dry, scatter chocolate sprinkles over the pretzels, if desired.

Try this, too...

These pretzels also taste good if they are covered with melted bitter (unsweetened) chocolate (with 70 percent cocoa content) instead of the mixture of icing sugar and cocoa.

Cocoa Walnut Cookies

The combination of cocoa and walnuts in these easy-to-make cookies ensures that they will quickly disappear from the jar.

250 g (1 cup/9 oz) butter, softened

275 g (1¼ cups/9¾ oz) white (granulated) sugar

250 g (2 cups/9 oz) plain (all-purpose) flour

230 g (1 cup/8 oz) ground walnuts

2 tablespoons cocoa powder

2 teaspoons ground cinnamon

2 teaspoons baking powder

1 egg white

80 walnut halves for decoration

MAKES 80

PREPARATION TIME 30 minutes plus chilling time overnight

COOKING TIME 12–15 minutes per tray

1 Use large baking trays and line with baking (parchment) paper. Using electric beaters, beat butter and sugar in a large bowl until the mixture is light and fluffy. Sift the flour; combine with walnuts, cocoa powder, cinnamon and the baking powder. Add to the butter mixture. Knead with floured hands to form a smooth dough.

2 Shape dough into 8 cylinders, each about 40 cm (16 in) long. Wrap cylinders in cling wrap; chill overnight in the refrigerator.

3 Preheat oven to 180°C (350°F, gas mark 4). On a floured work surface, cut each dough cylinder into 10 even pieces and shape into evenly sized balls. Place on baking trays. Make an indentation in the top of each ball for the walnuts.

4 Beat the egg white in a bowl; dip bottoms of walnut halves in it. Press the walnut halves into indentations. Bake cookies, a tray at a time, for 12–15 minutes until golden brown. Remove from oven, cool slightly; transfer to a wire rack to cool completely.

Vanilla Crescents

If you're in a hurry, chill the dough in the freezer for 1 or 2 hours instead of overnight.

275 g (2¼ cups/9½ oz) plain (all-purpose) flour

200 g (¾ cup/7 oz) butter, chilled and diced

100 g (½ cup/3½ oz) white (granulated) sugar

100 g (1 cup/3½ oz) ground almonds, plus 1 tablespoon

55 g (¼ cup/2 oz) caster (superfine) sugar

MAKES 75

PREPARATION TIME 40 minutes plus cooling time overnight

COOKING TIME 10–12 minutes per baking tray

1 Use large baking trays and line with baking (parchment) paper. Place flour, butter, sugar and 100 g almonds in a mixing bowl. Work by hand into a crumbly dough.

2 Place dough in a freezer bag; seal. Use a rolling pin to shape dough into a rectangle about 2.5 cm (1 in) thick. Chill overnight.

3 Preheat oven to 180°C (350°F, gas mark 4). Remove the dough from freezer bag and cut into 3 long strips. Cut each strip into 25 pieces (about 10 cm/4 in) long.

4 Shape pieces into crescents on a lightly floured work surface. Place on baking trays about 2 cm (¾ in) apart.

5 Bake the crescents, one tray at a time, for 10–12 minutes until pale yellow. Combine the sugar and remaining ground almonds; coat crescents in the mixture while still hot. Place on a wire rack to cool.

Piped Almond Circles

The dough must be just soft enough so that the cookies can easily be shaped with a piping bag.

250 g (1 cup/9 oz) butter, softened

200 g (1 cup/7 oz) white (granulated) sugar

2 egg yolks

1 tablespoon rum

150 g (1½ cups/5½ oz) ground almonds

350 g (2¾ cups/12 oz) flour

2–3 tablespoons milk

150 g (1 cup/5½ oz) good-quality chocolate

MAKES 70

PREPARATION TIME 45 minutes

COOKING TIME 12–15 minutes per baking tray

1 Use 2 large baking trays lined with baking (parchment) paper. Preheat oven to 180°C (350°F, gas mark 4). Cream butter, sugar, egg yolks and rum until light and fluffy. Combine the almonds and flour and stir in alternately with milk.

2 Spoon dough into a piping bag with a star nozzle. Pipe about 70 rounds of dough onto trays; place rounds 2.5 cm (1 in) apart; cookies should not be too thin or they will be more likely to break later. Bake, one tray at a time, for 12–15 minutes until golden. Cool on trays for a few minutes; transfer to a wire rack.

3 Melt chocolate in a bowl placed over a pan of gently simmering water. Dip one half of each cookie into the melted chocolate. Place on sheets of baking (parchment) paper and leave to set and dry.

Pecan Icebox Cookies

The ultimate standby. The dough is made ahead and kept in the freezer until you want to bake.

220 g (1 3/4 cups/7 1/2 oz) plain (all-purpose) flour

1/2 teaspoon ground cinnamon

1/4 teaspoon bicarbonate of soda (baking soda)

60 g (1/4 cup/2 1/4 oz) soft butter

140 g (2/3 cup/5 oz) white (granulated) sugar

85 g (1/3 cup/3 oz) light brown sugar

1 large egg

1 teaspoon vanilla essence (extract)

90 g (1/3 cup/3 1/4 oz) low-fat sour cream

40 g (1/3 cup/1 1/2 oz) chopped pecans, toasted

MAKES 72

PREPARATION TIME 20 minutes

COOKING TIME 20 minutes

1 Use large baking trays. Sift flour, cinnamon and bicarbonate of soda. With electric beaters, beat the butter and sugars on high speed in a large bowl until mixture is fluffy and pale, about 4 minutes. Add the egg and vanilla essence; beat until well combined. Stir in flour mixture with a wooden spoon; add the sour cream and pecans.

2 Tear off 50-cm (20-in) sheet of cling wrap and sprinkle lightly with flour. Transfer dough to cling wrap and shape into a log 38 cm (15 in) in length. Roll log tightly in the cling wrap and refrigerate until firm, about 2 hours. (Alternatively, wrap dough in heavy-duty foil and freeze for up to 1 month.)

3 Preheat oven to 190°C (375°F, gas mark 5). Slice dough into rounds about 3 mm (1/8 in) thick to make 72 cookies. Place 1 cm (1/2 in) apart on ungreased baking trays. Bake until crisp and golden brown around the edges, about 8 minutes, taking care not to overbake. If using frozen dough, increase baking time to 10 minutes. Transfer to wire racks to cool completely. Store in airtight containers.

Try this, too...

Love chocolate? At the beginning of Step 1, sift 40 g (1/3 cup/1 1/2 oz) unsweetened cocoa into the flour mixture. Increase butter to 90 g (1/3 cup/3 1/4 oz) and sour cream to 125 g (1/2 cup/4 1/2 oz).

Chocolate Oatmeal Crunch

These are good for the cookie jar and good for the lunchbox.

125 g (1 cup/4½ oz) plain (all-purpose) flour

½ teaspoon bicarbonate of soda (baking soda)

½ teaspoon salt

100g (1 cup/3½ oz) original rolled (porridge) oats

4 tablespoons butter

125 g (⅔ cup/4½ oz) light brown sugar

110 g (½ cup/3¾ oz) white (granulated) sugar

1 large egg

1 teaspoon vanilla essence (extract)

90 g (⅓ cup/3¼ oz) low-fat sour cream

130 g (¾ cup/4½ oz) dark (semisweet) chocolate chips

MAKES 36

PREPARATION TIME 15 minutes

COOKING TIME 20 minutes

1 Use 2 large baking trays. Line with baking (parchment) paper. Preheat oven to 190°C (375°F, gas mark 5). Sift flour, bicarbonate of soda and salt in a bowl. Add oats.

2 Place butter and sugars in a large bowl. Use electric beaters at high speed and beat until pale and fluffy. Add the egg and vanilla essence and beat until the mixture is light yellow and creamy, about 3 minutes. Add sour cream; use a wooden spoon to combine. Add the flour mixture all at once and mix until just combined. Don't overmix or the cookies may become tough. Stir in chocolate chips.

3 Heap teaspoonfuls of the dough 5 cm (2 in) apart on the baking trays. Bake until golden, for about 10 minutes. Cool on the trays for 2 minutes; transfer to wire racks to cool completely. Store in an airtight container for up to 2 weeks or freeze for up to 3 months.

Top Tip

The low-fat sour cream helps keep the melt-in-your-mouth quality high and the fat content low. The rolled (porridge) oats add an extra helping of heart-healthy goodness.

Gingernuts

Here's a healthier version of a traditional favourite. You can buy fancy-shaped cutters and let the children cut out gingerbread figures, stars or Christmas trees. Chopped dried fruit or nuts make good decorations.

85 g (²/₃ cup/3 oz) plain (all-purpose) flour

85 g (²/₃ cup/3 oz) plain wholemeal (all-purpose whole-wheat) flour

¹/₂ teaspoon bicarbonate of soda (baking soda)

2 teaspoons ground ginger

¹/₂ teaspoon ground cinnamon

60 g (¹/₄ cup/2¹/₄ oz) butter

80 ml (¹/₃ cup/2¹/₂ fl oz) dark corn syrup or golden syrup

MAKES 12

PREPARATION TIME 8–10 minutes

COOKING TIME 10–15 minutes

1 Use a large baking tray; grease lightly. Preheat oven to 190°C (375°F, gas mark 5). Sift plain and wholemeal flours, bicarbonate of soda, ginger and cinnamon into a bowl, tipping in any bran left in the sieve.

2 Place butter and syrup in a pan and melt over low heat, stirring occasionally. Pour mixture onto dry ingredients. Stir, working mixture into a firm dough.

3 Break off a walnut-sized lump of dough; roll into a ball in the palms of your hand. Flatten to 6 cm (2½ cm) in diameter and place on baking tray. Repeat with remaining dough. Alternatively, roll out dough on a floured work surface and cut out decorative shapes.

4 Bake for 8–10 minutes or until slightly risen and just browned. Cool on baking tray for 2–3 minutes or until cookies are firm enough to lift without breaking; transfer to a wire rack to cool completely. Store in an airtight tin for up to 5 days.

Try this, too...

For Oat and Orange Ginger Cookies, instead of using all wholemeal flour, use 45 g (¹/₃ cup/1½ oz) plain wholemeal flour and 50 g (½ cup/ 2 oz) rolled (porridge) oats. Add grated zest of 1 orange to melted butter mixture. Use 2 tbsp orange juice to bind butter mixture with dry ingredients. Work into a soft dough. Continue preparation as for the main recipe.

For Fruity Ginger Cookies, peel and grate 1 dessert apple; add to flour mixture with 60 g (½ cup/2¼ oz) sultanas (golden raisins) and the grated zest of 1 lemon. Shape and bake as before.

Top Tip

Golden syrup is used as a filling for tarts and as a topping for steamed and baked puddings in traditional English recipes. Dark corn syrup is an acceptable alternative.

Energy Bites

These nutty, moist cookies will cheer up a mid-morning coffee break or an after-school snack. They are satisfying and packed full of healthy ingredients to restore flagging energy levels.

60 g (½ cup/2¼ oz) hazelnuts (filberts), finely chopped

60 g (½ cup/2¼ oz) sunflower seeds, finely chopped

60 g (⅓ cup/2¼ oz) ready-to-eat dried apricots, finely chopped

55 g (⅓ cup/2 oz) pitted dried dates, finely chopped

1 tablespoon light brown sugar

50 g (⅓ cup/¾ oz) barley flakes

60 g (½ cup/2¼ oz) self-raising wholemeal (self-rising whole-wheat) flour

½ teaspoon baking powder

2 tablespoons sunflower oil

80 ml (⅓ cup/2½ fl oz) apple juice

MAKES 16

PREPARATION TIME 20 minutes

COOKING TIME 10–15 minutes

1 Use a large baking tray; grease lightly. Preheat oven to 190°C (375°F, gas mark 5). Mix hazelnuts, sunflower seeds, apricots and dates together in a large bowl. Add sugar, barley, flour and baking powder; stir to thoroughly combine.

2 Combine the sunflower oil and apple juice. Pour over the dry ingredients and stir until mixture is moistened and holds together.

3 With dampened fingers, scoop up a large walnut-sized piece of mixture and form it into a ball. Press to make a small, thick cookie about 5 cm (2½ in) in diameter and place on baking tray. Repeat with the remaining mixture.

4 Bake for 10–15 minutes or until slightly risen and just browned. Transfer to a wire rack to cool, then store in an airtight container for up to 4 days.

Try this, too...

Use unsalted cashew nuts instead of hazelnuts.

Use ready-to-eat chopped dried peaches and figs instead of the apricots and dates.

Substitute oat or wheat flakes for the barley flakes.

Chocolate Chip Cookies

Everyone loves choc-chip cookies. Not only are they simple to make, it's also easy to create variations by using different types of chocolate.

310 g (2½ cups/11 oz) plain (all-purpose) flour

1 teaspoon bicarbonate of soda (baking soda)

250 g (1 cup/9 oz) butter

115 g (½ cup/4 oz) caster (superfine) sugar

115 g (½ cup/4 oz) dark or light brown sugar

1 egg

1 teaspoon vanilla essence (extract)

300 g (2 cups/10½ oz) dark (semisweet) chocolate, chopped

MAKES 40

PREPARATION TIME 40 minutes

COOKING TIME 12 minutes per tray

1 Use 2 large baking trays. Grease the trays. Preheat oven to 180°C (350°F, gas mark 4).

2 Sift the flour and bicarbonate of soda onto a plate. Beat the butter and sugar in a small bowl until the mixture is light and fluffy. Add egg and vanilla essence; beat to combine. Transfer mixture to a large bowl. Add the flour mixture, stirring to combine, then stir in the chocolate. Roll level tablespoons of mixture into balls and place on the trays 2.5 cm (1 in) apart. Bake for about 12 minutes.

3 Cool cookies briefly on trays. Transfer to a wire rack to cool.

Try this, too...

For Chocolate Nut Cookies, halve the amount of chocolate used and add an equal weight of chopped walnuts, pecan nuts or macadamia nuts. Both chocolate and nuts should be chopped into fairly large pieces.

Toasted nuts give the best flavour. Preheat an oven to 180°C (350°F, gas mark 4), spread nuts in a single layer on a baking tray and bake until a light golden brown and fragrant. Stir occasionally with a wooden spoon to ensure even browning.

Vary the type of chocolate and try bitter (unsweetened) chocolate, milk (sweet) chocolate or white chocolate or a mixture. Use bars of chocolate, roughly chopped, or packaged chocolate chips. Bars are best if you like large chunks in your cookies.

For a coffee flavour, dissolve 1 tsp instant coffee powder in little water and add with the egg, omitting the vanilla essence.

Sift a little icing (confectioners') sugar over the cookies or a mix of icing sugar and unsweetened cocoa powder.

Top Tip

Choose the best-quality chocolate you can afford and store it in a cool, dry place. Chocolate may take on a whitish 'bloom', usually when the weather is hot or humid. Once melted, the chocolate takes on its customary appearance.

Fig Rolls

The sweetness and full flavour of dried figs go well with the crumbly pastry.

125 g (1 cup/4½ oz) plain (all-purpose) flour

110 g (¾ cup/3¾ oz) plain wholemeal (all-purpose whole-wheat) flour

160 g (⅔ cup/5½ oz) unsalted butter, cut into small pieces

65 g (⅓ cup/2¼ oz) light brown sugar

1 teaspoon vanilla essence (extract)

2 egg yolks

250 g (1⅓ cups/9 oz) ready-to-eat dried figs, finely chopped

2 tablespoons lemon juice

MAKES 20

PREPARATION TIME 35 minutes plus 30 minutes chilling

COOKING TIME 12–15 minutes

1 Use a large baking tray; grease. Sift flours into a mixing bowl, tipping in any bran left in the sieve. Rub in butter with fingertips until mixture resembles breadcrumbs. Add the sugar, vanilla essence and egg yolks; mix to a firm dough; add 1–2 tsp water, if needed. Combine ingredients in a food processor, if preferred. Wrap in cling wrap; chill for 30 minutes.

2 Place figs and 6 tbsp water in a small, heavy-based pan. Bring to the boil, reduce heat, cover and simmer gently for 3–5 minutes or until figs have plumped up slightly and absorbed the water. Transfer to a bowl and mash lightly with a fork to break up the pieces. Stir in lemon juice and leave to cool.

3 Preheat oven to 190°C (375°F, gas mark 5). Roll out the dough on a floured surface to a rectangle 50 x 15 cm (20 x 6 in). Cut dough in half lengthwise to make 2 strips.

4 Spoon half of the mashed figs evenly along each strip, close to one of the long sides. Bring the opposite long side up and over the filling to form a log shape; press edges of dough together to seal.

5 Slightly flatten each of the logs. Using a sharp knife, cut each log into 10 even pieces and transfer to the baking tray. Prick each piece several times with a fork. Bake for 12–15 minutes or until the pastry is slightly darkened in colour.

6 Transfer fig rolls to a wire rack to cool. They can be kept in an airtight container for 2–3 days. Do not mix them with other cookies or they may soften.

Top Tip

Dried fruits are a useful source of iron, particularly for those eating little or no red meat. Dried figs offer good amounts of calcium.

Cereal Bars

Naturally sweet and moist, these bars make a great addition to a packed lunch.
They are also a good way of getting the family to try some more unusual grains and seeds,
and add new healthy ingredients to the diet.

2 tablespoons sunflower seeds

2 tablespoons pumpkin seeds

2 tablespoons linseeds

2 bananas, about 300 g (10½ oz) in total, weighed with skins on

90 g (⅓ cup/3¼ oz) unsalted butter

60 ml (¼ cup/2 fl oz) light corn syrup or golden syrup

55 g (½ cup/2 oz) millet flakes

100 g (1 cup/3½ oz) original rolled (porridge) oats

110 g (⅔ cup/3¾ oz) pitted dried dates, roughly chopped

MAKES 14

PREPARATION TIME 25 minutes

COOKING TIME 30 minutes

Top Tip

The cereal bars can be frozen and will keep for 2 months. Wrap them individually in cling wrap or foil. Then, if you simply pack a frozen bar into a plastic container along with wrapped sandwiches, it will have thawed by lunchtime.

1 Use a 28 x 18 x 4 cm (11 x 7 x 1½ in) cake tin. Grease and line the base with baking (parchment) paper. Preheat oven to 180°C (350°F, gas mark 4). Roughly chop the three types of seeds. Peel the bananas and mash roughly.

2 Melt butter in a pan and stir in the corn syrup. Add the seeds and bananas, the millet flakes, oats and dates. Mix well and spoon into tin; level the surface.

3 Bake for about 30 minutes or until golden brown. Leave to cool in the tin for 5 minutes, then slice into 14 bars. Cool completely. The bars can be kept in an airtight container for up to 2 days.

Try this, too...

Instead of dates, use chopped ready-to-eat dried apricots or prunes or a mixture of chopped dried fruits.

Replace millet flakes with plain (all-purpose) flour, either white or wholemeal (whole-wheat).

Cranberry and Almond Biscotti

Biscotti means twice baked, a reference to the technique that gives these Italian cookies their characteristically hard texture. Traditionally, they are served after dinner with a glass of Vin Santo for dipping. They are also delicious with fresh fruit salad or a cup of coffee or tea.

55 g (⅓ cup/2 oz) blanched almonds

1 large egg

85 g (⅓ cup/3 oz) caster (superfine) sugar

125 g (1 cup/4½ oz) plain (all-purpose) flour, plus 1 tbsp

½ teaspoon baking powder

1 teaspoon ground cinnamon

55 g (⅓ cup/2 oz) dried cranberries

MAKES 20

PREPARATION TIME 30 minutes

COOKING TIME 30–40 minutes

1 Use a large baking tray; grease lightly. Preheat oven to 180°C (350°F, gas mark 4). Spread almonds in a baking tin; toast in the oven for 10 minutes or until lightly browned. Set aside to cool.

2 Place egg and sugar in a bowl and whisk with electric beaters until very thick and pale; beaters should leave a trail on the surface when lifted out. If using a rotary beater or hand whisk, set the bowl over a pan of almost boiling water, making sure water does not touch the base of the bowl.

3 Sift flour, baking powder and cinnamon onto a plate; sift again onto egg mixture. Carefully fold in, using a large metal spoon. Stir in almonds and cranberries to make a stiff dough.

4 Spoon dough onto baking tray and, with floured hands, form it into a neat brick shape about 25 x 6 x 2.5 cm (10 x 2¼ x 1 in). Bake for 20 minutes or until golden brown. Leave to cool on the baking tray for 5 minutes, then transfer to a board.

5 Using a serrated bread knife, cut the brick crosswise, slightly on the diagonal, into 20 slices. Place slices flat on baking tray and return to the oven. Bake for 10–15 minutes or until golden brown. Cool on tray for 5 minutes; transfer to wire rack to cool completely. Biscotti can be kept in an airtight container for up to 2 weeks.

Try this, too...

Substitute sultanas (golden raisins) for the cranberries.

For a stronger almond flavour, use ½ tsp almond essence (extract) instead of the cinnamon.

For Chocolate Biscotti, in place of cranberries, roughly chop 55 g (⅓ cup/2 oz) bitter (unsweetened) chocolate (at least 70 percent cocoa solids).

Top Tip

Almonds provide a good source of protein. They contain vitamin E and several B-group vitamins and also provide a valuable source of calcium for people on dairy-free diets. Fresh and dried cranberries are good sources of vitamin C.

Sunflower Cookies

These cookies make a healthy snack. You can use different seeds, chopped nuts
or a mixture to create a range of flavours.

250 g (2 cups/9 oz) plain
   (all-purpose) flour

1 teaspoon grated lemon zest

1 tablespoon honey

190 g (¾ cup/7 oz) butter, chilled

1 egg

150 g (1¼ cups/5½ oz)
   sunflower seeds

90 g (¼ cup/3¼ oz) honey

2–3 tablespoons cream

1 tablespoon lemon zest

MAKES 60

PREPARATION TIME 40 minutes

COOKING TIME 12–15 minutes per
   baking tray

1 Use 2 large baking trays lined with baking (parchment) paper. Preheat the oven to 180°C (350°F, gas mark 4). Place the flour, lemon zest, honey, 160 g (⅔ cup/5¾ oz) butter and the egg in a large bowl. Work into a crumbly dough; knead into a smooth dough with floured hands. Shape into a ball and wrap in cling wrap; chill for 30 minutes.

2 For the topping, in a saucepan, lightly toast sunflower seeds with honey, the remaining butter and the cream. Remove from heat and allow seeds to cool.

3 Roll out the dough on a floured work surface. Use a 5-cm (2-in) cookie cutter with scalloped edges and cut out about 60 cookies. Place on baking trays. Place 1 tsp topping on each cookie. Bake 12–15 minutes until golden brown. Place on a wire rack and sprinkle with lemon zest while still hot.

Top Tip

Instead of sunflower seeds, try pumpkin seeds, coarsely chopped hazelnuts (filberts) or walnuts or slivered almonds as a topping. Nuts, because of their oil content, can quickly turn rancid in a hot climate. Store them in the freezer, in an airtight container, to keep them as fresh as possible. Ideally, buy nuts as and when you need them to ensure the best quality.

Jam Stars

These attractive cookies are a favourite with children. Use jams of different flavours and colours to make them look even more appealing.

400 g (3¼ cups/14 oz) plain (all-purpose) flour

50 g (½ cup/2 oz) ground almonds

165 g (¾ cup/5¾ oz) caster (superfine) sugar

200 g (¾ cup/7 oz) butter

3 egg yolks

200 g (⅔ cup/7 oz) currant jam (jelly)

2–3 tablespoons icing (confectioners') sugar

MAKES 60–80

PREPARATION TIME 30 minutes plus 30 minutes cooling time

COOKING TIME 10–12 minutes per baking tray

1 Use large baking trays lined with baking (parchment) paper. Combine the flour, ground almonds and sugar. Dot little pieces of butter on top and add the egg yolks.

2 Mix with electric beaters for about 1 minute until crumbly, then press dough together by hand. Divide dough into 3 pieces; shape into balls and wrap in cling wrap; chill in refrigerator for 30 minutes.

3 Preheat oven to 200°C (400°F, gas mark 6). Roll out dough thinly on floured work surface or between 2 sheets of baking paper.

4 Cut out stars about 6 cm (2½ in) in diameter. Cut smaller stars out of the centre of half the stars. Bake all the stars for 10–12 minutes; place on a wire rack to cool.

5 Spread the cookies that have not had stars cut out of them thinly with jam. Sift the icing sugar thickly over the ones that have had stars cut out. Place an icing-sugar-coated cookie on top of each of the jam-covered ones. Dip remaining small stars in melted chocolate.

Brandy Snaps and Ginger Snaps

These thin, crisp biscuits are elegant to serve with coffee or tea or to accompany a fruit dessert.

FOR THE BRANDY SNAPS

125 g (½ cup/4½ oz) butter

115 g (½ cup/4 oz) caster (superfine) sugar

115 g (⅓ cup/4 oz) golden syrup or honey

1 tablespoon lemon juice

1 tablespoon brandy

125 g (1 cup/4½ oz) plain (all-purpose) flour, sifted

1 teaspoon ground ginger

310 ml (1¼ cups/10¾ fl oz) cream, whipped, for filling

MAKES 36

PREPARATION TIME 30 minutes

COOKING TIME 8–10 minutes per batch

FOR THE GINGER SNAPS

125 g (1 cup/4½ oz) self-raising (self-rising) flour

1 teaspoon bicarbonate of soda (baking soda)

¼ teaspoon salt

1 teaspoon ground ginger

1 teaspoon ground mixed spice (allspice)

45 g (¼ cup/1½ oz) rice flour

60 g (¼ cup/2¼ oz) butter

55 g (¼ cup/2 oz) caster (superfine) sugar

115 g (⅓ cup/4 oz) golden syrup or honey

MAKES 24

PREPARATION TIME 20 minutes

COOKING TIME 20–25 minutes

BRANDY SNAPS

1 Use 2 large baking trays; line with baking (parchment) paper. Preheat oven to 190°C (375°F, gas mark 5). Place butter, sugar, syrup, lemon juice and brandy in a pan over low heat until butter melts and sugar dissolves. Remove from heat, mix in the flour and ginger and leave to cool.

2 Put 6 teaspoonfuls of mixture on each tray, spacing them well apart to allow for spreading. Bake brandy snaps for 8–10 minutes or until lightly browned. To allow time for rolling, put the first tray into the oven 5 minutes ahead of the other.

3 Remove from oven; cool snaps on trays for a few seconds. Lift each one off with a palette knife and quickly roll it round the handle of a wooden spoon. (If they are too hard to roll, replace in the oven for a few seconds.) When firm, remove from handle; cool on a wire rack. Repeat with remaining mixture.

4 To fill, spoon the cream into a piping bag fitted with a small star nozzle and pipe into each end of the brandy snaps. Serve as soon as they are filled.

GINGER SNAPS

1 Preheat oven to 190°C (375°F, gas mark 5). Sift the flour and bicarbonate of soda, the salt, ginger and spice into a bowl. Stir in rice flour, rub in the butter and mix in the sugar. Warm syrup and stir in. Knead lightly in the bowl to form a smooth dough.

2 Shape the dough into walnut-sized balls and space well apart on greased baking trays. Bake each batch for 10–12 minutes or until golden. Cool on trays for 5 minutes, then transfer to a wire rack to cool.

Macaroons and Walnut Cookies

Crisp macaroons and walnut cookies make tempting nutty nibbles.

FOR THE MACAROONS

4 sheets of rice paper

125 g (1¼ cups/4½ oz) ground almonds

170 g (¾ cup/6 oz) caster (superfine) sugar

1 teaspoon cornflour (cornstarch)

2 egg whites, lightly beaten

¼ teaspoon vanilla essence (extract)

2 tablespoons chopped almonds

MAKES 24

PREPARATION TIME 15 minutes

COOKING TIME 15–20 minutes

FOR THE WALNUT COOKIES

185 g (1½ cups/6½ oz) plain (all-purpose) flour

125 g (½ cup/4½ oz) butter, at room temperature, in small pieces

110 g (½ cup/4 oz) dark brown sugar

2 teaspoons instant coffee powder or granules

30 g (¼ cup/1 oz) chopped walnuts

MAKES 24

PREPARATION TIME 30 minutes

COOKING TIME 20–30 minutes

MACAROONS

1 Use 2 large baking trays; line with rice paper. Preheat oven to 180°C (350°F, gas mark 4). Combine the almonds, sugar and cornflour in a mixing bowl. Add the egg whites and vanilla essence and beat well to make a fairly stiff mixture.

2 Put teaspoonfuls of mixture in little mounds on the rice paper, spacing them well apart. Or, place mixture in a piping bag fitted with a large, plain nozzle and pipe onto the paper. Press a split almond into the centre of each macaroon. Bake 15–20 minutes, or until pale golden brown. Remove from oven; leave to cool on the trays.

3 Tear off excess rice paper from base of each macaroon (the rice paper is edible).

WALNUT COOKIES

1 Use 2 large baking trays; grease lightly. Preheat oven to 160°C (315°F, gas mark 2–3). Sift flour into a bowl and add the butter. Reserve 1 tbsp sugar; add remainder with the coffee.

2 Rub mixture together until it resembles large breadcrumbs. Mould into small walnut-sized balls. Roll each ball in chopped walnuts.

3 Space the balls well apart on the baking trays and flatten with the bottom of a glass tumbler dipped in the reserved sugar.

4 Bake for 20–30 minutes or until the edges are lightly browned. Leave to cool a little before lifting onto a wire rack to cool completely.

Orange and Pecan Rounds

These are slice-and-bake cookies. The roll of dough is prepared in advance and kept in the refrigerator. Then, when you're ready to make cookies simply slice the roll into rounds, top with pecans and bake.

55 g ($^1/_3$ cup/2 oz) plain wholemeal (all-purpose whole-wheat) flour, plus extra for kneading

55 g ($^1/_2$ oz/2 oz) self-raising (self-rising) white flour

85 g ($^1/_3$ cup/3 oz) light brown sugar

55 g ($^1/_2$ cup/2 oz) ground rice

30 g ($^1/_4$ cup/1 oz) pecan nuts, chopped

Grated zest of 1 orange

80 ml ($^1/_3$ cup/2$^1/_2$ fl oz) sunflower oil

1 large egg

24 pecan nut halves to decorate

MAKES 24

PREPARATION TIME 15 minutes plus 2 hours chilling

COOKING TIME 8–10 minutes per tray

1 Use 2 large baking trays lined with baking (parchment) paper. Put flours, sugar, ground rice, nuts and orange zest in a bowl; stir until well combined.

2 Beat the oil and egg together in a small bowl. Add to the dry ingredients and combine with a fork until mixture comes together to make a dough.

3 Knead dough very lightly on a floured work surface until smooth. Roll into a sausage shape 30 cm (12 in) long; wrap in cling wrap and chill for 2 hours. Dough can be kept in the refrigerator for 2–3 days before baking.

4 Preheat oven to 180°C (350°F, gas mark 4). Unwrap dough and cut into 24 slices. Arrange the slices a little apart on baking trays and top each one with a pecan nut half, pressing it in lightly.

5 Bake for about 10 minutes or until firm to the touch and pale golden. Transfer to a wire rack to cool. Store in an airtight container for up to 5 days.

Try this, too...

Chopped hazelnuts (filberts) can be used in place of the pecans, with whole hazelnuts to decorate.

For Almond Polenta Cookies, mix 55 g ($^1/_3$ cup/2 oz) instant polenta (cornmeal) with 85 g ($^2/_3$ cup/3 oz) icing (confectioners') sugar and 125 g (1 cup/4$^1/_2$ oz) self-raising (self-rising) flour. Rub in 55 g ($^1/_4$ cup/2 oz) butter until mixture resembles fine breadcrumbs. Beat 1 egg with $^1/_2$ tsp almond essence (extract). Add to polenta mixture; mix to a soft dough. Continue as for the main recipe. Scatter flaked almonds on top before baking.

Top Tip

Sunflower oil is one of the most widely used vegetable oils because of its mild flavour. It works well in baked goods in place of saturated fats such as butter. It's a very good source of vitamin E—a powerful antioxidant. Polyunsaturated fats, such as are found in sunflower oil, are more susceptible to rancidity than saturated fats. However, the vitamin E content of sunflower oil helps to stop this oil going rancid.

Brownies

Few people can resist chocolate. Put it in a brownie and it gets even better.
Try serving this version as a quick and easy dessert with ice cream and chocolate sauce.

125 g (½ cup/4½ oz) butter,
at room temperature

200 g (1⅓ cups/7 oz) dark
(semisweet) chocolate, chopped

2 eggs

230 g (1 cup/8 oz) caster
(superfine) sugar

1 teaspoon vanilla essence (extract)

60 g (½ cup/2¼ oz) plain
(all-purpose) flour

2 tablespoons unsweetened cocoa
powder

100 g (1 cup/3½ oz) walnuts,
roughly chopped

MAKES 20–24

PREPARATION TIME 25 minutes

COOKING TIME 30 minutes

1 Use a 20-cm (8-in) square cake tin. Grease and line with baking (parchment) paper. Preheat oven to 180°C (350°F, gas mark 4). Melt the butter and 115 g (¾ cup/4 oz) of the chocolate in a bowl set over gently simmering water; remove from heat and leave to cool.

2 Whisk the eggs in a bowl with electric beaters. Gradually add the sugar; beat continuously until the mixture is thick and foamy and leaves a ribbon-like trail when the beaters are lifted. Add the vanilla essence and the chocolate mixture and blend in thoroughly. Sift flour and cocoa powder over the mixture and scatter in walnuts and the rest of the chocolate. Fold the mixture together with a large spoon.

3 Pour batter into the tin and bake for about 30 minutes or until the top is a rich brown. Place a piece of foil over the top if it looks to be in danger of burning. Cool brownies briefly in the tin; cut into squares. Cool brownies completely on a wire rack. Store in an airtight container; they will keep for 3–4 days.

Try this, too…

For a chocolate topping, beat 125 g (½ cup/4½ oz) butter with 90 g (¾ cup/3¼ oz) icing (confectioners') sugar until creamy. Beat in 1 tbsp water alternately with a further 30 g (¼ cup/1 oz) icing sugar. Beat in a few drops of vanilla essence (extract) and 30 g (¼ cup/1 oz) melted dark or white chocolate.

Add a dash of brandy or almond liqueur to the cake batter.

For Blondies, grease a 30- x 20-cm (12- x 8-in) baking tin. Place 360 g (2 cups/12½ oz) brown sugar and 160 g (⅔ cup/5½ oz) butter in a large bowl. Using electric beaters, beat until light and fluffy. Use a wooden spoon to stir in 2 eggs, one at a time, and ½ tsp almond or vanilla essence (extract). Then sift 185 g (1½ cups/6 oz) plain (all-purpose) flour, 1 tsp baking powder and ½ tsp bicarbonate of soda (baking soda); stir into the butter mixture. Chop 180 g (1¼ cups/6 oz) white chocolate; stir half into the mixture. Place mixture in tin. Sprinkle the top with the rest of the chopped chocolate. Bake 35–40 minutes. Cut into 18 squares when cool.

Top Tip

The hallmarks of a good brownie are a dense chocolate flavour and a fudge-like texture. The texture is achieved by the high proportion of sugar and butter to flour. A good-quality chocolate is important, too.

Sweet Almond Cakes

The ground almonds make these pretty little cakes very moist.
Strawberries add to the soft texture and complement the richness of the nuts.

6 egg whites

185 g (³/₄ cup/6¹/₂ oz) butter, melted

125 g (1 cup/4¹/₂ oz) ground almonds

240 g (1¹/₂ cups/9 oz) icing (confectioners') sugar

75 g (¹/₂ cup/2¹/₂ oz) plain (all-purpose) flour

150 g (1 cup/5¹/₂ oz) strawberries, thinly sliced

Extra icing (confectioners') sugar for dusting

MAKES 12
PREPARATION TIME 20 minutes
COOKING TIME 25 minutes

1 Use 1 x 12-hole (125 ml/¹/₂ cup/ 4 fl oz) muffin pan (see Top Tip). Grease pan and place on a baking tray. Preheat oven to 200°C (400°F, gas mark 6).

2 Place egg whites in a medium bowl; whisk lightly with a fork until combined. Add butter, ground almonds, sugar and flour. Stir with a wooden spoon until just combined.

3 Spoon mixture into prepared pan. Top with strawberry slices. Bake for about 25 minutes. Cool the cakes in the pan for 5 minutes; turn out onto wire rack to finish cooling. Dust with icing sugar.

Try this, too...

For a coffee flavour, dissolve 1 tbsp instant coffee granules in a little boiling water; add to the batter.

For a crunchy texture, chop 65 g (¹/₂ cup/2¹/₂ oz) pistachio nuts and add to the batter.

For Apple and Blueberry Friands, combine 75 g (¹/₂ cup/2¹/₂ oz) plain wholemeal (all-purpose whole-wheat) flour and 30 g (¹/₄ cup/1 oz) self-raising (self-rising) flour. Add 60 g (¹/₂ cup/2¹/₄ oz) sifted icing (confectioners') sugar and 100 g (1 cup/3¹/₂ oz) ground almonds. Add 80 ml (¹/₃ cup/2¹/₂ fl oz) milk, 60 ml (¹/₄ cup/2 fl oz) canola oil, 200 g (1 cup/7 oz) chopped, tart cooking apples and 85 g (¹/₂ cup/ 3 oz) blueberries and stir until just combined. Preheat oven to 200°C (400°F, gas mark 6). Beat 5 egg whites to soft peaks stage and carefully fold into mixture. Spoon into pan. Bake for 25–30 minutes. Leave in pan 10 minutes before turning out. Dust with icing sugar.

Top Tip

These little cakes are known as friands or financiers. The high proportion of ground almonds to flour makes them very moist and beautifully rich. They are most often made in oval or rectangular moulds or boat-shaped ones, but a standard muffin tin can be used.

fruit tarts
& cakes

Quick Cherry Streusel Cake

When you need a cake in a hurry, this is an excellent emergency recipe.
It tastes good eaten hot, straight from the oven, or cold.

FOR THE BASE

185 g (¾ cup/6½ oz) butter, chilled
and cut into cubes

185 g (1 cup/6½ oz) light brown
sugar

Few drops of vanilla essence (extract)

1 egg, lightly beaten

500 g (4 cups/1 lb 2 oz) plain
(all-purpose) flour

1½ tablespoons baking powder

FOR THE FILLING

About 600 g (3 cups/1 lb 5 oz)
cherries (fresh or canned)

90 g (1 cup/3¼ oz) flaked almonds

SERVES 8–10

PREPARATION TIME 25 minutes

COOKING TIME 25 minutes

1 Use a 25-cm (10-in) springform
tin. Grease tin; line base with
baking (parchment) paper. Preheat
oven to 200°C (400°F, gas mark 6).
For the base, place ingredients in a
bowl. Using electric beaters fitted
with dough hooks, mix until large
crumbs form. Or, rub the butter into
the dry ingredients with fingertips.

2 Spread a third of the streusel
mixture into the base of the
tin. Then press a third around the
side of the tin to make an edge.

3 Wash fresh cherries, remove
stalks and stones. Drain tinned
cherries well and stone. Spread the
fruit over streusel base; cover with
remaining streusel. Sprinkle with
almonds. Bake for 25 minutes.

Try this, too...

The streusel cake tastes delicious
with many seasonal fruits. Try
apricots, peaches, puréed plums
or stewed apples. Canned fruit
can also be used; just be sure to
drain off any excess juice.

Change the texture of the streusel
mixture by replacing a quarter of
the flour with an equal weight of
ground hazelnuts (filberts) and a
good pinch of ground cinnamon.

Blueberry Tart

The fluffy topping contrasts with the crunchy shortcrust pastry base in this easy-to-make tart that makes good use of your favourite seasonal berries.

FOR THE PASTRY

250 g (2 cups/9 oz) plain (all-purpose) flour

1 teaspoon baking powder

125 g (½ cup/4½ oz) butter, cut into small pieces

4 tablespoons white (granulated) sugar

1 egg, lightly beaten

FOR THE FILLING

500 ml (2 cups/17 fl oz) milk

125 g (1 cup/4¼ oz) semolina

3–4 tablespoons white (granulated) sugar

2 eggs, separated

1 teaspoon grated lemon zest

2 tablespoons brandy or rum

2 tablespoons sultanas (golden raisins)

About 600 g (4 cups/1 lb 5 oz) blueberries

SERVES 10–12

PREPARATION TIME 1 hour

COOKING TIME 10 minutes plus 15–20 minutes

1 Use a 25-cm (10-in) springform tin. Grease base of tin and line the base with baking (parchment) paper. Preheat oven to 160°C (315°F, gas mark 2–3). To make the pastry, sift flour and baking powder onto a work surface. Add butter, sugar and egg; knead to combine. Shape into a smooth ball, cover in cling wrap and chill for 30 minutes.

2 On a floured surface, roll pastry into a circle 30 cm (12 in) in diameter and use to line base and side of tin. Prick base several times with a fork. Chill pastry again for at least 20 minutes.

3 Cover pastry with baking paper. Half-fill tin with dried beans or rice; bake for 10 minutes. Remove beans and paper.

4 To make filling, bring milk to a boil. Add semolina and sugar in a trickle and simmer for 3 minutes. Quickly stir the egg yolks into the mixture and season to taste with lemon zest and brandy or rum. Add sultanas and leave them to plump up. Meanwhile, in a medium bowl, beat the egg whites until stiff peaks form. Using a metal spoon, gently fold them into the mixture.

5 Stir blueberries into semolina mixture. Spoon onto the pastry base and smooth the surface. Bake for 15–20 minutes or until just firm. Leave to cool in the tin. Serve with whipped cream.

Top Tip

Choose plump berries; those with a 'waxy' bloom are the freshest. To store, place unwashed berries in a single layer on a paper towel on a plate. Cover and refrigerate and use within 5 days.

Mixed Berry Flan

The flan base can be baked the day before it is needed. The creamy topping
and the mixed berries can be added the next day.

FOR THE BASE

90 g (⅓ cup/3¼ oz) butter,
  softened

60 g (⅓ cup/2 oz) brown sugar

2 tablespoons milk

Grated zest of 1 lemon

90 g (⅓ cup/3¼ oz) sour cream

100 g (⅔ cup/3½ oz) wholemeal
  (whole-wheat) flour

½ teaspoon baking powder

FOR THE FILLING

7 g (2 teaspoons) powdered clear
  gelatine

About 250 ml (1 cup/9 fl oz) milk

55 g (¼ cup/2 oz) white
  (granulated) sugar

Few drops of vanilla essence (extract)

Cold water and ice cubes

150 ml (⅔ cup/5 fl oz) cream, for
  whipping

About 600 g (2¾ cups/1 lb 5 oz)
  mixed fresh berries

SERVES 8–10

PREPARATION TIME 1½ hours plus
  chilling time

COOKING TIME 40 minutes

Top Tip

To add a special-occasion touch,
pipe rosettes of whipped cream
on the top of the flan, to decorate.
Use a mixture of seasonal berries
of your choice, or use a selection
of frozen berries that have been
completely defrosted and drained
of any excess juice.

1 Use a 28-cm (11-in) fluted flan
tin. Grease tin. Preheat oven to
160°C (315°F, gas mark 2–3). Place
butter and sugar in a bowl and beat
until light and fluffy. Stir in the milk
and half the lemon zest. Add sour
cream by the tablespoon; stir gently
to combine.

2 Combine the flour and baking
powder. Stir into sour cream
mixture until thoroughly combined.
Transfer mixture to the tin to cover
base and side; smooth surface with
a knife. Bake base for 40 minutes or
until a skewer inserted in the centre
comes out clean. Remove from oven
and leave in the tin for 10 minutes.
Turn out onto a wire rack to cool.

3 For the filling, pour the gelatine
over 60 ml (¼ cup/2 fl oz) cold
water; leave for 5 minutes. Place
milk, sugar, vanilla and remaining
lemon zest in a pan; bring to a boil.
Remove from heat.

4 Stir the gelatine into the hot
milk mixture. Place the water
and ice cubes in a bowl. Stand pan
in it and stir mixture constantly as
it cools, until it begins to thicken.

5 Whip cream until stiff. Wash
and trim berries and pat dry.
Stir whipped cream into the cooled
vanilla crème mixture and spoon
over the flan base. Refrigerate until
set. Arrange mixed berries on top
and serve.

Rhubarb Meringue Torte

For the best flavour, use fresh young rhubarb for this cake.

FOR THE BASE

3 eggs

Juice and zest of 1 small lemon

125 g (½ cup/4½ oz) butter, softened

115 g (½ cup/4 oz) caster (superfine) sugar

40 g (⅓ cup/1½ oz) cornflour (cornstarch)

155 g (1¼ cups/5½ oz) plain (all-purpose) flour

1 teaspoon baking powder

½ teaspoon ground cinnamon

FOR THE FILLING

500 g (4 cups/1 lb 2 oz) rhubarb

115 g (½ cup/4 oz) white (granulated) sugar

1 tablespoon honey

3 tablespoons apricot jam

25 g (1 oz/¼ cup) toasted flaked almonds

1 Use a 24-cm (9½-in) springform tin. Grease tin; line base with baking (parchment) paper. Preheat oven to 200°C (400°F, gas mark 6).

2 Separate 2 eggs, keeping egg whites for filling. Combine the whole egg, egg yolks and the other ingredients for the base in a bowl; beat with a wooden spoon until the mixture is smooth. Spoon into tin.

3 Peel and wash rhubarb and cut into 2.5-cm (1-in) pieces. Place over the base. Sprinkle with sugar, reserving 1 tbsp. Bake the torte for about 40 minutes.

4 Meanwhile, beat the egg whites until stiff peaks form, gradually adding the remaining sugar and the honey. Remove torte from oven and pipe meringue mixture onto it, first in a lattice pattern, then in rosettes.

5 Return torte to the oven and bake for further 15 minutes, until golden on top. Remove from the oven and stand the tin on a wire rack for a few minutes. Turn torte out onto rack and leave to cool completely.

6 Once cool, spread the apricot jam around the side and press the toasted flaked almonds onto it. This torte can be decorated with a few small pieces of lightly stewed rhubarb, if desired.

SERVES 8

PREPARATION TIME 25 minutes

COOKING TIME 40 minutes plus 15 minutes

Berry Cheese Tart

A very thin, crisp pastry case is filled with a creamy orange-flavoured filling
and covered with strawberries and blueberries. A sweet fruit glaze adds the finishing touch.
You can vary the fruits and berries used depending on the season.

FOR THE PASTRY

125 g (1 cup/4½ oz) plain
(all-purpose) flour

60 g (¼ cup/2 oz) unsalted butter,
at room temperature

2 tablespoons caster (superfine)
sugar

2 egg yolks

FOR THE FILLING

225 g (1 cup/8 oz) reduced-fat
soft cheese or ricotta

1 tablespoon clear honey

Grated zest of 1 orange

1 tablespoon orange juice

250 g (1⅔ cups/9 oz) ripe
strawberries, quartered

50 g (⅓ cup/2 oz) blueberries

4 tablespoons redcurrant jelly

SERVES 6

PREPARATION TIME 30 minutes plus
1½ hours for chilling and setting

COOKING TIME 15–20 minutes

1 Use a 20-cm (8-in) fluted flan tin with a loose base. Sift flour onto a work surface; make a well in the centre. Place butter, sugar and egg yolks in the well and, using the fingertips of one hand, work these ingredients together. Then draw in flour from the edge and work to a smooth paste. Wrap in cling wrap and chill for 30 minutes.

2 Roll out the dough on a floured surface to line base and side of tin. Chill for 30 minutes. Preheat the oven to 190°C (375°F, gas mark 5).

3 Line pastry case with baking (parchment) paper and fill with dried beans or rice. Bake for about 12 minutes or until lightly browned. Remove paper and beans; bake for a further 5 minutes or until cooked through. Allow pastry case to cool; carefully remove from tin.

4 For the filling, mix the cheese, honey, orange zest and juice together until smooth. Spoon the filling into the case and spread it evenly to the rim.

5 Arrange the berries on top of the filling. Gently heat the jelly until melted and smooth; brush it generously over berries. Refrigerate to cool and set. This dessert should be served within 2 hours of adding the filling.

Try this, too…

For Raspberry and Peach Tart, instead of the honey and orange juice, flavour cheese with 1 tsp rosewater, or to taste, and 1 tbsp caster (superfine) sugar. Replace strawberries and blueberries with 125 g (1 cup/4½ oz) raspberries and 3 ripe peaches, cut into neat slices. Use melted apricot jam for the glaze.

For Mango and Passionfruit Tart, instead of the orange zest and juice, flavour the cheese with the sieved pulp of 2 passionfruit. Replace berries with 1 large ripe mango cut into neat slices and glaze with melted apricot jam.

Topsy-turvy Apple Tart

This delectable tart is turned out upside-down to serve and resembles the French tarte tatin. The shortcrust pastry is made with reduced-fat soft cheese and butter and there is a lot of juicy fruit filling.

FOR THE PASTRY

115 g (1 cup/4 oz) plain (all-purpose) flour

30 g (2 tbsp/1 oz) unsalted butter, chilled and cut into cubes

30 g (1 oz) reduced-fat soft cheese

FOR THE FILLING

5 dessert apples, about 600 g (1 lb 5 oz) in total

50 g (¼ cup/1¾ oz) dark brown sugar

1 tablespoon lemon juice

30 g (¼ cup/1 oz) sultanas (golden raisins)

1 teaspoon ground mixed spice (allspice)

1 teaspoon finely grated lemon zest

FOR LEMON AND HONEY YOGURT

250 g (1 cup/9 oz) natural (plain) low-fat yogurt

1 tablespoon clear honey

1 teaspoon finely grated lemon zest

SERVES 4

PREPARATION TIME 45 minutes

COOKING TIME 20 minutes

1 Use a 23-cm (9-in) cake tin (not one with a loose base) or a pie plate. Sift flour into a large bowl and rub in butter and cheese until mixture resembles breadcrumbs. Sprinkle with 2 tbsp cold water and mix in, using a round-bladed knife, to form a soft dough. Gather into a smooth ball. Wrap in cling film and chill for 30 minutes.

2 Preheat oven to 200°C (400°F, gas mark 6). Peel and thickly slice the apples. Place sugar and lemon juice in a medium pan and heat, stirring, until sugar dissolves. Add apples; cover and cook over a low heat for 8–10 minutes, stirring occasionally, until the fruit is just softening but is not breaking up.

3 With a slotted spoon, transfer apples to the tin, slightly over-lapping the slices. Stir the sultanas, mixed spice and zest into the juice in the pan; simmer for 2–3 minutes. Pour mixture over the apples and set aside to cool slightly.

4 Roll out the dough on a lightly floured work surface to a round about 25 cm (10 in) in diameter. Place over the apple filling and tuck the edges down inside the tin. Bake for 20 minutes or until the pastry is golden brown.

5 Leave the tart to cool in the tin for 5–10 minutes, then carefully invert it onto a plate. Combine the yogurt, honey and lemon zest and serve with slices of the warm tart.

Try this, too...

If you're busy, make the pastry and the filling a day ahead. Assemble tart and bake just before serving.

Instead of lemon zest, use grated orange zest in the fruit filling and yogurt accompaniment.

For a Pear and Walnut Tart, use firm, ripe pears instead of apples. Add 30 g (¼ cup/1 oz) chopped pecans or walnuts with sultanas and lemon zest.

Spiced Apple and Blueberry Pie

Here's the easiest fruit pie you could hope to make. A crumbly, part-wholemeal shortcrust pastry is wrapped around a spiced mixture of apples and blueberries to make a rough parcel with an open top. There's no flan tin to line or pie dish to cover.

FOR THE PASTRY

85 g (2/3 cup/3 oz) plain (all-purpose) flour

75 g (1/2 cup/2 1/2 oz) plain wholemeal (whole-wheat) flour

1 teaspoon ground mixed spice (allspice)

85 g (1/3 cup/3 oz) unsalted butter, chilled and diced

30 g (1/4 cup/1 oz) icing (confectioners') sugar, sifted

1 egg yolk

FOR THE FILLING

4 cooking apples, about 600 g (1 lb 5 oz) in total

100 g (2/3 cup/3 1/2 oz) blueberries

45 g (1/4 cup/1 1/2 oz) dark brown sugar

1 teaspoon ground cinnamon

1/4 teaspoon freshly grated nutmeg

1 egg white, lightly beaten

SERVES 6

PREPARATION TIME 20 minutes plus at least 30 minutes for chilling

COOKING TIME 30–35 minutes

1 To make the pastry, sift white and wholemeal flours and the spice into a bowl; tip in the bran left in the sieve. Rub in the butter until the mixture resembles fine breadcrumbs. Stir in sugar.

2 Mix the egg yolk with 1 tbsp cold water. Add to the flour mixture and mix to form a soft dough, adding a few drops more water, if needed. Gather dough into a small ball; wrap in cling wrap and chill for at least 30 minutes.

3 Preheat oven to 190°C (375°F, gas mark 5). Peel and slice the apples and mix with blueberries. Combine the sugar, cinnamon and nutmeg. Reserve 1 tbsp and stir the rest into the fruit.

4 Roll out dough on a non-stick baking sheet to make a 30-cm (12-in) round and brush all over with some of the egg white.

5 Pile fruit mixture in the middle of the pastry, then draw the edges up over the fruit, leaving the centre open. Brush case with the remaining egg white and sprinkle with the reserved spiced sugar.

6 Bake for 30–35 minutes or until the pastry is golden brown and the apples are tender. Serve warm with vanilla yogurt, if liked.

Try this, too...

For a pastry with more texture, roll out the dough on a surface lightly sprinkled with fine oatmeal.

To make a deep-dish pie, replace blueberries with blackberries, and sprinkle the fruit with the sugar and 1 tsp ground allspice. Place fruit in a deep 23-cm (9-in) pie dish. Brush rim with water. Roll out the pastry to cover the dish. Place over filling and press edges to the rim to seal. Crimp edges and brush pastry with egg white. Sprinkle with sugar and a pinch of ground allspice. Preheat oven to 190°C (375°F, gas mark 5) and cook pie for 30–35 minutes or until pastry is golden brown.

Apple and Grape Pie

The pastry top with its tangy lemon icing complements the sweet, juicy filling
of apples and grapes braised in white wine.

FOR THE PASTRY

500 g (4 cups/1 lb 2 oz) plain
(all-purpose) flour

¼ teaspoon baking powder

140 g (⅔ cup/5 oz) white
(granulated) sugar

2 eggs

250 g (1 cup/9 oz) butter, softened

FOR THE FILLING

8 cooking apples, about 1 kilo
(2 lb 4 oz) in total

125 g (¾ cup/5 oz) grapes

125 ml (½ cup/5 fl oz)
white wine

1 tablespoon white (granulated)
sugar

1 teaspoon ground cinnamon

1 egg yolk

2 tablespoons lemon juice

60 g (½ cup/2¼ oz) icing
(confectioners') sugar

1 Use a 28-cm (11¼-in) springform tin. Sift flour and baking
powder into a large bowl. Make a
well in the centre; place the sugar,
eggs and butter in it. Using the
fingertips of one hand, draw all the
ingredients in the centre together,
then draw in flour from the edge to
make a soft dough. Knead well and
gather into a smooth ball. Wrap in
cling wrap and chill for 30 minutes.

2 Preheat oven to 200°C (400°F,
gas mark 6). Peel, halve and
core apples. Remove grape stems.
Combine the apples, grapes, white
wine, sugar and cinnamon in a pan.
Simmer gently over medium heat
for 5 minutes. Leave to cool for a
few minutes.

3 Roll out two-thirds of the dough
on a floured surface. Grease tin.
Line with pastry, shaping an edge
about 2.5 cm (1 in) high. Prick base
several times with a fork. Bake for
10 minutes.

4 Spread fruit mixture on pastry
base. Roll out remaining pastry
and place on top of filling. Brush
with egg yolk and bake 25 minutes.
Leave to cool. Mix lemon juice and
icing sugar together to make a fairly
runny consistency. Drizzle over pie.

SERVES 10–12

PREPARATION TIME 40 minutes

COOKING TIME 10 minutes plus
25 minutes

Latticed Apple Pie

The lattice pattern is a classic decoration for shortcrust pies. It works well not only on fruit such as apples, cherries or plums, but also on a poppyseed mixture or jam.

FOR THE PASTRY

250 g (2 cups/9 oz) plain (all-purpose) flour

1/2 teaspoon baking powder

150 g (2/3 cup/5 1/2 oz) butter

2 tablespoons honey

2 egg yolks

2 tablespoons water

FOR THE FILLING

6 apples, about 600 g (1 lb 5 oz) in total

1 teaspoon lemon juice

125 ml (1/2 cup/4 fl oz) cream

2 eggs

3 egg yolks

1 teaspoon vanilla essence (extract)

3 tablespoons sugar

70 g (2/3 cup/2 1/2 oz) ground almonds

SERVES 10–12

PREPARATION TIME 45 minutes

COOKING TIME 10 minutes plus 20 minutes

1 Use a 26-cm (10½-in) spring-form tin. Grease tin. To make the pastry, sift the flour and baking powder into a bowl. Add remaining ingredients; knead to form a dough. Gather into a smooth ball, wrap in cling wrap and chill for 30 minutes.

2 Set about one-fifth of pastry aside. Roll out the rest of the pastry to line the base of the tin and to make an edge 2.5 cm (1 in) high. Prick the base several times with a fork. Chill for 20 minutes.

3 Preheat oven to 180°C (350°F, gas mark 4). Cover pastry base with baking (parchment) paper and dried beans. Bake for 10 minutes.

4 Peel, core and slice the apples. Drizzle with lemon juice.

5 Set 1 tbsp cream aside and mix remaining cream, eggs, 2 egg yolks, vanilla and sugar together. Add the almonds.

6 Fill the pastry case with apples. Pour cream mixture over fruit.

7 Increase oven temperature to 200°C (400°F, gas mark 6). Cut remaining pastry into thin strips and arrange on top of filling in a lattice pattern. Combine remaining egg yolk and cream and brush the lattice with the mixture. Bake for 20 minutes. Serve hot or cold.

Viennese Apple Strudel

A covering of wafer-thin strudel pastry ensures that fruit such as apples, sour cherries and apricots retain their juice and flavour when cooked.

FOR THE PASTRY

250 g (2 cups/9 oz) plain (all-purpose) flour

1 tablespoon oil

1 egg

1 tablespoon butter

FOR THE FILLING

125 g (½ cup/4½ oz) butter

4 tablespoons fresh breadcrumbs

85 g (⅔ cup/3 oz) sultanas (golden raisins)

7 cooking apples, about 2 kilos (4lb 8 oz) in total

85 g (½ cup/3 oz) chopped almonds

1 teaspoon ground cinnamon

115 g (½ cup/4 oz) caster (superfine) sugar

2 tablespoons icing (confectioners') sugar

MAKES 1 large or 2 small strudels

PREPARATION TIME 1½ hours

COOKING TIME 30–40 minutes

1 To make the pastry, sift the flour onto a work surface and make a well in the centre. Place the oil, egg and 125 ml (½ cup/4 fl oz) lukewarm water in it. Using a flat-bladed knife, start from outer rim and work the flour into the liquid ingredients. Electric beaters can be used, if preferred.

2 Knead for about 10 minutes to make a smooth dough. Shape into a ball. Heat a bowl and invert it over the dough, leaving it for about 45 minutes. Maintain temperature of the bowl by repeatedly covering it with a warm, damp cloth.

3 To make the filling, melt all but 1 tbsp of butter in a pan. Add breadcrumbs and fry until golden. Cover sultanas with warm water and let soak for 15 minutes; drain. Peel and core apples; slice thinly. Combine sultanas, apples, almonds, cinnamon, sugar and breadcrumbs in a bowl.

4 Preheat oven to 200°C (400°F, gas mark 6). Spread out a clean cloth kitchen towel, sprinkle thickly with flour and place the dough on it. Roll dough out very thinly.

5 Melt 1 tbsp butter and brush the dough with it. Dust hands with flour and slide them under the pastry into a position that makes it possible to stretch the dough well in all directions. The dough must be stretched so thinly that the pattern of the towel is visible through it.

6 Spread filling over the pastry, keeping clear of the sides and lower edge. Begin at the narrow end of towel and carefully roll strudel up, using the towel to help. Firmly press the edge and sides together. Leave whole or cut in half.

7 Grease a baking tray; carefully place strudel on it and bake for 30–40 minutes. Sprinkle with icing sugar while still warm.

Top Tip

Apples supply vitamin C as well as some potassium. It's best to eat the peel to get the full measure of fibre. Some of the fibre in apples is pectin, which is thought to help lower blood cholesterol. It is best to store apples in the refrigerator because they tend to deteriorate quickly at room temperature; the flesh turns mushy and the apples lose some of their vitamin content.

Apricot Chocolate Roll

This combination of chocolate, cream and apricots is a sumptuous treat.
The flavour of fresh summer apricots is hard to beat.

FOR THE CAKE

3 eggs

85 g (⅓ cup/3 oz) caster (superfine) sugar

45 g (⅓ cup/1½ oz) plain (all-purpose) flour

½ teaspoon baking powder

2 tablespoons cocoa powder

FOR THE FILLING AND DECORATION

125 ml (½ cup/4 fl oz) cream, for whipping

350 g (1⅔ cups/12 oz) cream cheese

2–3 tablespoons white (granulated) sugar

1 tablespoon apricot or orange liqueur

300 g (10 oz) apricots (about 8 apricots)

Icing (confectioners') sugar, for dusting

SERVES 6–8

PREPARATION TIME 30 minutes

COOKING TIME 12–14 minutes

1 Use a 33- x 23-cm (13- x 9-in) Swiss roll tin. Grease tin; line with baking (parchment) paper. Preheat oven to 200°C (400°F, gas mark 6). Beat eggs and sugar with electric beaters until very pale and fluffy. Sift dry ingredients onto the mixture and fold in carefully using a metal spoon. Spread mixture onto baking paper. Bake 12–14 minutes, then remove from oven, cover with a kitchen towel and leave to cool. Turn out onto a towel dusted with icing sugar. Peel off baking paper.

2 Whip cream until stiff. Beat the cream cheese, sugar and liqueur in a bowl with a wooden spoon until smooth. Fold in the cream. Spread over sponge, leaving 2.5 cm (1 in) at the far long edge uncovered.

3 Pour boiling hot water over the apricots; skin, halve and stone. Cut apricots into small pieces and sprinkle them over cream mixture.

4 Starting from a long side, roll up sponge using towel to help. Place roll on a tray lined with foil and chill in freezer for 20 minutes. To serve, dust with icing sugar.

Top Tip

Dried apricots can be used instead of fresh in this recipe. Soak about 180 g (1 cup/6 oz) dried apricots in water overnight. In a pan, cook the drained apricots for 10 minutes with 90 ml (⅓ cup/3 fl oz) orange juice and a little sugar.

Fig Tart with Orange Yogurt

The delicious taste, texture and colour of fresh figs are shown off to advantage.
Either greenish-yellow or dark purple-skinned figs can be used. Peel figs if the skin tastes bitter.

FOR THE BASE

2 eggs

85 g (⅓ cup/3 oz) caster (superfine) sugar

90 g (¾ cup/3¼ oz) plain (all-purpose) flour

1 egg white

FOR THE FILLING

1 orange

8 ripe figs

250 g (1 cup/9 oz) natural (plain) yogurt

1 tablespoon icing (confectioners') sugar

60 ml (¼ cup/2 fl oz) tablespoons orange liqueur

SERVES 8

PREPARATION TIME 40 minutes plus 1 hour cooling time

COOKING TIME 25 minutes

1 Use a 22-cm (8½-in) springform tin. Grease tin; line base with baking (parchment) paper. Separate eggs. Beat yolks and 1 tbsp warm water for 3 minutes with electric beaters. Add sugar and beat until mixture is very pale and creamy.

2 Preheat oven to 180°C (350°F, gas mark 4). Sift the flour onto egg mixture and fold in carefully. Beat egg whites until stiff, then pile them on the mixture and fold in.

3 Place mixture in tin; smooth surface. Bake for 25 minutes until golden. Remove from tin and place on a wire rack to cool.

4 Grate the zest of the orange and squeeze the juice. Wash figs; cut each one into 8 segments.

5 Combine yogurt with icing sugar and zest. Combine juice and orange liqueur.

6 Place tart base on a serving platter. Drizzle juice mixture over it, then spread with yogurt. Arrange fig segments on top. Cover tart with cling wrap and place in the refrigerator for 1 hour. Remove and serve as soon as possible.

Top Tip

A hot minted chocolate drink goes well with this tart. Place 1 tbsp mint leaves in a bowl. Boil 250 ml (1 cup/9 fl oz) water and pour it over the leaves; let stand for about 10 minutes. Heat 375 ml (1½ cups/ 13 fl oz) milk. Break 100 g (⅔ cup/ 3½ oz) dark (semisweet) chocolate into pieces; add to hot milk. Stir until the chocolate has dissolved. Strain the mint and add the liquid to chocolate milk. Reheat. Sweeten to taste with sugar.

Crunchy Apricot Tart

Make the most of apricots when they're in season by using them in this attractive tart.
It has a sweet orange shortcrust base and is topped with a crumbly oat and nut mixture.
Serve slightly warm for dessert or with morning coffee or afternoon tea.

FOR THE PASTRY

125 g (1 cup/4½ oz) plain (all-purpose) flour

60 g (¼ cup/2 oz) unsalted butter, chilled and cut into small pieces

30 g (¼ cup/1 oz) icing (confectioners') sugar

Finely grated zest of 1 orange

1 tablespoon orange juice

1 egg yolk

FOR THE FILLING

500 g (1 lb 2 oz) ripe apricots, stoned and quartered (about 10 apricots)

3 tablespoons orange juice

½ teaspoon ground mixed spice (allspice)

1 tablespoon clear honey

FOR THE TOPPING

50 g (½ cup/1½ oz) original rolled (porridge) oats

2 tablespoons sultanas (golden raisins)

2 tablespoons hazelnuts (filberts), chopped

1 tablespoon each sunflower and sesame seeds

1 tablespoon clear honey

1 tablespoon fresh orange juice

SERVES 6

PREPARATION TIME 35–40 minutes plus cooling and 30 minutes chilling

COOKING TIME 30 minutes

1 Use a 23-cm (9-in) non-stick flan tin with a loose base. For the pastry, sift flour into a bowl. Add butter; rub in with fingertips until the mixture resembles fine crumbs. Stir in the sugar and zest. Lightly beat orange juice with egg yolk. Add to flour mixture; mix in using a round-bladed knife to form a soft dough. Draw into a smooth ball, wrap in cling wrap and chill for 30 minutes.

2 To make filling, place apricots in a heavy-based pan with the orange juice and mixed spice and bring to a boil. Cover tightly and cook on low heat for 20–25 minutes, stirring occasionally, until mixture is thick. Allow to cool; stir in honey.

3 Preheat oven to 190°C (375°F, gas mark 5). Roll out pastry on a lightly floured surface to line tin. Prick base with a fork. Line the case with baking (parchment) paper and half-fill with dried beans or rice.

4 Bake pastry for 10 minutes; remove beans and paper. Bake a further 5 minutes, then set aside. Reduce oven temperature to 180°C (350°F, gas mark 4).

5 To make the topping, combine the oats, sultanas, hazelnuts, sunflower and sesame seeds. Mix honey with orange juice; stir into the oat mixture.

6 Spread the cooled apricot filling evenly over the tart case. Spoon oat mixture on top and press down lightly. Bake 12–15 minutes or until topping is pale golden. Serve warm.

Try this, too...

For a Plum Muesli Tart, flavour the pastry with lemon zest and juice instead of orange. For the filling, use halved and stoned plums or damsons instead of apricots, and poach with 80 ml (⅓ cup/2½ fl oz) apple juice and ½ tsp ground star anise. Cool and then stir in the honey. For the topping, mix 50 g (½ cup/1½ oz) rolled (porridge) oats, 1 small apple, peeled and coarsely grated, and a few dried cranberries and flaked almonds. Bake as for the main recipe.

Apricot Danish

Layers of filo pastry encase a cream-cheese filling topped with apricot purée and nuts.

140 g (³/₄ cup/5 oz) dried apricots, chopped

115 g (¹/₂ cup/4 oz) brown sugar, plus extra 2 tablespoons

125 ml (¹/₂ cup/4 fl oz) water

2 teaspoons vanilla essence (extract)

¹/₂ teaspoon ground ginger

115 g (¹/₂ cup/4 oz) low-fat cream cheese

6 gingersnaps, crushed

12 sheets frozen filo pastry, thawed

3 tablespoons unsalted butter, melted

3 tablespoons chopped hazelnuts (filberts) or walnuts

70 g (2¹/₂ oz/¹/₃ cup) apricot preserve

1 tablespoon icing (confectioners') sugar

SERVES 8

PREPARATION TIME 25 minutes

COOKING TIME 45 minutes

1 Combine the apricots, half the brown sugar and all the water in a pan. Slowly bring to a simmer; cook 10 minutes or until soft. Place in food processor, add 1 tsp vanilla essence and process until smooth.

2 Place remaining brown sugar, the ground ginger, remaining vanilla and all the cream cheese in a bowl. Use electric beaters to mix thoroughly. Combine gingersnap crumbs and the 2 tbsp brown sugar in a small bowl.

3 Place filo on a work surface and cover with a damp cloth towel. Spray a baking sheet with non-stick cooking spray. Lay 2 sheets of filo on the sheet and brush with melted butter. Sprinkle with 1 tbsp ginger-snap crumbs. Repeat the layering with more filo, butter and crumbs, reserving a little melted butter.

4 Preheat oven to 190°C (375°F, gas mark 5). Spoon the cream-cheese mixture down the centre of the dough in a strip 4 cm (1½ in) wide; stop about 2.5 cm (1 in) short of the narrow ends. Spoon apricot in 2 strips 4 cm (1½ in) wide, one on either side of the cheese. Roll the long sides of the pastry in towards the centre until they just begin to cover the apricot. Roll narrow sides in just to the filling; press firmly to seal. If not firmly sealed, the filo may start to unfold as it bakes. The finished size should be about 33 x 17 cm (13 x 6½ in).

5 Brush the crust with remaining butter; sprinkle chopped nuts over filling. Bake for 30–35 minutes or until golden and crisped. In the meantime, melt apricot preserve in 1 tbsp water in a small saucepan over low heat. Brush preserve over warm cooked pastry and sprinkle with icing sugar to serve.

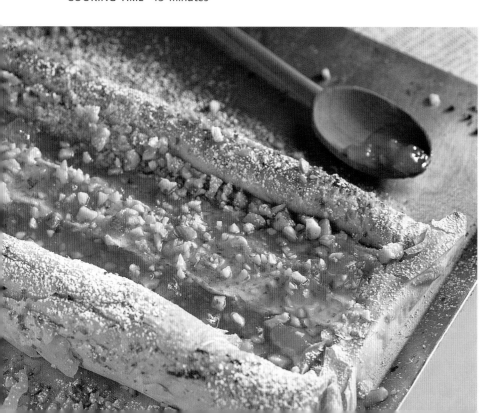

Blueberry Coffee Cake

Brown sugar, berries and cinnamon add great flavour to this melt-in-your-mouth snack.

400 g (2½ cups/14 oz) fresh or frozen blueberries

60 g (⅓ cup/2¼ oz) soft brown sugar

1 teaspoon ground cinnamon

125 g (½ cup/4½ oz) butter

220 g (1 cup/8 oz) caster (superfine) sugar

1 large egg and 1 large egg white

1 tablespoon grated lemon zest

310 g (2½ cups/11 oz) self-raising (self-rising) flour

310 ml (1¼ cups/11 fl oz) reduced-fat milk

SERVES 16

PREPARATION TIME 20 minutes

COOKING TIME 40 minutes

1 Use a 33- x 23-cm (13- x 9-in) baking pan; grease and flour pan. Preheat oven to 180°C (350°F, gas mark 4). In a small bowl, toss 310 g (2 cups/7 oz) blueberries in the brown sugar and cinnamon.

2 Using electric beaters at high speed, cream butter and sugar in a large bowl until light and fluffy; about 4 minutes. Add egg and egg white and beat for 2 minutes; add lemon zest. Reduce speed to low. In 3 batches, add flour alternately with the milk. Stop beating occasionally to scrape down the side of the bowl. Do not overbeat.

3 Spread half the batter into pan; sprinkle with blueberry mixture. Spoon remaining batter on top and spread evenly. Swirl a knife through the batter several times, then top mixture with remaining blueberries.

4 Bake for 40–45 minutes or until a skewer inserted in the centre comes out with moist crumbs on it. Cool in the pan on a wire rack for 15 minutes. Cut into 16 pieces and serve warm or at room temperature.

Top Tip

Traditional coffee cake recipes often use at least 2 eggs. Using 1 egg plus an egg white ensures that the cake has a light, delicate texture and a lower fat content. Reduced-fat milk trims back more of the fat and cholesterol content.

Quince Tart

A quince is a large, pear-shaped, yellow-skinned fruit with a distinctive, mellow flavour.
Use 3 or 4 firm pears or tart apples, if preferred.

FOR THE PASTRY

1 lemon

150 g (1 cup/5 ½ oz) wholemeal
   (whole-wheat) flour

55 g (¼ cup/2 oz) white
   (granulated) sugar

70 g (⅓ cup/2 ½ oz) butter,
   softened

FOR THE FILLING

About 500 g (1 lb 2 oz) quinces

1 orange

125 ml (½ cup/4 fl oz) apple juice

30 g (2 tbsp) white (granulated)
   sugar

90 g (¾ cup/3 oz) slivered almonds

2 eggs

150 g (⅔ cup/5 oz) cream cheese
   or mascarpone cheese

1 tablespoon honey

1 teaspoon ground cinnamon

1 Use a 26-cm (10½-in) spring-form tin. Grate half the lemon. Place zest, flour, sugar, 2 tbsp water and the butter in a bowl and knead to a smooth dough; add more water if needed. Line the tin with pastry, shaping an edge 2.5 cm (1 in) high. Chill for 30 minutes.

2 Preheat oven to 200°C (400°F, gas mark 6). Quarter, peel and core quinces; cut into slices 1 cm (½ in) thick. Peel a few thin strips of zest from the orange. Cut orange in half; squeeze out the juice. Bring juice, zest, apple juice and sugar to a boil. Add quince slices and poach over low heat for 15 minutes. Strain, retaining the liquid; allow to cool. Discard zest.

3 Sprinkle the almonds over the pastry base. Pre-bake pastry for 15 minutes. Reduce heat to 180°C (350°F, gas mark 4). Place quinces on pastry base. Whisk the reserved cooled cooking liquid with the eggs and cream cheese; pour over the fruit. Bake for a further 30 minutes.

4 Combine honey and cinnamon. Spread over tart. Leave tart in the turned-off oven for 10 minutes. Remove sides of springform tin. Let tart cool on the base of the tin.

SERVES   8–10

PREPARATION TIME   45 minutes

COOKING TIME   15 minutes plus
   30 minutes

Pear Tart

The delicate flavour of fresh pears is worth waiting for each year.
Although the pears must be ripe, they should be firm enough to slice cleanly and neatly.

FOR THE PASTRY

90 g (¹⁄₃ cup/3¹⁄₄ oz) butter, softened

200 g (1¹⁄₄ cups/6¹⁄₂ oz) plain (all-purpose) flour

40 g (3 tbsp/1¹⁄₂ oz) sugar

1 egg yolk

2 tablespoons rum or apple juice

FOR THE FILLING

2 apples

6 ripe pears

Juice of 1 large lemon

85 ml (¹⁄₃ cup/2¹⁄₂ fl oz) water or pear juice

Pinch each of ground cinnamon and ground cloves

30 g (¹⁄₄ cup/1 oz) chopped pistachio nuts

SERVES 8–10

PREPARATION TIME 35 minutes

COOKING TIME 20 minutes plus 15 minutes

1 Use a 26-cm (10-in) springform tin. Lightly grease tin. For the pastry, place the butter, flour, sugar, egg yolk and rum or apple juice in a bowl; mix lightly. Knead ingredients together by hand or use the dough hooks of an electric mixer.

2 Flour hands and knead dough on a floured board until shiny. Shape into a smooth ball and wrap in cling wrap. Chill for 30 minutes.

3 Meanwhile, peel, quarter and core the apples and 2 pears and cut into pieces.

4 Place apple and pear pieces in a saucepan with the lemon juice, water or pear juice, ground cinnamon and ground cloves.

5 Cover the pan; simmer mixture over low heat until fruit is soft. Cook, uncovered, for 15 minutes until fruit has reduced to a purée. Remove pan from heat. Leave the mixture to cool.

6 Preheat oven to 180°C (350°F, gas mark 4). Roll pastry into a round to fit the base and side of the tin. Spread the fruit purée over the pastry base and pre-bake for about 20 minutes.

7 Meanwhile, peel, quarter and core the remaining pears and cut into neat slices. Arrange over the puréed fruit in the pastry case. Sprinkle the pistachio nuts over the top. Bake for a further 15 minutes. Cool before serving.

Top Tip

An iced-chocolate drink goes well with this pear tart. Place 2 tbsp commercially prepared, bottled, thick chocolate sauce per serving in a tall glass and swirl around to coat the inside. Fill the glass two-thirds full with cold milk. Top with a scoop of vanilla ice cream and a dollop of stiffly whipped cream. Dust with cocoa powder.

Tipsy Orange Cake

Store this cake in an airtight container and let it stand for a couple of days.
You'll be rewarded with a full orange flavour.

FOR THE CAKE

3 eggs, separated, and 1 egg yolk

200 g (¾ cup/7 oz) butter, softened

225 g (1 cup/8 oz) caster (superfine) sugar

2 teaspoons grated orange zest

210 g (1⅔ cups/7 oz) plain (all-purpose) flour

3 teaspoons baking powder

FOR THE GLAZE

125 ml (½ cup/4 fl oz) freshly squeezed orange juice

3 tablespoons orange liqueur

110 g (½ cup/4 oz) white (granulated) sugar

1 teaspoon grated orange zest

1 Use a 24-cm (9½-in) springform tin. Grease the base or line with baking (parchment) paper. Preheat oven to 180°C (350°F, gas mark 4).

2 To make the cake, beat the egg whites until stiff. Using electric beaters, beat the butter, sugar, 4 egg yolks and orange zest in a medium bowl until the mixture is light and fluffy, about 5 minutes.

3 Sift flour and baking powder; stir into the butter mixture a tablespoon at a time. Fold egg white into mixture with a metal spoon.

4 Transfer mixture to the tin and smooth the top. Bake cake for 35–40 minutes until golden brown. Leave in the tin.

5 Stir ingredients for the glaze in a small saucepan over low heat until sugar dissolves. Prick hot cake a few times with a fork and drizzle with glaze. Stand tin on a wire rack and leave cake to cool completely.

Try this, too...

To make a Tipsy Lemon Cake, use lemon juice and zest and a lemon or almond-flavoured liqueur.

SERVES 8

PREPARATION TIME 20 minutes

COOKING TIME 35–40 minutes

108

Large Orange Tart

This delicious tart is just the right size for a big party. It's simple and quick
to prepare, making it an ideal recipe for a busy cook.

FOR THE PASTRY

250 g (2 cups/9 oz) plain
(all-purpose) flour

55 g (¼ cup/2 oz) caster
(superfine) sugar

125 g (½ cup/4½ oz) butter,
softened

1 teaspoon baking powder

1 egg

FOR THE FILLING

3 large oranges

2 egg yolks

75 g (⅓ cup/3 oz) caster
(superfine) sugar

14 g (1 tablespoon) powdered clear
gelatine

500 ml (2 cups/17 fl oz) fresh
orange juice

185 ml (½ cup/4 fl oz) cream,
for whipping

1 Use a large baking tray; grease
lightly. Mix pastry ingredients
in a bowl; knead to make a dough.
Knead into a smooth ball, wrap in
cling wrap and chill for 30 minutes.

2 Preheat oven to 180°C (350°F,
gas mark 4). Roll out pastry on
a floured surface into a circle 35 cm
(14 in) in diameter. Place on baking
tray; prick several times with a fork.
Bake for 15 minutes. Remove to a
platter while still warm.

3 Peel 3 oranges, removing all
the white pith. Hold oranges
over a bowl to catch any juice;
segment the fruit by slicing neatly
between the membranes. Beat egg
yolks and sugar until very pale and
creamy. Arrange two-thirds of the
orange segments over base.

4 Soak the gelatine in cold water.
Bring 2 tbsp orange juice to the
boil and dissolve gelatine in it. Stir
into the remaining juice and add to
egg mixture, stirring all the time.
Chill until mixture begins to set.

5 Meanwhile, whip cream until
stiff. When the mixture has set
a little, fold in the cream. Place a
piece of baking (parchment) paper
5 cm (2 in) high around the pastry
base to support the filling while it
sets. Spread the filling onto the tart
and refrigerate until set. Remove
paper collar. Decorate the tart with
the remaining orange segments.

SERVES 12–16

PREPARATION TIME 15 minutes

COOKING TIME 30 minutes

Mexican Banana Cake

This distinctive cake is made with a fragrant banana and sweet potato purée.
It is served as a dessert in Mexico.

500 g (1 lb 2 oz) sweet potatoes
500 g (1 lb 2 oz) bananas
500 ml (2 cups/17 fl oz) milk
1 vanilla bean
3 eggs
110 g (½ cup/3 oz) white
    (granulated) sugar
160 g (⅔ cup/6 oz) butter, softened
60 ml (¼ cup/2 fl oz) rum
420 g (1⅓ cups/15 oz) raspberry
    jam

SERVES 6–8
PREPARATION TIME 40 minutes
COOKING TIME 1 hour

1 Use a 20-cm (8-in) springform tin. Peel sweet potatoes and bananas and slice into rounds.

2 Place the potato and banana slices in a large pan and cover with the milk; top up with water if there is not enough milk. Bring to the boil. Cook slices over low heat for 20 minutes or until cooked and softened.

3 Drain potato and banana in a sieve. Purée in a blender; set aside. Preheat oven to 200°C (350°F, gas mark 4).

4 Slice the vanilla bean in half lengthwise and scrape out the seeds with a sharp knife. In a small bowl, beat the eggs and sugar with electric beaters until the mixture is pale and fluffy.

5 Add 125 g (½ cup/4½ oz) butter, the rum, the vanilla seeds and the purée to the egg mixture. Stir until combined and smooth.

6 Grease springform tin with the remaining butter. Place in an ovenproof dish which is larger and a little higher than the springform tin. Pour lukewarm water into the dish, filling it to just over one-third full. Bake cake for 40 minutes.

7 Remove cake from oven and allow to cool in the tin. Turn out onto a serving platter. Heat jam over a low heat and brush over the cake. Serve immediately.

Top Tip

It's important that the springform tin used to bake this cake in can be relied upon not to leak. If you have doubts, use a soufflé mould.

Banana Cream Pie

The wafer crust contrasts beautifully with the creamy interior of this pie.

48 vanilla wafers (about 225 g/8 oz)

2 tablespoons honey

115 g (½ cup/4 oz) white (granulated) sugar

40 g (⅓ cup/1½ oz) plain (all-purpose) flour

750 ml (3 cups/26 fl oz) milk

2 egg yolks and 1 whole egg

1 tablespoon butter

1 tablespoon vanilla essence (extract)

6 large bananas

60 ml (¼ cup/2 fl oz) orange juice

2 tablespoons apricot preserve

SERVES 8

PREPARATION TIME 30 minutes plus chilling

COOKING TIME 15 minutes

1 Use a 23-cm (9-in) pie plate. Grease lightly. Preheat oven to 180°C (350°F, gas mark 4). Place the wafers, honey and 2 tbsp water in a food processor; process to make fine crumbs. Press into pie plate to form a crust. Bake until set, about 10 minutes. Cool on a wire rack.

2 Whisk the sugar and flour in a saucepan until blended. Whisk in the milk slowly and bring to a simmer over medium heat. Whisk egg yolks and egg in a bowl; whisk in 250 ml (1 cup/9 fl oz) of the hot milk mixture. Return the mixture to pan (this avoids curdling). Cook, whisking, until mixture comes to a full boil and thickens. Remove from heat, then whisk in the butter and vanilla. Cool for 15 minutes.

3 Slice bananas; toss with orange juice. Line crust with one-third of the bananas and top with half of the filling. Repeat, then arrange the remaining bananas on top; overlap slices to make a spiral design. Melt the apricot preserve and brush over bananas. Let cool for 30 minutes at room temperature. Chill for at least 4 hours or overnight before serving.

Pineapple Tart

You can tell when pineapples are ripe by the fact that the inside leaves of the crown are easy to pull out and the fruit exudes an intense aroma.

FOR THE PASTRY

1 lemon

250 g (2 cups/9 oz) plain (all-purpose) flour

3 tablespoons sugar

125 g (½ cup/4½ oz) butter

1 egg, lightly beaten

FOR THE FILLING

1 egg yolk

1 vanilla bean

2 eggs

80 g (⅓ cup/2¾ oz) caster (superfine) sugar

125 ml (½ cup/4 fl oz) cream

1 ripe pineapple

4 tablespoons redcurrant jelly

85 g (¼ cup/3 oz) apricot jam

250 ml (1 cup/9 fl oz) apple juice

40 g (¼ cup/1½ oz) chopped almonds

SERVES 12

PREPARATION TIME 1 hour

COOKING TIME 25 minutes

1 Use a 26-cm (10½-in) spring-form tin. Grease tin. To make the pastry, grate 1 tbsp lemon zest. Place flour, sugar, butter, egg, zest and 2–3 tbsp water in a bowl and combine.

2 Work ingredients together by hand or use an electric mixer fitted with dough hooks. Flour work surface and hands and knead dough for a few minutes until shiny. Form into a smooth ball and wrap in cling wrap. Chill for 30 minutes.

3 Preheat oven to 200°C (400°F, gas mark 6). Roll pastry into a round large enough to line the base of the tin and create an edge about 2.5 cm (1 in) high. Place in tin.

4 To make filling, brush pastry base with the egg yolk. Slice vanilla bean in half lengthwise and scrape out seeds. Combine the eggs, half the sugar, the vanilla seeds and cream in a bowl, then spread mixture over the pastry base. Bake for 25 minutes.

5 Meanwhile, peel and slice the pineapple and remove woody centre of each slice. Remove cake from oven and let cool. Cover with pineapple slices.

6 Using a teaspoon, fill the centre of each pineapple slice with a little redcurrant jelly.

7 Combine apricot jam, the apple juice and the remaining sugar in a small saucepan; stir over low heat until smooth; strain. Brush the mixture over the cake and sprinkle the chopped almonds around the edge before the glaze sets.

Top Tip

To cut pineapple, first remove the spiky crown by grasping it in your hand and twisting firmly. If you need slices, first pare off the skin with a sharp knife, then slice the fruit. Cut out the woody core after slicing. If a recipe requires that the fruit is chopped, cut the pineapple into four lengthwise and slice the skin off the fruit before chopping.

113

Glazed Mango Sponge

In this unusual upside-down cake, juicy slices of mango are topped with a simple, light sponge mixture flavoured with lime and coconut. After baking, the cake is turned out so that the fruit is on top. It is then dredged with icing sugar and caramelised to a golden brown under a hot grill.

1 ripe mango

170 g (³/₄ cup/6 oz) caster (superfine) sugar

2 eggs, lightly beaten

125 g (¹/₂ cup/4¹/₂ oz) natural (plain) yogurt

125 ml (¹/₂ cup/4 fl oz) sunflower oil

Finely grated zest of 1 lime

185 g (1¹/₂ cups/6¹/₂ oz) plain (all-purpose) flour

2 teaspoons baking powder

30 g (¹/₃ cup/1 oz) desiccated (sweetened shredded) coconut

2 tablespoons icing (confectioners') sugar, sifted

SERVES 8

PREPARATION TIME 20 minutes

COOKING TIME 50 minutes

1 Use a 18-cm (7-in) square, deep tin with a loose base or a 20-cm (8-in) round, deep cake tin. Grease tin and line the base with baking (parchment) paper. Preheat oven to 180°C (350°F, gas mark 4).

2 Peel the mango. Cut the flesh away from the stone and slice thinly. Arrange over the bottom of the prepared cake tin.

3 Place sugar, eggs, yogurt, oil and lime zest in a large bowl and stir until smooth and mixed thoroughly. Sift flour and baking powder and fold into the mixture, alternating with the coconut.

4 Spoon mixture over the sliced mango and smooth the top. Bake for 50 minutes or until golden brown and firm to the touch. Check after 30 minutes and cover with foil if the cake is browning too quickly.

5 Leave cake in the tin for about 15 minutes, then turn out onto the rack of a grill tray, mango-side up. Peel off baking paper. Preheat grill. Dust cake thickly with icing sugar and place under the hot grill for 3–4 minutes or until the sugar has melted and is golden. Leave to cool on the rack.

6 Transfer the cake to a plate for serving. Any leftover cake can be covered with cling film and kept in the refrigerator for 2–3 days.

Try this, too...

For a Chocolate, Pear and Walnut Upside-down Cake, instead of mango use 2 ripe but firm pears, peeled, cored and sliced. Use 3 tbsp cocoa powder in place of the 3 tbsp of the plain flour, and fold in 30 g (¹/₄ cup/1 oz) finely chopped walnuts instead of the desiccated coconut.

For a Peach Sponge, halve and stone 3 ripe, firm peaches. Turn peach halves rounded side up and slice each one into 6 or 7 wedges; do not cut all the way through. Arrange sliced side up in a greased and lined 23-cm (9-in) springform tin. Place 125 g (¹/₂ cup/4¹/₂ oz) softened unsalted butter, 115 g (¹/₂ cup/4 oz) dark brown sugar, 50 g (¹/₃ cup/1³/₄ oz) wholemeal (whole-wheat) flour, 40 g (¹/₃ cup/1¹/₂ oz) self-raising (self-rising) flour, 1 tsp baking powder, 30 g (¹/₄ cup/1 oz) ground almonds, 1 tbsp milk and 2 eggs in a large mixing bowl. Beat for 2 minutes or until thoroughly combined. Spoon mixture into tin. Bake as for the main recipe.

Fruity Lemon Cheesecake

Enjoy this thin but dense Italian-style cheesecake with a cup of tea
or as a dessert. Unlike many cheesecakes, this one isn't baked with a butter-rich
crust and it uses lower-fat ricotta rather than rich cream cheese.

3 tablespoons semolina

40 g (⅓ cup/1 ½ oz) sultanas
(golden raisins)

60 ml (¼ cup/2 fl oz) brandy

340 g (1 ⅓ cups/12 oz) ricotta
cheese

3 large egg yolks

85 g (⅓ cup/3 oz) caster
(superfine) sugar

60 ml (¼ cup/2 fl oz) lemon juice

1 ½ teaspoons vanilla essence
(extract)

Finely grated zest of 2 large lemons

FOR THE TOPPING

2 oranges

2 satsumas or mandarins

1 lemon

4 tablespoons lemon marmalade

SERVES 8

PREPARATION TIME 20 minutes
plus 30 minutes for soaking and
2–3 hours for cooling

COOKING TIME 35–40 minutes

1 Use a 20-cm (8-in) non-stick,
sandwich tin with a loose base.
Line base with baking (parchment)
paper. Grease the paper and side of
tin. Place 1 tbsp semolina in the tin;
tilt tin to coat base and side and
tap out any excess. Place sultanas
in a bowl and add brandy. Leave to
soak for 30 minutes or until most of
the brandy has been absorbed.

2 Preheat oven to 180°C (350°F,
gas mark 4). Press the ricotta
through a sieve into a bowl. Add
the egg yolks, sugar, juice, vanilla
and remaining semolina and beat
to combine. Stir in the lemon zest
and the sultanas with any brandy
that remains.

3 Spoon mixture into tin; smooth
surface. Bake for 35–40 minutes
or until top is browned and edge is
shrinking away from the tin. Switch
off the oven. Leave cake to cool for
about 2 hours with the door ajar.

4 Peel oranges, satsumas and
lemon, removing all the white
pith. Cut between the membranes
to segment the fruit. Then melt
marmalade in a small saucepan
over very low heat.

5 Remove cheesecake carefully
from the tin and place on a
serving platter. Brush with a little
melted marmalade, arrange citrus
segments on top and glaze with
remaining marmalade. Leave to
set before serving.

Try this, too…

Replace the sultanas with finely
chopped dried apricots or sour
cherries soaked in orange juice.

Blueberry and Orange Tart

Pepper may seem a strange ingredient, but it actually heightens the blueberry flavour. The dough for the tart shell is made with healthy monounsaturated olive oil instead of butter.

185 g (1½ cups/6½ oz) plain (all-purpose) flour

40 g (⅓ cup/1½ oz) icing (confectioners') sugar

2 teaspoons grated orange zest

½ teaspoon baking powder

60 ml (¼ cup/2 fl oz) olive oil, plus 2 tablespoons

2 tablespoons orange juice plus 60 ml (¼ cup/2 fl oz)

About 700 g (3½ cups/1 lb 8 oz) fresh or frozen blueberries

8 tablespoons white (granulated) sugar

½ teaspoon ground pepper

⅛ teaspoon ground nutmeg

30 g (¼ cup/1 oz) cornflour (cornstarch)

SERVES 8

PREPARATION TIME 30 minutes plus standing and chilling time

COOKING TIME 30 minutes

1 Use a 23-cm (9-in) flan tin with a loose base. Combine the flour, icing sugar, orange zest and baking powder in a large bowl. Add oil and 2 tbsp orange juice; stir to combine. Flour hands and work surface and knead dough to form a ball. Flatten into a disc and wrap in cling wrap. Chill for 30 minutes.

2 Preheat oven to 180°C (350°F, gas mark 4). Press dough into the tin to line base and side. Prick base several times with a fork. Line with baking (parchment) paper; fill with dried beans or rice. Bake case for 15 minutes; remove paper and beans. Bake a further 10 minutes or until golden. Cool on a wire rack.

3 Combine the blueberries, the remaining orange juice, 6 tbsp sugar, the pepper and the nutmeg in a pan; bring to the boil. Reduce heat; simmer for 5 minutes.

4 Combine the remaining 2 tbsp sugar and the cornflour. Add to the berries and cook for 2 minutes or until the berry mixture is thick.

5 Cool the blueberry mixture to room temperature, then spoon into the baked shell. Chill the tart for 1 hour before serving.

Summer Fruit Swiss Roll

Fresh summer fruits such as strawberries, peaches and nectarines taste sumptuous with cream. Here, these aromatic fruits are combined with cream plus yogurt to make a delicious filling for a light-as-air, fat-free sponge.

FOR THE CAKE

3 large eggs

115 g (½ cup/4 oz) caster (superfine) sugar

125 g (1 cup/4½ oz) plain (all-purpose) flour

1 tablespoon lukewarm water

FOR THE FILLING

150 ml (½ cup/5 fl oz) cream, for whipping

1 teaspoon vanilla essence (extract)

90 g (⅓ cup/3¼ oz) natural (plain) yogurt

150 g (1 cup/5 oz) strawberries, sliced

1 ripe peach or nectarine, chopped

FOR DECORATION

2–3 tablespoons icing (confectioners') sugar, sifted

Few slices of strawberry and peach or nectarine

SERVES 8

PREPARATION TIME 30 minutes

COOKING TIME 10–12 minutes

1 Use a 33- x 23-cm (13- x 9-in). Swiss roll tin Grease; line with baking (parchment) paper. Preheat oven to 200°C (400°F, gas mark 6).

2 Place eggs and sugar in a large bowl. Use an electric mixer and beat until very thick and pale and the mixture leaves a trail on the surface when beaters are lifted out. If using a hand whisk, set the bowl over a pan of almost boiling water, making sure that the water does not touch the base of the bowl.

3 Sift half the flour over the egg mixture and gently fold it in with a large metal spoon. Sift the remaining flour over the top and fold it in with the lukewarm water.

4 Pour mixture into the tin; give tin a gentle shake to spread the mixture evenly into the corners. Bake for 10–12 minutes or until the sponge is well risen, springs back when pressed gently with a finger and is pale gold in colour.

5 Turn out onto a sheet of baking paper slightly larger than the sponge. Peel off lining paper. Trim the crusty edges of the sponge with a sharp knife; make a score mark 2.5 cm (1 in) from one of the short edges (this will make the sponge easier to roll up).

6 Roll up loosely from the short side, with the paper inside, and place seam-side down on a wire rack to cool.

7 When sponge is cold, carefully unroll it and remove the paper. Whip cream and vanilla essence until soft peaks form, then fold in the yogurt. Spread over the sponge, leaving a 1-cm (½-in) border all the way around. Scatter fruit over the cream. Carefully re-roll the sponge and place it seam-side down on a serving plate.

8 Put 2.5-cm (1-in) wide strips of baking paper diagonally, at an equal distance apart, over the cake. Dust with the icing sugar to create a striped effect. Carefully remove the paper. Decorate with the extra fruit. Keep roll in the refrigerator until ready to serve. This sponge is best eaten within a day of making.

Try this, too...

For a simple Jam Swiss Roll, follow recipe to the end of step 6, then spread 5 tbsp warmed jam over the sponge and roll up. Sprinkle with caster sugar.

For a Chocolate and Raspberry Swiss Roll, replace 3 tbsp of the flour with 3 tbsp cocoa powder. Use 175 g (1½ cups/6 oz) fresh raspberries in the filling instead of strawberries and peaches. Decorate with icing sugar and cocoa powder.

Pear and Redcurrant Filo

The bright red juice of the currants tints the pears and looks attractive under the pastry lattice. Although redcurrants only have a short season, they freeze well. You can substitute another red-berried fruit, if they are not available.

2 tablespoons redcurrant jelly

1 teaspoon lemon juice

3 ripe but firm pears, about 170 g (6 oz) each

125 g (1 cup/4 1/2 oz) redcurrants

3 sheets filo pastry, each 30 x 50 cm (12 x 20 in) in size, about 90 g (3 1/4 oz) in total

20 g (3/4 oz) unsalted butter, melted

40 g (1/4 cup/1 1/2 oz) ground almonds

SERVES 6

PREPARATION TIME 25 minutes

COOKING TIME 15–20 minutes

1 Use a 23-cm (9-in) non-stick flan tin with a loose bottom. Preheat the oven to 200°C (400°F, gas mark 6) and put a baking sheet in to heat. For the filling, place the redcurrant jelly and lemon juice in a small saucepan and heat gently until melted. Remove from heat.

2 Peel pears and slice thinly. Add to the jelly glaze; toss gently to coat. Stir in the redcurrants.

3 Lay 2 sheets of filo on top of each other. (Cover third sheet with a damp cloth kitchen towel to prevent it from drying out.) Cut into quarters. Separate the 8 pieces and brush lightly with butter. Use to line the tin; overlap them slightly, scrunching and tucking in edges.

4 Sprinkle tart case with ground almonds. Top evenly with the pear and redcurrant mixture.

5 Cut the remaining sheet of filo in half crosswise; brush lightly with butter. Place one half on top of the other. Cut into 10 strips about 2.5 cm (1 in) wide and trim excess pastry. Twist doubled strips gently and arrange in a lattice pattern over the filling. Neatly tuck in the ends.

6 Place the tin on the hot baking sheet. Bake for 15–20 minutes or until pastry is crisp and golden brown. Serve warm.

Try this, too...

To make a Pear and Raspberry Filo Lattice, use raspberries instead of redcurrants. Instead of redcurrant jelly for the glaze, use seedless raspberry jam.

For a Mango and Cape Gooseberry Filo Tart, sprinkle the tart case with 30 g (1/3 cup/1 oz) desiccated (shredded) coconut. Peel and dice 2 ripe mangoes; mix with 100 g (1 cup/3 1/2 oz) cape gooseberries, halved. Toss the fruit gently with 2 tbsp each of lime juice and soft brown sugar, then spoon into the pastry case and spread evenly. Top with pastry lattice. Bake as for main recipe.

Top Tip

Pears contain very little vitamin C. However, in this recipe they are combined with redcurrants, which are a useful source of vitamin C. Pears do offer good amounts of potassium as well as soluble fibre.

Redcurrants contain more beta-carotene than white currants but less than blackcurrants.

Plum Cobbler

This version of an old-fashioned favourite dessert features walnuts in the topping for a crunchy texture and nutty flavour. The topping is arranged over the plums in strips to form a lattice pattern.

About 800 g (1 lb 12 oz) plums, halved or quartered

Grated zest and juice of 1 large orange

1 cinnamon stick

2 tablespoons light brown sugar

FOR THE TOPPING

200 g (1²/₃ cups/7 oz) self-raising (self-rising) flour

1 teaspoon baking powder

30 g (2 tbsp/1 oz) unsalted butter, chilled and diced

30 g (2 tbsp/1 oz) light brown sugar

1 tablespoon chopped walnuts

100 ml (3½ fl oz) skimmed milk plus 1 tablespoon for brushing

SERVES 6

PREPARATION TIME 45 minutes

COOKING TIME 25–30 minutes

1 Use a 1.2-litre (5-cup/44-fl oz) ovenproof dish. Preheat oven to 180°C (350°F, gas mark 4). Put the plums, orange zest, juice, cinnamon stick and sugar in the dish and mix well. Gently shake the dish so the fruit settles evenly.

2 To make the topping, sift flour and baking powder in a mixing bowl. Rub in butter until mixture resembles fine breadcrumbs. Stir in the sugar and chopped walnuts. Make a well in the centre, add milk and mix to a soft (not sticky) dough.

3 Transfer the dough to a lightly floured work surface and knead briefly. Roll out to a rectangle about 1 cm (½ in) thick and a little wider than the diameter of the dish. With a sharp knife or pastry wheel, cut dough into strips 2 cm (¾ in) wide.

4 Dampen the rim of the dish with water. Arrange the strips over the fruit in a lattice pattern, pressing each end onto the rim of the dish and trimming the ends neatly. Brush the lattice with the extra milk.

5 Bake for 25–30 minutes or until the topping is golden and the fruit is tender. Serve hot or warm. Remove cinnamon before serving.

Try this, too...

Make the cobbler with a mixture of apples and plums or with the traditional blackberry and apples. Apples with raspberries and pears with berries are two other good combinations.

For a Strawberry and Rhubarb Cobbler, replace plums with 400 g (14 oz) each chopped rhubarb and whole strawberries, and flavour with the orange zest and 2 tbsp redcurrant jelly. Add chopped toasted hazelnuts (filberts) to the topping in place of walnuts. Roll out the dough to an 18-cm (7-in) round that is 1 cm (½ in) thick and cut into rounds using a 3-cm (1¼-in) fluted cutter. Arrange the rounds on top of the fruit, slightly overlapping, brush with milk and bake as in the main recipe.

Raspberry Brownie Cake

Raspberries and chocolate have a natural affinity that's hard to beat.

2 tablespoons vegetable oil

2 tablespoons unsweetened cocoa powder

1 egg

140 g (¾ cup/5 oz) brown sugar

60 g (½ cup/2¼ oz) plain (all-purpose) flour

¼ teaspoon bicarbonate of soda (baking soda)

30 g (¼ cup/1 oz) coarsely chopped pecans

375 g (3 cups/13 oz) raspberries

1 tablespoon cornflour (cornstarch) mixed with 2 tablespoons water

SERVES 8

PREPARATION TIME 15 minutes

COOKING TIME 30 minutes

1 Spray a 20-cm (8-inch) round cake tin with non-stick cooking spray. Preheat oven to 180°C (350°F, gas mark 4). Combine the oil, cocoa powder, egg, 60 ml (¼ cup/2 fl oz) water, 90g (½ cup/3¼ oz) of the sugar, all the flour and bicarbonate of soda in a large bowl. Combine. Fold in the nuts; pour batter into the tin and bake for 20 minutes or until a metal skewer inserted into the centre comes out clean. Cool in the tin on a wire rack.

2 Meanwhile, combine half the raspberries and the remaining sugar in a pan and cook, stirring, for 4 minutes or until the berries are juicy. Stir in cornflour mixture. Cook, stirring for another 4 minutes or until thickened. Strain through a sieve to remove the seeds. Cool for 10 minutes. Spoon over the brownie base and arrange the remaining raspberries on top.

Fruit Turnovers

With their spicy fruit filling, these little pies are just right to hold in the hand.
They're perfect for a picnic or a winter barbecue.

FOR THE PASTRY

375 g (3 cups/13 oz) plain
(all-purpose) flour

160 g (²⁄₃ cup/5½ oz) butter,
chopped

185 ml (¾ cup/6 fl oz) chilled water

125 g (½ cup/4½ oz) white
vegetable fat

FOR THE FILLING

4 large cooking apples, peeled,
cored and sliced

125 g (¾ cup/4½ oz) each of
roughly chopped ready-to-eat
stoned dates and prunes

1 tablespoon fresh orange juice

55 g (¼ cup/2 oz) brown sugar

½ teaspoon ground cinnamon

1 egg, beaten

2–3 tablespoons caster (superfine)
sugar

MAKES 12

PREPARATION TIME 45 minutes plus
30 minutes chilling time

COOKING TIME 20–25 minutes

1 To make pastry, sift flour into a bowl and rub in half the butter. Add water and mix to a soft dough. On a lightly floured surface, roll the dough into a rectangle about 5 mm (¼ in) thick. Dot half the remaining butter over the top two-thirds of the rectangle, then fold the bottom third up and over the centre third. Then bring the top third down so that it covers the bottom third. Press edges together with the rolling pin.

2 Give the dough a quarter turn to the left so that the side joins are to the bottom and top. Roll out again into a rectangle 5 mm (¼ in) thick. Dot vegetable fat over the top two-thirds of pastry; fold and turn as before. Repeat, using remaining butter. Wrap in cling wrap and chill for 30 minutes.

3 To make the filling, place the apples, dates, prunes, orange juice, sugar and cinnamon in a pan. Cook gently, covered, for 8 minutes. Remove from heat; cool. Preheat oven to 220°C (425°F, gas mark 7).

4 Cut dough in half, roll out one piece to 35 x 25 cm (14 x 9 in) in size. Cut in half lengthwise and into 3 crosswise to make 6 pieces, each 12 cm (4½ in) square. Spoon half the filling onto the centre of the squares, dividing it up equally. Brush the edges with a little beaten egg, then fold each square in half diagonally to enclose the filling and to form a triangle. Press the edges together well to seal and decorate with a fork. Put the turnovers on a baking sheet and refrigerate while making 6 more in the same way with remaining dough and filling.

5 Brush the turnovers with the remaining beaten egg; sprinkle with sugar. Bake for 20–25 minutes or until well risen, crisp and golden. Cool briefly on wire racks.

Spiced Plum Tart

The simplicity of this recipe belies the sophistication of the combined flavours.
Full-fat cream cheese and sour cream can be used instead of the low-fat versions.

125 g (1 cup/4½ oz) plain
(all-purpose) flour, plus 1 extra
tablespoon

3 teaspoons white (granulated) sugar

2 tablespoons unsalted butter,
chopped

1½ tablespoons low-fat cream
cheese

1½ tablespoons low-fat sour cream

1 egg white, lightly beaten

650 g (1lb 7 oz) purple plums, cut
into 5 mm (¼ in) wedges

80 g (⅓ cup/3 oz) light brown
sugar

¼ teaspoon ground ginger

Pinch of black pepper

SERVES 6

PREPARATION TIME 30 minutes plus
1 hour chilling

COOKING TIME 40 minutes

1 Use a baking tray. Combine the
flour (reserving 1 tbsp) and the
sugar in a large mixing bowl. Cut in
the chopped butter and the cream
cheese with 2 knives until mixture
resembles coarse crumbs. Combine
sour cream and 1 tbsp iced water in
a small bowl; stir into flour mixture
just until combined. Flatten dough
into a round, wrap in cling wrap
and refrigerate for at least 1 hour.

2 Preheat oven to 190°C (375°F,
gas mark 5). Roll out dough on
a floured surface to a 33-cm (13-in)
round. Place on a baking tray and
roll the edges over once to form a
neat edge.

3 Brush dough with the beaten
egg white. Arrange the plums
on top in overlapping concentric
circles. Combine the sugar, ginger,
pepper and the remaining flour in
a small bowl. Sprinkle evenly over
the plums. Bake for 40 minutes or
until the plums are tender and the
crust is golden.

special
occasions

Chocolate Mousse Tart

Spectacular and sensational—chocolate and special occasions were made for each other.

215 g (1¾ cups/7½ oz) chocolate graham cracker or digestive biscuit crumbs (about 9 large crackers)

1 large egg white

2 tablespoons honey

7 g (2 tsp/¼ oz) powdered clear gelatine

225 g (1 cup/8 oz) caster (superfine) sugar

125 g (1 cup/4½ oz) unsweetened cocoa powder, plus extra for dusting

80 ml (⅓ cup/2½ fl oz) milk, warmed

1 teaspoon vanilla essence (extract)

375 ml (1½ cups/13 fl oz) cream, for whipping

85 g (⅔ cup/3 oz) dark (semisweet) chocolate, for curls

SERVES 8

PREPARATION TIME 20 minutes

COOKING TIME 10 minutes plus chilling

1 Use a 25-cm (10-in) non-stick tart tin with a removable base. Grease lightly. Preheat the oven to 180°C (350°F, gas mark 4). Combine the crumbs, egg white and honey. Press crumb mixture onto bottom and side of tart tin to make a crust. Bake 10 minutes. Cool.

2 Put 3 tbsp water in a saucepan; sprinkle on gelatine. Leave for 1 minute. Stir over a low heat until gelatine dissolves, about 2 minutes. Remove from heat.

3 Mix sugar and cocoa in a large bowl. Stir in milk and vanilla essence until cocoa dissolves. Stir in the gelatine. Cool.

4 Whip cream until stiff. Fold three-quarters of the whipped cream into cooled cocoa mixture until blended. Pour into the crust. Swirl remaining whipped cream in the centre. Refrigerate for 2 hours or overnight to let mousse set.

5 Dust with cocoa powder and decorate with chocolate curls. To make curls, the chocolate must be at room temperature. Draw the blade of a vegetable peeler across it, pressing down firmly. Lift curls into place with a skewer.

Top Tip

Gelatine must be softened and dissolved with care because it can easily become lumpy when added to other mixtures. Sprinkle powder evenly on top of liquid to soften. Do not stir gelatine while it is in the process of dissolving.

Mocha Cream Roll

You can also decorate this deliciously moist sponge roll with
mocha chocolate beans or chocolate shavings.

FOR THE CAKE

3 eggs

90 g (½ cup/3¼ oz) sugar

1 teaspoon grated orange zest

1 tablespoon orange juice

90 g (¾ cup/3¼ oz) plain
(all-purpose) flour

½ teaspoon baking powder

FOR THE FILLING AND DECORATION

100 g (⅔ cup/3 oz) mocha-flavoured
chocolate

420 ml (1⅔ cups/14½ fl oz) cream,
for whipping

1 tablespoon cold instant coffee

2 tablespoons icing (confectioners')
sugar

Cocoa powder, for dusting

Chocolate flowers and leaves

1 Use a 33- x 23-cm (13- x 9-in)
baking tray. Line with baking
(parchment) paper. Preheat oven
to 180°C (350°F, gas mark 4).

2 Beat eggs, sugar, orange zest
and juice until fluffy. Sift flour
and baking powder over the egg
mixture; fold in with a whisk.

3 Spread mixture evenly on tray;
bake for 12–14 minutes or until
golden brown. Remove from oven,
turn out onto baking paper (leaving
tray on top of sponge); cool.

4 Melt chocolate in a bowl over
gently simmering water; cool.
Whip cream until stiff. Gradually
stir in chocolate, coffee and icing
sugar. Place about 6 tbsp chocolate
cream in a piping bag fitted with a
star nozzle.

5 Remove tray and top sheet
of paper from sponge. Spread
three-quarters of chocolate cream
over sponge. Using bottom sheet of
baking paper to help keep the roll
neat, roll up sponge; work from a
long side.

6 Spread remaining chocolate
cream over roll and pipe small
rosettes on the top. Dust with the
cocoa powder and decorate with
chocolate flowers and leaves.

SERVES 8

PREPARATION TIME 45 minutes

COOKING TIME 12–14 minutes

Lemon Meringue Pie

This old favourite contrasts the sweetness of meringue with the tartness of lemons.
The pie is delicious served warm or cold.

FOR THE PASTRY

165 g (1⅓ cups/5¾ oz) plain (all-purpose) flour

2 tablespoons icing (confectioners') sugar

150 g (⅔ cup/5½ oz) butter, chilled and cubed

1½ tablespoons iced water

FOR THE FILLING

170 g (¾ cup/6 oz) caster (superfine) sugar

60 g (½ cup/2¼ oz) cornflour (cornstarch)

Finely grated zest of 3 lemons

80 ml (⅓ cup/2½ fl oz) lemon juice, strained

185 ml (¾ cup/6 fl oz) water

3 egg yolks

FOR THE MERINGUE

3 egg whites

Pinch of cream of tartar

80 g (⅓ cup/2¾ oz) caster (superfine) sugar

SERVES 6

PREPARATION TIME 30 minutes

COOKING TIME 35 minutes plus 3 hours for chilling

1 Use a 25-cm (10-in) pie plate. To make the pastry, process the flour in a food processor with icing sugar and butter until the mixture resembles coarse breadcrumbs. Add iced water; process just until the mixture comes together in a ball.

2 Turn pastry out onto a lightly floured work surface; knead it gently until smooth and press into a 15-cm (6-in) disc. Wrap in cling wrap and chill for 30 minutes.

3 To make the lemon filling, put the caster sugar and cornflour in a saucepan. Combine the lemon zest and lemon juice and the water and add to the pan. Stir constantly over a medium heat until mixture comes to the boil. Remove from the heat, add egg yolks and mix well to combine. Transfer filling to a bowl and cover with cling wrap; chill for 2 hours.

4 Preheat oven to 180°C (350°F, gas mark 4). Roll out pastry to a 33-cm (13-in) round about 5 mm (¼ in) thick. Pierce the base several times with a fork. Chill the case for 15 minutes.

5 Line the pastry with baking (parchment) paper and half-fill with dried beans or rice. Bake for 15 minutes. Remove the paper and beans or rice and cook for a further 10 minutes or until light golden and aromatic. Leave pastry case to cool, then spoon the filling into it, smoothing the top with the back of a spoon.

6 To make the meringue topping, whisk the egg whites in a bowl with the cream of tartar until soft peaks form. Add sugar, a spoonful at a time, beating well after each addition. The meringue should be thick and shiny.

7 Spread the meringue over the lemon filling, making sure it forms a seal all around the pastry shell to prevent filling overheating (which could cause it to separate). Bake for 10 minutes or until the meringue is a light golden colour.

Pavlova

This impressive dessert is easy to make. Once you have prepared the meringue mixture, bake it immediately; otherwise it will collapse and begin to 'weep'.

FOR THE MERINGUE

8 egg whites

375 g (1⅔ cups/13 oz) caster (superfine) sugar

2 teaspoons vanilla essence (extract)

2 teaspoons brown vinegar

Large pinch of salt

2 teaspoons cornflour (cornstarch)

FOR THE FILLING

310 ml (1¼ cups/10¾ fl oz) cream, for whipping

250 g (1⅔ cups/9 oz) strawberries, halved

2 bananas, peeled and sliced

90 g (⅓ cup/3¼ oz) passionfruit pulp

1 Use a large baking tray; line with baking (parchment) paper. Mark a 23-cm (9-in) circle on it as a guide for the meringue. Preheat oven to 180°C (350°F, gas mark 4).

2 In a large, dry bowl, beat the egg whites with electric beaters on high speed until soft peaks form. Gradually add the sugar and beat continuously until mixture is firm and glossy and sugar has dissolved. Beat in vanilla, then the vinegar and salt. Sift the cornflour and fold in.

3 Using a spatula, spread mixture over marked circle. Straighten sides, making them higher than the centre. Bake for 10 minutes in the centre of the oven.

4 Reduce temperature to 120°C (235°F, gas mark ½). Bake for a further hour. Remove pavlova from oven and leave to cool completely. Whip the cream until firm; chill.

5 Just before serving, top pavlova with whipped cream. Decorate with strawberries and banana and drizzle passionfruit pulp over the top. Or, decorate with 3 peeled and sliced kiwi fruit, arranged in rounds; top with the passionfruit pulp.

SERVES 8–10

PREPARATION TIME 20 minutes

COOKING TIME 1 hour 10 minutes

Top Tale

Australia and New Zealand each staked claims for the pavlova's invention. Recipes for a fruit-filled meringue began to appear in New Zealand in 1926, at a time when acclaimed ballerina Anna Pavlova was taking the country by storm. Australia came in second with Bert Sachse, a chef at the Esplanade Hotel in Perth, claiming to have created the dessert in 1935, after Pavlova stayed at the hotel.

Cream Profiteroles

It's a good idea to make an extra batch of the choux pastry cases and freeze them.
You can thaw them when needed. Heat briefly and then fill.

FOR THE PASTRY

250 ml (1 cup/9 fl oz) water

90 g (1/3 cup/3 1/4 oz) butter

125 g (1 cup/4 1/2 oz) plain
   (all-purpose) flour

4 eggs

1 teaspoon vanilla essence (extract)

Grated zest of 1/2 lemon

Pinch of sugar

1 egg yolk, for brushing

2 teaspoons cream

FOR THE FILLING

185 ml (3/4 cup/6 fl oz) cream,
   for whipping

3 tablespoons icing (confectioners')
   sugar

1 teaspoon vanilla essence (extract)

MAKES 12

PREPARATION TIME 35 minutes

COOKING TIME 35–40 minutes

1 Use a large baking tray and line with baking (parchment) paper. Preheat the oven to 200°C (400°F, gas mark 6).

2 Pour water into a saucepan, add butter and bring to a boil. Tip in flour all at once; stir vigorously with a wooden spoon until dough comes together and a white film forms on base of pan. Remove pan from heat; leave dough to cool briefly. Beat in whole eggs one at a time; add the vanilla, lemon zest and sugar.

3 Spoon dough into a piping bag fitted with a large star nozzle; pipe 12 rosettes onto the baking tray. Combine egg yolk and cream; brush over the profiteroles. Bake for 35–40 minutes until golden. Remove from oven; cool on a wire rack. Cut profiteroles in half horizontally.

4 For the filling, whip the cream until stiff; stir in 2 tbsp icing sugar and the vanilla essence. Top each profiterole half with cream and sandwich 2 together. Dust with the remaining icing sugar.

Carrot and Brazil Nut Cake

Bake a carrot cake and you'll get your children to eat vegetables without even noticing.
The creamy icing is lighter in fat than a traditional one because it uses ricotta cheese.

175 g (1 ½ cups/6 oz) self-raising
  wholemeal (self-rising whole-
  wheat) flour

175 g (1 ½ cups/6 oz) self-raising
  (self-rising) flour

1 teaspoon ground cinnamon

100 g (⅔ cup/½ oz) brazil nuts

60 g (½ cup/2 oz) raisins

140 g (⅔ cup/5 oz) light brown
  sugar

200 ml (¾ cup plus 1 tablespoon/
  7 fl oz) sunflower oil

4 large eggs

200 g (1 ⅓ cups/7 oz) carrots
  (about 3 carrots), finely grated

Finely grated zest and juice of
  ½ orange

FOR THE ICING

250 g (1 cup/9 oz) ricotta cheese

55 g (¼ cup/2 oz) icing
  (confectioners') sugar, sifted

Finely grated zest of ½ orange

SERVES 12

PREPARATION TIME 30 minutes plus
  cooling time

COOKING TIME 50 minutes

1 Use a 20-cm (8-in) round, deep cake tin and line the base with baking (parchment) paper. Grease lightly. Preheat oven to 180°C (350°F, gas mark 4).

2 Sift the flours and cinnamon into a large bowl, tipping in any bran left in the sieve. Coarsely chop about two-thirds of the brazil nuts; stir into flour with the raisins. Slice remaining nuts thinly, lengthwise; set aside.

3 In another bowl, beat sugar and oil with a wooden spoon until well combined. Beat in the eggs one at a time. Stir in the grated carrots and orange zest and juice. Using a large metal spoon, fold the carrot mixture into the flour mixture, just until combined. Do not overmix.

4 Spoon mixture into tin. Bake for 50 minutes or until risen and firm to the touch. Leave the cake in the tin for 5 minutes, then turn out onto a wire rack and peel off the baking paper. Leave to cool.

5 To make the icing, beat ricotta, sugar and orange zest in a bowl with a wooden spoon. Spread icing on top of cold cake; top with the reserved sliced nuts, placing them so that they stick up at different angles. Cake will keep, covered, in the refrigerator for up to 3 days.

Try this, too...

Substitute cashew or macadamia nuts for the brazil nuts.

To make a Passion Cake, drain a can of pineapple in natural juice, about 260 g (1 cup/9 oz), and chop finely. Pat the pineapple between sheets of paper towels to absorb excess moisture. Stir into mixture with 150 g (1 cup/5½ oz) grated carrots (about 2 carrots). Omit the orange juice and zest; use pecan nuts instead of brazil nuts.

Top Tip

Wholemeal flour is a useful source of many of the B vitamins, plus iron and zinc. It also provides good amounts of fibre, particularly the insoluble variety.

Carrots provide one of the richest sources of the antioxidant beta-carotene; this helps to protect cells against damage by free radicals. While most vegetables are more nutritious eaten raw, carrots have more to offer when cooked. This is because cooking breaks down the tough cell membranes and makes it easier for the body to absorb the beta-carotene.

Italian Cake with Red Fruits

This unusual flourless cake makes an excellent dessert. Italian arborio (risotto) rice is cooked slowly in milk until tender and creamy. It is then mixed with eggs, nuts, lemon and rum and baked in the oven. An accompanying red fruit salad adds a dash of colour.

625 ml (2½ cups/21 fl oz) milk

Strip of lemon zest

165 g (¾ cup/5½ oz) arborio rice

115 g (¾ cup/4 oz) pine nuts

115 g (¾ cup/4 oz) blanched almonds

3 large eggs, separated

80 g (⅓ cup/2¾ oz) caster (superfine) sugar

Grated zest of 1 lemon

1 tablespoon dark rum

Icing (confectioners') sugar, sifted, to decorate

FOR THE FRUIT SALAD

300 g (2 cups/10 oz) strawberries

125 g (1 cup/4 oz) raspberries

250 g (1¼ cups/9 oz) cherries, pitted

SERVES 8–10

PREPARATION TIME 1¼ hours plus chilling overnight

COOKING TIME 40 minutes

1 Use a 20-cm (8-in) springform tin. Grease tin; line base with baking (parchment) paper. Heat the milk and zest in a heavy-based pan; bring to a boil. Stir in the rice, then reduce heat so that the milk barely simmers. Cook, uncovered, stirring frequently, for 40 minutes or until the rice is very soft and the mixture is thick and creamy.

2 Spoon the rice mixture into a large bowl; leave to cool. Preheat oven to 180°C (350°F, gas mark 4).

3 Spread pine nuts and almonds in separate baking tins; toast in oven for about 10 minutes or until lightly browned. Roughly chop the almonds.

4 Remove the lemon zest from the rice. Using a wooden spoon, beat in the egg yolks one at a time. Beat in caster sugar, grated lemon zest and rum. Add the nuts.

5 In a separate bowl, whisk egg whites until stiff peaks form. Gently fold into rice mixture using a large metal spoon. Spoon mixture into the tin. Bake for 40 minutes or until a skewer inserted in the centre comes out clean.

6 Leave the cake to cool in the tin. Wrap in cling wrap (still in the tin); chill overnight. Refrigerate for up to 48 hours, if necessary.

7 To make the red fruit salad, purée half the strawberries in a food processor or blender or rub through a sieve with the back of a wooden spoon. Cut the remaining strawberries into halves; stir into the purée with the raspberries and cherries. Spoon into a bowl.

8 Unmould cake onto a serving plate and peel off the lining paper. Dust cake with icing sugar. Serve with fruit salad.

Try this, too...

To make a chocolate version, cook rice with the lemon zest, as in main recipe. Then remove from heat, discarding the zest. While the mixture is still hot, add 50 g (⅓ cup/2 oz) grated dark (semi-sweet) chocolate (containing at least 70 percent cocoa solids); stir until melted. Cool, then stir in 2 tbsp cold espresso coffee. Continue as for the main recipe.

Golden Syrup Tart

This simple, classic English tart is a must for those with a sweet tooth.
It can also be made with dark corn syrup.

FOR THE PASTRY

185 g (1½ cups/6½ oz) plain (all-purpose) flour

60 g (¼ cup/2¼ oz) butter

30 g (2 tbsp/1 oz) lard or white vegetable fat

1 egg, beaten

FOR THE FILLING

235 g (⅔ cup/8½ oz) golden syrup or dark corn syrup

Finely grated zest of 1 small lemon

2 teaspoons lemon juice

40 g (½ cup/1½ oz) soft white (fresh) breadcrumbs

SERVES 6

PREPARATION TIME 45 minutes

COOKING TIME 25–30 minutes plus 30 minutes for chilling

1 Use a 23-cm (9-in) pie plate. Sift the flour into a bowl and rub in the butter and lard until mixture resembles fine breadcrumbs. Mix to a firm dough with the egg. Turn out onto a lightly floured work surface; knead briefly until smooth. Wrap in cling wrap and chill for 30 minutes.

2 Preheat oven to 200°C (400°F, gas mark 6). Place syrup, lemon zest and juice in a small saucepan and heat gently for 1–2 minutes to thin the syrup. Remove from heat, stir in the breadcrumbs. Leave the filling to cool.

3 Roll the dough out fairly thinly to line the pie plate, pressing the dough down gently. Trim off the surplus from around the edge and prick the base lightly with a fork. Knead the trimmings again, roll out and cut out small shapes such as hearts with a fancy pastry cutter.

4 Spread the syrup mixture in the lined pie plate, leaving a narrow border around the edge. Brush the shapes with water and arrange them around the edge of the pastry. Place the plate on a baking tray and bake in the centre of the oven for 25–30 minutes, or until the pastry is cooked. Serve tart warm or cold, with whipped cream or custard.

Top Tip

When measuring golden syrup, run the measuring cup under hot water first, then add the syrup. The warmth of the container will make it easy to pour the syrup out.

Pumpkin Pie

This traditional American pie dates back to colonial times.

FOR THE PASTRY

125 g (1 cup/4½ oz) plain
  (all-purpose) flour

30 g (¼ cup/1 oz) self-raising
  (self-rising) flour

2 tablespoons icing (confectioners')
  sugar

125 g (½ cup/4½ oz) butter,
  chopped

2 tablespoons water

FOR THE FILLING

2 eggs

55 g (¼ cup/2 oz) brown sugar

2 tablespoons maple syrup

250 g (1 cup/9 oz) cooked mashed
  pumpkin (about 350 g/12 oz
  uncooked)

125 ml (½ cup/4 fl oz) cream

1 teaspoon ground cinnamon

½ teaspoon ground nutmeg

1 Use a 23-cm (9-in) pie plate. Sift the flours and icing sugar into a bowl. Add butter and rub in with fingertips until mixture resembles fine breadcrumbs. Add water and mix to form a ball, adding extra water, if necessary. Knead gently on floured work surface until smooth; cover in cling wrap and refrigerate for 30 minutes.

2 Preheat oven to 180°C (350°F, gas mark 4). Roll dough onto a lightly floured work surface until large enough to line pie plate. Line plate and trim edge. Use scraps of pastry to make a double edge for the rim. Trim and pinch the rim.

3 Place pie plate on baking tray. Line pastry case with baking (parchment) paper; fill with dried beans or rice. Bake for 10 minutes. Remove paper and beans; bake for a further 10 minutes or until pastry is lightly browned; cool.

4 To make the filling, beat eggs, sugar and maple syrup in a small bowl with electric beaters until thick. Stir in the pumpkin, cream and spices.

5 Pour filling into pastry case; bake in moderate oven for about 50 minutes or until filling is set; cool. Lightly dust with extra sifted icing sugar, if desired.

Try this, too...

Canned pumpkin produces a good result and is quick to use when you don't have time to make the filling yourself.

SERVES 6–8

PREPARATION TIME 20 minutes plus chilling

COOKING TIME 1¼ hours

Spiced Flan

A flan can be both a pastry-based tart and a baked custard, like a crème caramel.
This one is the latter—a feather-light custard made from butternut pumpkin (squash),
eggs and sour cream, fragrantly spiced and flavoured with orange.

1 butternut pumpkin (acorn or butternut squash), about 450 g/1 lb)

Grated zest and juice of 1 large orange

2 eggs, lightly beaten

100 g (½ cup/3½ oz) light brown sugar

1 teaspoon ground cinnamon

½ teaspoon ground ginger

¼ teaspoon freshly grated nutmeg

¼ teaspoon salt

1 tablespoon brandy (optional)

150 g (⅔ cup/5½ oz) sour cream

Icing (confectioners') sugar, for dusting

Extra sour cream, for serving

SERVES 6

PREPARATION TIME 30 minutes plus at least 1 hour cooling

COOKING TIME 25–30 minutes

1 Use a 23-cm (9-in) flan dish or non-metallic pie plate. Peel the pumpkin and cut into chunks; discard seeds. Place in a saucepan with the orange juice. Bring to the boil, then lower the heat and cook gently, covered, for 20–25 minutes or until tender. Drain, discarding the remaining juice. Purée finely in a food processor or mash well. Preheat oven to 180°C (350°F, gas mark 4).

2 Beat the eggs with the orange zest, sugar, cinnamon, ginger, nutmeg, salt, brandy, if using, and the sour cream. Add the pumpkin and mix well.

3 Bake for 25–30 minutes or until just set. Loosen the edges with a round-bladed knife, then leave to cool for 1 hour. Serve slightly warm. Alternatively, cover and chill before serving. Dust flan lightly with icing sugar and serve with sour cream.

Try this, too...

For a Souffléd Spiced Flan, in step 2, separate the eggs and beat yolks with orange zest, the sugar, ½ tsp cinnamon, 1 tsp mixed spice, the salt and the brandy, if using. Mix with puréed pumpkin. Whisk egg whites until soft peaks form. Fold into pumpkin mixture with sour cream. Pour into a 23-cm (9-in) ovenproof dish, 5-cm (2-in) deep. Scatter 30 g (¼ cup/1 oz) chopped pecan nuts over the top. Bake as for the main recipe, until slightly puffy and pale golden. Serve hot, dusted with icing sugar and with the extra sour cream.

Top Tip

Food terminology can be confusing and can often vary from country to country. Butternut pumpkin is the term used in Australia (where this recipe originated). For people in the USA and Canada, butternut or acorn squash can be used.

Butternut pumpkin (squash) is a good source of the antioxidant beta-carotene, as indicated by the bright orange colour of the flesh.

Pumpkin seeds are high in iron, magnesium, zinc and phosphorus.

Raspberry Torte

This can be made with other seasonal berries. Peaches or canned pineapple are also suitable.

FOR THE SPONGE

55g (¼ cup/2 oz) caster (superfine) sugar

1 teaspoon vanilla essence (extract)

2 eggs

60 g (½ cup/2¼ oz) plain (all-purpose) flour

¼ teaspoon baking powder

FOR THE PASTRY

125 g (1 cup/4½ oz) plain (all-purpose) flour

½ teaspoon baking powder

60 g (¼ cup/2¼ oz) butter

2 tablespoons white (granulated) sugar

1 egg yolk

FOR CHOCOLATE LAYER AND FILLING

50 g (⅓ cup/2 oz) dark (semisweet) chocolate

600 g (4¾ cups/1 lb 5 oz) fresh or frozen raspberries

115 g (½ cup/4 oz) sugar

350 g (1⅓ cups/12 oz) natural (plain) yogurt

80 ml (⅓ cup/2½ fl oz) lemon juice

14 g (1 tbsp/½ oz) powdered clear gelatine

375 ml (1½ cups/13 fl oz) cream, for whipping

FOR THE GLAZE AND DECORATION

60 ml (¼ cup/2 fl oz) redcurrant juice

60 g (¼ cup/2¼ oz) raspberry jam, warmed and strained

50 g (½ cup/2 oz) flaked almonds

1 Use 2 x 28-cm (11-in) spring-form tins. Grease the base and side of one tin. Preheat oven to 180°C (350°F, gas mark 4). To make the sponge, beat the sugar, vanilla essence, eggs and 1 tbsp cold water until fluffy.

2 Mix flour and baking powder. Sift over egg mixture and fold in with a whisk. Spread the sponge mixture in the greased tin, building it up a little at the sides. Bake for 20–25 minutes. Remove the tin from the oven. Loosen side with a knife. Turn sponge layer out onto baking (parchment) paper; do not remove the base of the tin. Let sponge cool.

3 For the pastry, combine all the ingredients in a bowl; knead into a smooth dough. Shape into a ball, press flat, wrap in cling wrap and chill for 30 minutes. Grease base of the second springform tin. Roll out pastry to line base of tin and prick several times with a fork. Bake for 12–15 minutes. Remove from the oven; cool on a wire rack. Remove from the tin.

4 To make the chocolate layer, melt chocolate in a bowl over simmering water and spread over cooled pastry base. Remove base of tin and baking paper from sponge base. Place sponge on top of pastry base with top facing downwards. Place a cake ring around the two.

5 To make the filling, purée half the raspberries, pressing them through a sieve with the back of a spoon (allow frozen berries to thaw briefly). Combine the purée, sugar, yogurt and lemon juice.

6 Sprinkle gelatine over 60 ml (¼ cup/2 fl oz) warm water in a small saucepan; stir over a low heat until dissolved. Stir into raspberry mixture; chill.

7 Beat cream until stiff. As soon as raspberry mixture begins to set, stir in the cream and pour onto the sponge base; smooth the top. After a few minutes, spread the rest of the raspberries on the raspberry mixture. (Place frozen berries on top while they are still frozen).

8 To make glaze, combine juice and jam. Spoon carefully onto raspberries so that lukewarm glaze does not mix with cream mixture.

9 Cover torte and chill for at least 2 hours. Remove cake ring just before serving. Toast almonds in a pan, cool briefly and press onto the side of the torte.

SERVES 12–16

PREPARATION TIME 1 hour plus 2 hours cooling time

COOKING TIME 35–40 minutes

143

Crème Torte with Fruit

This sumptuous torte is deceptive. It looks as though it requires a high level of culinary skill, but it couldn't be simpler. Change the fruit to whatever is in season or to your taste. Or, you can use very well drained fruit from a can.

FOR THE SPONGE

6 eggs

100 g (½ cup/3½ oz) caster (superfine) sugar

1 teaspoon vanilla essence (extract)

80 g (½ cup/2¾ oz) wholemeal (whole-wheat) flour

40 g (¼ cup/1½ oz) rice flour

1 teaspoon baking powder

FOR THE FILLING AND THE TOPPING

125 ml (½ cup/4 fl oz) milk

1 teaspoon vanilla essence (extract)

2 eggs, separated

3 tablespoons sugar

2 teaspoons rice flour

125 g (½ cup/4½ oz) natural (plain) yogurt

2 tablespoons orange marmalade

300 g (1½ cups/10½ oz) mixed fruit (such as peaches, bananas, honeydew melon and apricots), chopped

185 ml (¾ cup/6 fl oz) cream, for whipping

1 tablespoon unsalted pistachio nuts

SERVES 16

PREPARATION TIME 1 hour

COOKING TIME 30–35 minutes

1 Use a 26-cm (10½-in) spring-form tin and line with baking (parchment) paper. Preheat oven to 180°C (350°F, gas mark 4). To make the sponge, separate the eggs and beat the whites with 60 ml (¼ cup/2 fl oz) cold water until semi-stiff. Add the sugar and vanilla and beat until stiff and shiny. Stir in the yolks one at a time.

2 Mix the flours with the baking powder. Sift over egg mixture; fold in with a whisk. Spoon mixture into tin; smooth the top. Bake for 30–35 minutes. Remove from oven; leave in tin for 10 minutes. Remove cake from tin, place on a wire rack and allow to cool completely.

3 To make the filling, bring milk to a boil with the vanilla. With electric beaters, beat egg yolks and 2 tbsp sugar in a saucepan until fluffy. Add rice flour. Pour hot milk into the rice flour mixture, stirring. Place the pan over medium heat and heat, stirring constantly with a wooden spoon until thick.

4 Half-fill a bowl with cold water and a few ice cubes. Place pan in it and stir mixture until it is cold. Beat the egg whites until stiff. Fold yogurt and the marmalade into the cold crème mixture, then fold in the egg whites.

5 Slice cake into 3 and place one layer on a plate. Spread half the crème over it. Top with second layer of cake and cover with remaining crème. Top with third layer.

6 Decorate the top with the fruit. Whip cream until stiff, sweeten with remaining sugar and pour into a piping bag. Pipe swirls of cream around the edge of the cake. Chop pistachios and sprinkle on the top. Decorate with mint leaves, if liked.

Try this, too...

To make a Chocolate Sponge with Berries, bake a sponge cake with flour, rice flour and 2 heaped tbsp cocoa powder. Prepare crème as described in main recipe. Stir in 55 g (⅓ cup/2 oz) chopped dark (semisweet) chocolate with the egg whites. Fill the cake with the chocolate mixture and cover the top with blueberries, strawberries raspberries and blackberries. Pipe on cream swirls and grate dark chocolate over the top.

Meringues

A variety of flavours for the fillings makes these meringues all the more attractive for a special occasion.

FOR THE MERINGUES

4 egg whites

285 g (1 ¼ cups/10 oz) caster (superfine) sugar

170 ml (⅔ cup/5 ½ fl oz) cream, for whipping

Icing (confectioners') sugar, for decoration

FOR THE LEMON FLAVOURING

Finely grated zest of 1 lemon

1 tablespoon lemon juice

1 tablespoon icing (confectioners') sugar

FOR THE VANILLA FLAVOURING

¼ teaspoon vanilla essence (extract)

1 teaspoon icing (confectioners') sugar

FOR THE COFFEE FLAVOURING

1 ½ tablespoons strong black coffee

1 tablespoon icing (confectioners') sugar

FOR THE LIQUEUR FLAVOURING

Finely grated zest of 1 small orange

1 tablespoon Cointreau or Grand Marnier

1 teaspoon icing (confectioner's) sugar

MAKES 8

PREPARATION TIME 15 minutes

COOKING TIME 2–3 hours (the time needed to dry the meringues will vary from oven to oven)

1 Use 2 large baking trays. Line with baking (parchment) paper. Preheat oven to 110°C (225°F, gas mark ½).

2 Using a large, dry mixing bowl, whisk the egg whites until stiff but not dry. Add sugar, a tablespoon at a time, whisking until all of it is incorporated and the mixture is thick and glossy.

3 Use 2 tablespoons to form neat oval shapes; place 16 spoonfuls of the mixture on the trays, spacing them 2.5 cm (1 in) apart. Bake for 2–3 hours or until lightly coloured on the outside and still slightly soft, like marshmallow, in the centre.

4 Remove from the oven, allow to cool on the baking trays, then store in an airtight container until ready to fill.

5 For the filling, whisk chosen flavouring into the cream until thick but not buttery. Sandwich the meringues together with the cream, place on a large serving dish and sift icing sugar lightly over them.

Mango Cream Torte

The ripeness of the mango is crucial to the fruity aroma of the cream.
Ripe mangoes are fragrant and have a taut skin which yields slightly when gently pressed.

200 g (1²/₃ cups/7 oz) plain (all-purpose) flour

¹/₂ teaspoon baking powder

100 g (¹/₃ cup/3¹/₂ oz) butter

90 g (¹/₂ cup/3¹/₄ oz) white (granulated) sugar

1 egg

2 ripe mangoes

2 tablespoons lemon juice

2 egg yolks

125 ml (¹/₂ cup/4 fl oz) apple juice

10 g (3 teaspoons/¹/₄ oz) powdered clear gelatine

50 g (¹/₃ cup/1³/₄ oz) dark (semisweet) chocolate

500 ml (2 cups/17 fl oz) cream, for whipping

Few drops of vanilla essence (extract)

30 g (¹/₄ cup/1 oz) coarsely grated chocolate of your choice

1 Use a 26-cm (10¹/₂-in) spring-form tin. Preheat oven to 180°C (350°F, gas mark 4). Place the flour, baking powder, butter, 2 tbsp sugar, the egg and 2 tbsp water in a bowl and knead to make a firm dough. Shape into a ball and cover in cling wrap; chill for 30 minutes. Roll out the pastry to line the base and side of the tin. Bake for 15–20 minutes. Remove pastry base from tin; cool. Place a cake ring around it.

2 Peel mangoes. Slice flesh away from stone and cut into small cubes; mix with the lemon juice. Set 12 cubes aside and purée the remaining flesh with the egg yolks and remaining sugar. Heat 3 tbsp apple juice and dissolve gelatine in it. Stir into the mango cream with remaining apple juice. Chill.

3 Melt the chocolate in a bowl set over simmering water; spread over the pastry base. Whip 375 ml (1¹/₂ cups/13 fl oz) cream until stiff, fold into the setting mango cream and pour over the pastry base.

4 Cover the torte in cling wrap and chill overnight. Just before serving, whip the remaining cream with a few drops of vanilla until stiff; pipe onto cake. Decorate with 12 reserved mango cubes and the coarsely grated chocolate.

SERVES 12

PREPARATION TIME 45 minutes plus 12 hours cooling time

COOKING TIME 15–20 minutes

Charlotte Russe

This fabulous dessert is worth the time it takes to prepare. But make things easier for yourself by baking a double quantity of the sponge and shortcrust pasty bases and freezing half of them. Then, next time, all you have to do is thaw them, prepare the crème and fill and decorate.

FOR THE PASTRY

60 g (¼ cup/2 oz) butter, chilled

90 g (¾ cup/3 ¼ oz) plain (all-purpose) flour

1 egg yolk

FOR THE SPONGE

3 eggs

1½ tablespoons water

60 g (¼ cup/2 oz) sugar

85 g (⅔ cup/3 oz) plain (all-purpose) flour

1 tablespoon cornflour (cornstarch)

2 tablespoons rum

FOR THE CRÈME

14 g (1 tablespoon/½ oz) powdered clear gelatine

Grated zest and juice of 1 lemon

4 egg yolks

170 g (¾ cup/6 oz) caster (superfine) sugar

1 teaspoon vanilla essence (extract)

1 tablespoon orange juice

375 ml (13 fl oz/1 ½ cups) white wine

250 ml (1 cup/9 fl oz) cream, for whipping

FOR DECORATION

120 g (⅔ cup/4 oz) preserved fruit

2 tablespoons apricot jam

80 ml (⅓ cup/2½ fl oz) cream, for whipping

28 lady finger biscuits

Icing (confectioners') sugar, sifted

1 Use 2 large baking trays. Cut the butter into small pieces and place in a bowl. Add the flour and egg yolk. Knead into a smooth dough; add a little water or flour as needed. Wrap in cling wrap; chill for 30 minutes.

2 To make sponge, beat eggs and water with electric beaters for about 3 minutes or until fluffy. Add sugar and beat a further 5 minutes, or until mixture is pale. Sift flour and cornflour; add to egg mixture in several batches.

3 Preheat oven to 200°C (400°F, gas mark 6). Cut out 4 circles of baking (parchment) paper each 20 cm (8 in) in diameter and place 2 circles on each baking tray. Divide cake mixture evenly between them.

4 Bake sponge bases for about 5 minutes. Remove from oven and trim edges smoothly using a 20-cm (8-in) cake ring as a guide. Peel off paper. Leave sponge bases to cool on a wire rack, then drizzle with the rum.

5 Place pastry on a lightly floured work surface; roll out to a circle 20 cm (8 in) in diameter. Grease 1 baking tray. Place the pastry on tray and prick several times with a fork. Bake for 10–12 minutes.

6 To make crème, dissolve the gelatine in 60 ml (¼ cup/2 fl oz) water. Heat gently to dissolve. Place the lemon zest and juice, egg yolks, sugar, vanilla, orange juice and wine in a saucepan. Heat gently, stirring constantly until mixture thickens a little; do not allow it to boil. Stir in the gelatine mixture.

7 Remove pan from heat; place in a dish of cold water to stop the cooking process. Stir until cold. Whip cream until stiff. When the crème begins to set, fold in cream.

8 Drain fruit and cut into small pieces. Place pastry base on a serving platter and put a cake ring around it. Spread jam on the base. Place a sponge layer on top; cover with a quarter of the crème. Place second sponge layer on top. Spread with crème. Cover with fruit.

9 Cover with more crème and top with third sponge layer. Spread with remaining crème and smooth the top. Cover with the final sponge layer. Chill for 1 hour. Whip cream until stiff. Remove cake ring. Coat the side of the cake with the cream and firmly press lady finger biscuits onto it. Dust top with icing sugar.

SERVES 12–14

PREPARATION TIME 1 ¼ hours plus 1 hour cooling time

COOKING TIME 20 minutes

Wine Crème Torte

The creamy filling for this melt-in-the-mouth treat can be flavoured with
white grape juice and a little lemon juice instead of wine.

FOR THE BASE

200 g (1²⁄₃ cups/7 oz) plain
(all-purpose) flour

100 g (¹⁄₃ cup/3 ¹⁄₂ oz) butter

3 tablespoons sugar

1 egg

FOR THE FILLING AND DECORATION

60 ml (¹⁄₄ cup/2 fl oz) apple jelly

4 egg yolks

150 g (²⁄₃ cup/5 ¹⁄₂ oz) caster
(superfine) sugar

1 teaspoon grated lemon zest

80 ml (¹⁄₃ cup/2 ¹⁄₂ fl oz) each of
lemon and orange juice

375 ml (1 ¹⁄₂ cups/13 fl oz) white
wine

10 g (3 teaspoons/¹⁄₄ oz) powdered
clear gelatine

500 ml (2 cups/17 fl oz) cream, for
whipping

Icing (confectioners') sugar

16 small cookies

1 Use 2 large baking trays; line
with baking (parchment) paper.
Place flour, butter, sugar and egg in
a bowl and knead to form a dough.
Chill for 30 minutes. Preheat oven
to 180°C (350°F, gas mark 4). Roll out
dough to a size large enough to be
able to cut out 2 x 26-cm (10½-in)
rounds of dough. Place on the trays
and prick several times with a fork.
Bake 15–20 minutes. Leave to cool;
trim edge neatly.

2 Cover one layer with jelly; place
a cake ring around it. Beat egg
yolks with 115 g (½ cup/4 oz) sugar,
the zest and the juices in a bowl set
over gently simmering water until
mixture is the consistency of thick
cream. Heat 60 ml (¼ cup/2 fl oz)
wine and sprinkle on gelatine to
dissolve. Stir into crème mixture
with remaining wine. Cover; chill.

3 Whip the cream until stiff and
sweeten a quarter of it with the
remaining sugar. Place in a piping
bag. Fold the remaining cream into
setting wine crème. Pour mixture
onto cake base. Chill.

4 Cut second pastry layer into
16 pieces and place on top of
crème. Chill for 6 hours. Sift icing
sugar over and decorate with piped
cream rosettes and cookies.

SERVES 16

PREPARATION TIME 50 minutes plus
at least 6½ hours cooling time

COOKING TIME 15–20 minutes

Pear Tartlets

These attractively shaped tartlets are ideal served warm as a dinner-party
dessert with whipped cream or ice cream.

3 sheets fresh or frozen puff pastry,
   about 400 g/14 oz

1 egg yolk

FOR THE FILLING

6 firm pears

1 tablespoon lemon juice

125 ml (½ cup/4 fl oz) white wine

150 g (1½ cups/5½ oz) ground
   almonds

2 tablespoons honey

80 ml (⅓ cup/2½ fl oz) cream

12 cloves and 12 pumpkin seeds

2 tablespoons fresh currant jelly

MAKES 12

PREPARATION TIME 30 minutes

COOKING TIME 15–20 minutes

1 Use a large baking tray and line with baking (parchment) paper. Preheat oven to 220°C (425°F, gas mark 7). Place pastry sheets beside one another; thaw if necessary.

2 For the filling, peel, halve and core the pears. Bring the pear halves to a boil in a pan with the lemon juice and wine. Cover and stew over a low heat for 5 minutes. Remove from heat and drain pears.

3 Combine almonds, honey and cream. Roll out pastry 3 mm (⅛ in) thick on a lightly floured work surface. Cut into 12 pear-shaped pieces with stems; they should be 2.5 cm (1 in) larger all round than the pear halves.

4 Shape remaining pastry into leaves and press onto stems. Place pear-shaped pastry pieces on baking tray and prick several times with a fork. Spread almond filling in the middle of each pastry; leave a 1-cm (½-in) wide margin.

5 Make several incisions along the length of the round side of each pear or score with the tines of a fork; place the fruit flat side down on almond filling. Place the cloves in the pears for the blossoms and pumpkin seeds as stems. Combine egg yolk with 2 tsp water and brush over the edges of the pastries. Bake for 15–20 minutes; coat with jelly while still warm.

151

Strawberry Shortcake

This streamlined version of an American classic makes an impressive
summer dessert. It is based on a quick, light scone mixture and is filled with yogurt,
whipped cream and lots of juicy fresh strawberries…simply irresistible!

250 g (2 cups/9 oz) self-raising
(self-rising) flour

1 teaspoon baking powder

90 g (⅓ cup/3¼ oz) unsalted
butter, cut into small pieces

3 tablespoons caster (superfine)
sugar

1 egg, beaten

80 ml (⅓ cup/2½ fl oz) milk

½ teaspoon vanilla essence (extract)

1 teaspoon icing (confectioners')
sugar

FOR THE FILLING

350 g (2⅓ cups/12 oz) strawberries

90 ml (⅓ cup/3 fl oz) cream, for
whipping

90 g (⅓ cup/3¼ oz) natural (plain)
yogurt

SERVES 8

PREPARATION TIME 15 minutes

COOKING TIME 10–15 minutes

Top Tip

Rinse strawberries in cold water,
then hull them. If you hull them
before rinsing, they will absorb
excess water. To hull a strawberry,
remove both the leafy cap and the
white 'core' attached to the cap.
Use a small paring knife to dig it
out quickly.

Whipping the cream incorporates
air into it and increases its volume,
thus making a modest amount go
quite a long way.

1 Use a baking tray and grease
lightly. Preheat oven to 220°C
(425°F, gas mark 7). Sift flour and
baking powder into a bowl. Rub in
the butter until mixture resembles
fine breadcrumbs. Stir in the sugar.
Make a well in the centre.

2 Combine the beaten egg, milk
and vanilla essence and pour
into the dry ingredients. Gradually
stir dry ingredients into the liquid;
draw together with your hands into
a soft dough. Pat into a smooth ball;
place on a floured work surface.

3 Roll out the dough into a 19-cm
(7½-in) round. Place on baking
tray; bake 10–15 minutes or until
well risen, firm and browned on the
top. Slide the shortcake onto a wire
rack and leave to cool.

4 Using a large serrated knife,
slice shortcake horizontally in
half. Cut the top layer into 8 equal
wedges. Trim a fraction off each so
that there is a little space between
them when you place them on top
of the shortcake. Place bottom layer
on a serving plate.

5 For the filling, reserve 8 whole
strawberries; hull the remainder
and slice thickly. Whip cream until
soft peaks form. Stir yogurt; gently
fold it into the cream until blended.

6 Spread cream mixture thickly
over the bottom shortcake layer
and cover with sliced strawberries,
pressing them into the cream.

7 Sift icing sugar over the shortcake wedges and place on top
of the shortcake. Slice the reserved
strawberry lengthwise, leaving the
slices attached at the stalk end. Fan
them out slightly and place one on
each shortcake wedge. This cake is
best eaten within a few hours of
being assembled.

Try this, too…

For Spiced Shortcake add 1 tsp
ground cinnamon to the scone
mixture with the caster sugar.
Stone and slice 225 g (1⅓ cups/
8 oz) ripe plums. Reserve 8 slices
for decoration. Place remainder
on top of cream. Reserve 8 blackberries from 225 g (1⅓ cups/8 oz)
and press the remainder into the
cream with the plums. Finish as
in the main recipe, decorating the
top of the shortcake wedges with
the reserved plum slices and
blackberries.

Christening Cake

This beautifully iced and decorated fruitcake is a wonderful, traditional way
to welcome a new member of the family.

500 g (2½ cups/1 lb 2 oz) butter

285 g (1¼ cups/10 oz) caster (superfine) sugar

8 eggs, separated

500 g (4 cups/1 lb 2 oz) plain (all-purpose) flour

1 teaspoon each of ground cinnamon and mace

125 ml (½ cup/4 fl oz) brandy or whisky

375 g (3 cups/13 oz) sultanas (golden raisins)

125 g (1 cup/4½ oz) slivered almonds

550 g (3 cups/1 lb 4 oz) chopped mixed peel

FOR THE ALMOND PASTE

375 g (3 cups/13 oz) icing (confectioners') sugar

450 g (4½ cups/1 lb) ground almonds

8 egg yolks

1 teaspoon vanilla essence (extract)

1 tablespoon rosewater

125 ml (½ cup/4 fl oz) apricot jam, heated and sieved

FOR THE ICING AND DECORATION

6 egg whites, lightly whisked

1.1 kg (9 cups/2 lb 7 oz) icing (confectioners') sugar, sifted

3 teaspoons lemon juice

Fresh flower heads: miniature roses, freesias, violets or rose petals

1 small egg white, lightly beaten

4 teaspoons rosewater

About 170 g (¾ cup/6 oz) caster (superfine) sugar

THE CAKE

1 Use a 23-cm (9-in) square cake tin. Grease and line with baking (parchment) paper. Preheat oven to 180°C (350°F, gas mark 4). Beat the butter until soft and creamy, then add sugar and beat until mixture is very light and fluffy.

2 Whisk the egg whites until soft peaks form. Gradually beat into creamed mixture. Whisk yolks until pale, thick and creamy; then beat gradually into the butter mixture.

3 Sift flour and spice into the bowl and, using a large metal spoon, carefully fold them into the mixture. Gently mix in the brandy or whisky, then gently fold in the sultanas and slivered almonds.

4 Spoon a third of the mixture into the tin, spread evenly and sprinkle with half the peel. Spoon in half the remaining mixture and sprinkle with remaining peel. Spread the last of the mixture on top.

5 Bake in the centre of the oven for 1¼–1½ hours, until a skewer inserted into the centre of the cake comes out clean. Remove from the oven, leave in the tin for 1 hour to cool. Remove from tin and transfer to a wire rack to cool completely.

THE ALMOND PASTE

1 To make the almond paste, sift icing sugar into a bowl. Add the almonds; mix to a stiff paste with egg yolks, vanilla and rosewater.

Turn out onto a work surface lightly dusted with icing sugar and knead briefly until smooth. Roll out to a 38-cm (15-in) square.

2 Place cake on a 28-cm (11¼ in) cake board and brush apricot jam over all surfaces. Carefully lift the paste onto the cake; smooth it evenly over the top and down the sides. Trim off the excess around the base. Leave overnight in a cool place to dry.

THE ICING

1 To make the icing, put the egg whites in a bowl and gradually beat in the icing sugar, beating well until the mixture is smooth. Stir in the lemon juice.

2 Using a palette knife, spread an even layer of icing over the top of the cake. Pull a ruler, preferably a metal one, across the top of the cake to smooth the icing. Trim the excess icing from the edges. Spread a coat of icing over one side of the cake, then pull a cake scraper along the side to smooth it. Repeat with the other sides.

3 Leave the cake overnight to dry. Meanwhile, put the remaining icing in a clean bowl, cover surface closely with cling wrap, cover bowl and refrigerate.

4 Next day, trim the rough icing from around the top edge and corners of the cake with a sharp knife. Beat chilled icing mixture

and coat the cake as before. Repeat twice more, leaving each coat to dry overnight before adding the next. Reserve remaining icing for piping decorative borders of your choice around the cake's edges.

THE DECORATION

1 To make the decoration, select 18 to 24 of the most perfect flower heads. Depending on their size, leave them whole or separate the petals.

2 Blend egg white smoothly with the rosewater. Using a clean, fine paintbrush, paint each flower lightly and evenly with the mixture. Immediately sift lightly with caster sugar all over.

3 Dry the flowers on a wire rack for 2–3 days in a warm place.

4 Spoon some of the remaining icing into a piping bag fitted with a small star nozzle; pipe a decorative border around the top

and bottom edges of the cake. Use stars or shells, or a double shell edge as shown in the picture.

5 Leave overnight to dry. Tie a ribbon around cake. Decorate the top with the sugared flowers.

SERVES 40

PREPARATION TIME about 7 hours over 7–8 days

COOKING TIME 1 1/4–1 1/2 hours

holiday baking

Panettone

The yeast dough for this Italian specialty is unusually runny, which makes the cake
all the more moist and light. Mini-panettone can be baked successfully in muffin pans.

125 g (1 cup/4½ oz) sultanas
(golden raisins)

2 tablespoons rum

150 g (⅔ cup/5½ oz) butter, plus
extra for brushing

400 g (3¼ cups/14 oz) plain
(all-purpose) flour

½ teaspoon salt

125 ml (½ cup/4 fl oz) milk

14 g (½ oz) dry (powdered) yeast

60 g (⅓ cup/2¼ oz) white
(granulated) sugar

1 teaspoon vanilla essence (extract)

4 eggs and 2 egg yolks

50 g (¼ cup/1¾ oz) glacé
(candied) cherries, cut in
small pieces

55 g (⅓ cup/2 oz) each of
blanched almonds, candied
orange peel and candied lemon
peel, finely chopped

105 g (⅓ cup/3½ oz) apricot jam

125 g (1 cup/4½ oz) icing
(confectioners') sugar

1–2 tablespoons lemon juice

SERVES 16

PREPARATION TIME 40 minutes plus
1½–2 hours resting time

COOKING TIME 60–70 minutes

1 Use a 22-cm (8½-in) springform tin. Soak the sultanas in rum for about 20 minutes until plump. Melt butter and allow to cool.

2 To make the dough, place flour and salt in a mixing bowl and pour butter around the edge. Heat milk until lukewarm, stir in yeast, sugar, vanilla essence, eggs and egg yolks and add mixture to the bowl. Knead dough for about 5 minutes with the dough hooks of an electric mixer or by hand.

3 Work glacé cherries into the dough with the almonds, peel and drained sultanas. Cover with a cloth and leave in a warm place to rise for 40 minutes.

4 Grease springform tin thickly with butter. Fold a double layer of baking (parchment) paper into a 30- x 35-cm (12- x 14-in) strip and make into a ring using a paper clip. Press ring around the inside of the tin to increase its height.

5 Beat dough vigorously with a wooden spoon, cover and let rise again for 10 minutes. Preheat oven to 200°C (400°F, gas mark 6). Place dough in the tin. Cover and leave to rise until it is almost the height of the baking paper ring.

6 Bake panettone on the lowest oven shelf for 60–70 minutes until brown; brush with soft butter 2 or 3 times during cooking. After 30 minutes, check that the top is not browning too fast; cover with baking paper, if necessary. The cake is cooked when a skewer inserted in the centre comes out clean.

7 Remove from the oven; leave to cool for 5 minutes. Place on a wire rack and loosen the side of the tin. Leave to cool completely. Remove paper and tin just before serving. Warm and strain the jam and brush over the cake. Combine icing sugar and lemon juice and spread lightly over the panettone.

Top Tale

Panettone is a cake associated with Milan. It is usually prepared and enjoyed at Christmas. There are many stories about its history, each claiming to be the definitive one. However, its exact origins are unknown. Panettone tastes good served with crema di mascarpone, a mixture of mascarpone cheese, eggs and a sweet liqueur such as almond liqueur.

Christmas Stollen

Stollen is shaped with tapered ends and a ridge down the centre,
symbolising the infant Jesus in swaddling clothes.

310 g (2½ cups/11 oz) sultanas (golden raisins)

115 g (¾ cup/4 oz) currants

2 tablespoons rum

10 g (¼ oz) dry (powdered) yeast

2 teaspoons sugar

250 ml (1 cup/9 fl oz) lukewarm milk

750 g (6 cups/1 lb 10 oz) flour, plus extra for kneading

120 g (⅔ cup/4¼ oz) white (granulated) sugar

Pinch of salt

2 teaspoons finely grated lemon zest

6 drops bitter almond essence (extract)

Pinch each of ground cardamom and ground mace

250 g (1 cup/9 oz) butter, melted

95 g (½ cup/3½ oz) candied lemon peel, finely diced

100 g (1 cup/3½ oz) ground almonds

60 g (¼ cup/2¼ oz) butter, for spreading

Icing (confectioners') sugar, for dusting

SERVES 18

PREPARATION TIME 40 minutes plus 1½–2 hours resting time

COOKING TIME 45–55 minutes

1 Soak the sultanas and currants in rum for 20 minutes. Drain in a sieve. Stir the yeast, sugar and 60 ml (¼ cup/2 fl oz) milk in a bowl. Leave to rise at room temperature for 15 minutes.

2 Place 500 g (4 cups/1 lb 2 oz) flour in a bowl. Make a well in the centre. Place sugar, salt, lemon zest, almond essence, spices and melted butter on top of the flour.

3 Pour the yeasty milk mixture into the well. Starting from the centre, work ingredients together. Add the remaining flour and knead dough vigorously until it is smooth and no longer sticks to the sides of the bowl. Add the drained sultanas and currants with the candied peel and almonds and knead to combine. Cover the dough with a cloth; leave to rise in a warm place for 1 hour.

4 Lightly flour a work surface. Knead and punch down the dough for about 10 minutes; it is ready when it feels elastic and is no longer sticky. Roll out the dough into a 35-cm (14-in) circle. Fold one side over to just beyond the centre to make the traditional shape.

5 Line a baking tray with baking (parchment) paper. Place the stollen on it, cover with a cloth and leave to rise in a warm place until it has increased by half its original size, both in height and in width. Preheat oven to 250°C (500°F, gas mark 9).

6 Place stollen in preheated oven. Reduce the oven temperature to 160°C (315°F, gas mark 2–3). Bake for 45–55 minutes.

7 Melt the butter in a small pan and brush generously over the stollen while it is still hot from the oven. Dust thinly with icing sugar and allow to cool completely. Wrap in foil and store for 2–3 weeks. Sift a thick layer of icing sugar over the top before serving.

Sugar Nut Bars

This is the ideal recipe for Christmas cooks in a hurry.
Simply roll out the mixture, bake it as a sheet and then cut into slices.

150 g (¾ cup/5½ oz) brown sugar

235 g (⅔ cup/8½ oz) honey

55 g (⅓ cup/2 oz) each of candied lemon and orange peel, finely chopped

310 g (2½ cups/11 oz) plain (all-purpose) flour

100 g (⅔ cup/3½ oz) coarsely chopped almonds

1 teaspoon grated lemon zest

1 teaspoon baking powder

¼ teaspoon each of grated nutmeg and ground cloves

1 teaspoon ground cinnamon

90 g (¾ cup/3 oz) icing (confectioners') sugar

2–3 tablespoons Kirsch

1 Use a 30- x 20-cm (12- x 8-in) deep baking tray. Line the base and sides with baking (parchment) paper. Place sugar and honey in a pan, bring to a boil and boil until sugar has dissolved. Allow mixture to cool.

2 Place honey mixture in a bowl. Add peel, flour, almonds, zest, baking powder and spices. Knead mixture into a sticky dough using electric beaters with dough hooks fitted or knead by hand. Smooth the dough into a ball.

3 Roll out the dough on a lightly floured work surface to 1 cm (½-in) thick, large enough to fit the baking tray. Place dough on the tray, cover with a cloth kitchen towel and leave in a cool place overnight.

4 Preheat oven to 200°C (400°F, gas mark 6). Bake the cookies for 15–20 minutes. While still hot, brush with a mixture of icing sugar and Kirsch. Slice into 2.5- x 5-cm (1- x 2-in) rectangles. Leave to cool.

MAKES 50

PREPARATION TIME 20 minutes plus overnight cooling and resting

COOKING TIME 15–20 minutes

Spice Cookies

In this classic festive recipe, almonds are used in place of flour to produce delicious chewy cookies with a bit of crunch to them.

100 g (²⁄₃ cup/3½ oz) blanched almonds

200 g (2 cups/7 oz) ground almonds

55 g (¹⁄₃ cup/2 oz) each of candied lemon peel and candied orange peel, finely chopped

1 teaspoon grated lemon zest

½ teaspoon each of ground cloves, ground cinnamon and ground ginger

3 eggs

225 g (1¼ cups/8 oz) brown sugar

1 Use 2 large baking trays; line with baking (parchment) paper. Preheat oven to 150°C (300°F, gas mark 2). Chop one quarter of the almonds in halves; toast lightly on a baking tray for 10 minutes. Cool.

2 Coarsely chop the remaining blanched almonds. Combine the chopped and ground almonds with the peel, zest and spices.

3 Place eggs and sugar in a bowl over hot, but not boiling water; whisk for 6–8 minutes with a hand whisk until thick and creamy.

4 Using a whisk, fold the almond mixture into the egg mixture. Drop tablespoonfuls of the mixture onto trays, piling it up a little in the centre of each cookie.

5 Decorate cookies with toasted halved almonds. Bake for about 20 minutes (this is more of a drying process in a cool oven), one tray at a time; the cookies should remain soft. Remove from oven, place on a wire rack overnight to cool and dry.

Try this, too...

For Glazed Cherry Cookies, cook as for main recipe; omit almonds for decoration. Mix 150 g (1¼ cups/ 5½ oz) icing (confectioners') sugar and 2–3 tbsp rum or lemon juice; spread over hot cookies. Decorate with glacé (candied) cherries.

MAKES 40

PREPARATION TIME 35 minutes

COOKING TIME 20 minutes per baking tray plus overnight cooling

163

Vanilla Cookies

These look pretty if the baked objects and scenes are painted with coloured icing.

2 eggs

225 g (1 cup/8 oz) white (granulated) sugar

1 teaspoon vanilla essence (extract)

250 g (2 cups/9 oz) plain (all-purpose) flour

Generous pinch of baking powder and bicarbonate of soda (baking soda)

MAKES 80

PREPARATION TIME 45 minutes plus 2 hours cooling time plus resting time overnight

COOKING TIME 35 minutes per baking tray

1 Use 2 baking trays. Line with baking (parchment) paper. Beat eggs, sugar and vanilla with electric beaters until pale and fluffy. Mix remaining dry ingredients and fold into egg mixture. Add a little more flour if the mixture is sticky.

2 Wrap in cling wrap and chill for about 2 hours. Roll out dough on a lightly floured work surface to 5 mm (¼ in) thick.

3 Moisten a mould on the picture side with water and carefully dust with flour. Press mould firmly onto the dough so that the picture is stamped on it. Repeat across the rest of the dough. Dust mould each time before stamping.

4 Make cookies by cutting along the edges of the pictures. Place on baking trays; leave overnight to dry. Preheat oven to 150°C (300°F, gas mark 2). Bake cookies, one tray at a time for about 25 minutes; do not let them brown. Turn cookies onto a wire rack to cool. Paint with coloured icing, if desired.

Lemon Cookies

Other candied peel such as pineapple, pawpaw or mango can be used in this recipe.

1 lemon

4 eggs and 6 egg yolks

500 g (2¼ cups/1 lb 2 oz) white (granulated) sugar

500 g (5 cups/1 lb 2 oz) ground almonds

55 g (⅓ cup/3½ oz) candied orange and lemon peel, finely chopped (combined weight)

1 teaspoon ground cinnamon

Pinch of ground cloves

2 pinches bicarbonate of soda (baking soda)

500 g (4 cups/1 lb 2 oz) plain (all-purpose) flour

55 g (½ cup/2 oz) icing (confectioners') sugar

1 Use 2 baking trays. Finely grate zest of half the lemon; squeeze the juice of the whole lemon. Place eggs, yolks and sugar in a bowl and beat with electric beaters until pale and fluffy.

2 Stir almonds, lemon zest and juice (reserve 1 tbsp), the peel, spices and bicarbonate of soda into the egg mixture. Add the flour and knead to a smooth dough. Wrap in cling wrap and chill for 30 minutes.

3 Roll out the dough on a lightly floured work surface to 5 mm (¼ in) thick. Cut out 70 4- x 8-cm (1½- x 3-in) rectangles. Cover with a cloth and leave for 3 hours.

4 Preheat oven to 180°C (350°F, gas mark 4). Line baking trays with baking (parchment) paper. Place cookies on the trays 2.5 cm (1 in) apart; bake for 20–25 minutes until light brown. Turn onto a wire rack. Ice with the combined icing sugar and lemon juice when cool.

MAKES 70

PREPARATION TIME 25 minutes plus 3 hours resting time

COOKING TIME 20–25 minutes per baking tray

German Spiced Cookies

These are called spekulatius cookies in Germany. If you do not have specially shaped moulds, roll out the dough as a sheet and cut into squares.

200 g (1 ½ cups/7 oz) plain (all-purpose) flour

¼ teaspoon baking powder

100 g (⅓ cup/3 ½ oz) butter, chopped

100 g (½ cup/3 ½ oz) brown sugar

1 egg yolk

1–2 tablespoons milk

1 teaspoon ground mixed spice (allspice)

1 teaspoon vanilla essence (extract)

30 g (⅓ cup/2 oz) flaked almonds

Cornflour (cornstarch), for shaping

MAKES 40

PREPARATION TIME 45 minutes plus 30 minutes cooling time

COOKING TIME 10–15 minutes per baking tray

Top Tip

Look in specialty cookware stores for rolling pins and moulds carved with festive scenes and designs.

1 Use 2 large baking trays. Line with baking (parchment) paper. Place flour, baking powder, butter, sugar, egg yolk, milk, mixed spice and vanilla in a bowl; knead into a dough. Shape into a ball and wrap in cling wrap; chill for 30 minutes.

2 Preheat oven to 180°C (350°F, gas mark 4). Sprinkle baking paper with flaked almonds.

3 Lightly flour work surface. Roll out pastry to 5 mm (¼ in) thick; cut into pieces to fit figures in the spekulatius moulds. Dust moulds with cornflour and press the pastry into them.

4 Turn moulds over and strike so that the pastry shapes fall out. Place on baking trays. Remove any remaining cornflour by brushing the pastry with a little water.

5 Bake 10–15 minutes (this will depend on size and thickness of cookies) or until golden. Remove from oven. Cool on a wire rack.

Try this, too...

For Marzipan-filled Cookies (small cookies in the photo), knead 350 g (1¾ cups/12 oz) plain (all-purpose) flour, 2 tsp baking powder, 155 g (⅔ cup/5½ oz) each of butter and brown sugar, 2 tsp mixed spice and 310 g (3 cups/11 oz) ground almonds into a dough. Form into a ball and chill. Preheat oven to 180°C (350°F, gas mark 4), line tray with baking paper. Finely crumble 310 g (11 oz) marzipan paste with a fork. Work to a spreadable mass with 210 g (1¾ cups/7½ oz) icing (confectioners') sugar and 5 tbsp orange juice. Roll out dough into 2 sheets of equal size. Put 1 sheet on baking tray. Spread with the marzipan mixture; put second sheet on top and press the edges together. Brush with a mixture of beaten egg yolk and 2 tsp water. Prick dough with a fork. Top with halved blanched almonds. Bake for 40 minutes until golden. Cut into 60 rectangles while warm.

Nutty Macaroons

With their cheerful cherry decoration, these little macaroons look very festive.
They're packed with flavour, too.

2 egg whites

140 g (¾ cup/5 oz) caster (superfine) sugar

75 g (⅔ cup/2½ oz) ground hazelnuts (filberts)

75 g (⅔ cup/2½ oz) ground almonds

85 g (⅔ cup/3 oz) grated dark (semisweet) chocolate

85 g (⅔ cup/3 oz) sultanas (golden raisins)

1 teaspoon grated lemon zest

1 tablespoon rum

½ teaspoon ground cinnamon

100 g (¾ cup/3½ oz) plain (all-purpose) flour

125 g (1 cup/4½ oz) icing (confectioners') sugar

2 tablespoons lemon juice

15 red glacé (candied) cherries, cut in halves

MAKES 30
PREPARATION TIME 35 minutes
COOKING TIME 12–15 minutes

1 Use 2 baking trays. Preheat the oven to 160°C (315°F, gas mark 2–3); line baking tray with baking (parchment) paper.

2 Beat egg whites with electric beaters until very stiff. Add half the sugar, a little at a time, beating until mixture is shiny and the sugar has dissolved.

3 Using a large whisk, fold in the remaining sugar, the ground nuts, chocolate, sultanas, zest, rum, cinnamon and flour, taking care that the beaten egg whites retain their shape and stiffness. Using a teaspoon, shape 30 walnut-sized mounds of mixture and place on baking trays.

4 Cook for 12–15 minutes (the low temperature will dry the macaroons out rather than actually bake them); when done, the insides should still be soft. Transfer to a wire rack.

5 Combine the icing sugar and lemon juice in a small bowl. Cover macaroons thinly with icing while still hot; decorate each one with half a glacé cherry.

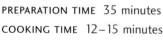

Top Tip

To make a luxury version of these macaroons, after they have cooled and been iced, coat the bases with melted chocolate and leave to set.

Shortbread Shapes

Turn a simple recipe into something special just by using differently shaped cookie cutters. Children love cutting out the stars, hearts and rounds.

400 g (3¼ cups/14 oz) plain (all-purpose) flour

185 g (¾ cup/7 oz) butter, chopped

100 g (¾ cup/3½ oz) icing (confectioners') sugar

1 egg and 1 egg yolk

Pinch of salt

2 teaspoons cream

Sugar sprinkles, glacé (candied) cherries and blanched almonds, for decoration

MAKES 50

PREPARATION TIME 30 minutes plus 30 minutes cooling time

COOKING TIME 10–15 minutes per baking tray

1 Use 2 baking trays; line with baking (parchment) paper. Sift flour onto a work surface; make a well in the centre. Place the butter, icing sugar, whole egg and salt in the well. Starting from the centre, work the ingredients into a smooth dough. Roll into a ball, wrap in cling wrap and chill for 30 minutes.

2 Preheat oven to 200°C (400°F, gas mark 6). Roll out the dough thinly on a lightly floured work surface. Use shaped cookie cutters to cut out 50 shortbread shapes.

3 Place shapes 2.5 cm (1 in) apart on trays. Brush with combined egg yolk and cream. Top with sugar sprinkles or chopped glacé cherries. Bake shortbread, one tray at a time, for 10–15 minutes until golden.

Santa Cookies

Served fresh from the oven with a cup of hot chocolate spiced with cinnamon, these festive figures won't last long. It is best to bake a double quantity and freeze one portion without the icing. Thaw shortly before serving, then ice and reheat briefly.

80 ml (⅓ cup/2 fl oz) vegetable oil

1 teaspoon salt

500 g (4 cups/1 lb 2 oz) plain (all-purpose) flour

200 ml (¾ cup/7 fl oz) milk

10 g (¼ oz) dry (powdered) yeast

60 g (⅓ cup/2¼ oz) white (granulated) sugar

2 eggs

1 teaspoon vanilla essence (extract)

FOR DECORATION

A selection of cashew nuts, pumpkin seeds, hazelnuts (filberts), poppyseeds and almonds

FOR THE GLAZE

200 g (1⅔ cups/7 oz) icing (confectioners') sugar

1 tablespoon clear berry jam (jelly)

2–3 drops red food colouring

1 egg white

MAKES 14

PREPARATION TIME 1 hour plus 1½ hours resting time

COOKING TIME 15–20 minutes per baking tray

1 Use 2 baking trays. Line with baking (parchment) paper. To make the dough, mix oil with salt and flour in a bowl. Heat milk until lukewarm. Stir the yeast, sugar and eggs into 170 ml (⅔ cup/5½ fl oz) milk and pour into flour mixture.

2 Knead to form a smooth dough, if necessary adding just enough of the remaining milk to make the dough soft and very slightly sticky. Shape dough into a ball, cover with a cloth and let rise in a warm place for 30 minutes.

3 Knead the dough on a lightly floured work surface for about 5 minutes. Roll out dough to make 2 rectangles, each 15 x 30 cm (6 x 12 in). Cut out 14 triangles of equal size and place on baking trays.

4 Brush the dough triangles with milk. Decorate the faces using nuts and seeds. Cover and let rise for 30–40 minutes.

5 Preheat oven to 200°C (400°F, gas mark 6). Bake cookies, one tray at a time, for 15–20 minutes or until golden brown. Place on a wire rack.

6 Combine 50 g (⅓ cup/2 oz) icing sugar, the jam and the food colouring. Use to paint hats on the Santas. Beat egg white until stiff; beat in the remaining icing sugar until the mixture is very shiny and forms peaks.

7 Pour icing into a piping bag and pipe wavy lines for the beards and hat trim. Leave to dry at room temperature or in an oven heated to 70°C (150°F, gas mark ¼).

Try this, too...

To make Dough Boys, make dough as for main recipe; roll out 2.5 cm (1 in) thick. Cut out 4 dough boys. Decorate with raisins for the eyes, mouth and buttons. Brush with a mixture of 2 tbsp milk and 1 tbsp sugar. Bake as described in main recipe for 15–20 minutes.

Fruit Bread

Wrapped in foil and tied with Christmas ribbon, this loaf makes an ideal gift during the Advent and Christmas season.

200 g (2⅔ cups/7 oz) dried pears

125 g (⅔ cup/4½ oz) dried figs

60 g (⅓ cup/2¼ oz) fresh dates

250 g (1¾ cups/9 oz) hazelnuts (filberts)

60 g (⅓ cup/2¼ oz) each of candied lemon and candied orange peel

60 g (½ cup/2¼ oz) sultanas (golden raisins)

6 tablespoons pear brandy

1 teaspoon each of ground cinnamon and mixed spice (allspice)

½ teaspoon ground coriander

¼ teaspoon each of fennel seeds and aniseed

100 g (⅔ cup/3½ oz) wholemeal (whole-wheat) rye flour

50 g (⅓ cup/1¾ oz) wholemeal (whole-wheat) flour

125 ml (½ cup/4 fl oz) milk

10 g (¼ oz) dry (powdered) yeast

2 tablespoons butter

1 tablespoon lemon juice

30 g (¼ cup/1 oz) blanched almonds

2 tablespoons milk, extra

MAKES 1 loaf

PREPARATION TIME 1 hour plus overnight soaking plus 2¼ hours resting time

COOKING TIME 1 hour

1 Place dried fruit in a pan and cover with water. Cover; leave to soak overnight. Boil the fruit for 20 minutes; drain. Cut dried fruit into medium-sized pieces.

2 Discard the date seeds and cut the dates into strips lengthwise. Coarsely chop the hazelnuts; finely chop the candied peel.

3 Mix all the fruit in a bowl with sultanas, pear brandy, spices, fennel seeds and aniseed. Cover and set aside.

4 Mix the flours in a bowl. Make a well in the centre. Heat milk to lukewarm. Sprinkle yeast over 2 tbsp milk; leave for 5 minutes to dissolve, stirring once.

5 Pour dissolved yeast into well; cover with a little flour. Cover with a cloth and leave to rise in a warm place for 15 minutes.

6 Melt butter in a saucepan. Add the remaining milk, butter and lemon juice to flour mixture. Knead to a smooth dough; it should not be sticky. Cover dough and let rise in a warm place for around 1½ hours, until doubled in size.

7 Knead fruit mixture into dough. Place dough on a lightly floured work surface and shape into a loaf. Let rise for another 30 minutes.

8 Grease a baking tray. Preheat the oven to 180°C (350°F, gas mark 4).

9 Decorate loaf with blanched almonds and brush top with a little of the extra milk. Bake on the lower shelf of the oven for 1 hour, brushing with milk several times during the cooking.

Top Tip

This loaf tastes best if the flavours mature for a while. Wrap it in foil after cooling and store for 1 week.

Christmas Shapes

Together with red and gold balls, stars, candles and all the other
trimmings, these honey cookies are very eye-catching on the Christmas tree.
Make some for the tree and some for eating!

FOR THE DOUGH

260 g (¾ cup/9 oz) clear honey

115 g (½ cup/4 oz) brown sugar

1 teaspoon vanilla essence (extract)

1 egg

2 tablespoons rum

250 g (2 cups/9 oz) plain
(all-purpose) flour

250 g (2½ cups/9 oz) rye flour

1 teaspoon baking powder

1 tablespoon ground cinnamon

Pinch each of salt, grated nutmeg
and ground cloves

1 teaspoon grated lemon zest

FOR DECORATION

60 ml (¼ cup/2 fl oz) cream

Glacé (candied) cherries

Blanched almonds, cut in halves

Coloured sugar pearls

MAKES 100

PREPARATION TIME 45 minutes

COOKING TIME 20–25 minutes per
baking tray

1 Use 2 baking trays; line with baking (parchment) paper. Heat honey and sugar in a pan over low heat. Pour into a mixing bowl, add vanilla essence, egg and rum and beat until fluffy. Stir flours, baking powder, salt, spices and zest into the honey mixture. Knead well and form into a ball.

2 Preheat oven to 200°C (400°F, gas mark 6). Place dough on a lightly floured work surface and roll out 1 cm (½ in) thick. Use a variety of Christmas-themed cookie cutters and cut out about 100 cookies.

3 Place cookies about 1 cm (½ in) apart on the trays. Brush with cream, then decorate with the glacé cherries, almonds and sugar pearls. Use a knitting needle to make holes in the cookies you intend to hang on the Christmas tree; don't make them too small as they will close up a little during cooking.

4 Bake cookies for 20–25 minutes. Remove from oven and leave to harden for a short time while still on the trays. Then lift carefully with a palette knife and cool completely on a wire rack.

5 Thread coloured ribbon through the cookies that are to decorate the tree. Store the remainder in air-tight tins or freezer containers so they do not become moist and soft.

Top Tip

Experiment with different types of honey. Those with a strong flavour work particularly well. If honey has turned solid in the jar, place the jar in hot water. Make sure the water is no hotter than 30°C (70°F), as overheating the honey causes the loss of important nutrients.

Oatmeal Macaroons

These crunchy, munchy morsels are very easy to make.
Let the children help with a batch.

65 g (¼ cup/2¼ oz) butter

150 g (1½ cups/5½ oz) original rolled (porridge) oats

1 egg

55 g (¼ cup/2 oz) brown sugar

½ teaspoon ground cinnamon

Pinch of ground cloves

115 g (½ cup/4 oz) dried apricots or dried pitted dates, chopped in small pieces

1 teaspoon grated lemon zest

MAKES 35

PREPARATION TIME 30 minutes

COOKING TIME 15–18 minutes per baking tray

1 Use 2 baking trays; line with baking (parchment) paper. Preheat oven to 180°C (350°F, gas mark 4). Melt butter in a pan, add rolled oats and brown them lightly; stir constantly. Transfer to a large plate and allow to cool.

2 Beat egg, sugar and spices with electric beaters until very fluffy. Stir in the oats, dried fruit and the lemon zest.

3 Using a moistened teaspoon, form mixture into 35 walnut-sized mounds and place on baking trays about 5 cm (1 in) apart; the macaroons expand as they cook.

4 Bake the cookies, one tray at a time, on the top shelf of the oven for 15–18 minutes until light brown. Place on a wire rack to cool.

Coconut Kisses

These very pretty cookies have a name to match.
Add cocoa powder to some of the mixture to make different colours.

3 egg whites

75 g (⅓ cup/2½ oz) white (granulated) sugar

½ teaspoon lemon juice

85 g (⅔ cup/3 oz) icing (confectioners') sugar

225 g (2¼ cups/8 oz) desiccated coconut

100 g (⅔ cup/3½ oz) chopped dark (semisweet) chocolate

MAKES 50

PREPARATION TIME 20 minutes

COOKING TIME 12–15 minutes per baking tray

1 Use 2 large baking trays; line with baking (parchment) paper. Preheat oven to 160°C (315°F, gas mark 2–3).

2 Beat egg whites in a large bowl with electric beaters until stiff. Gradually add the sugar and lemon juice; beat well. The mixture should be shiny and the sugar dissolved.

3 Mix icing sugar with desiccated coconut and carefully fold into the egg white mixture. Take care to fold in just enough so that mixture is neither crumbly nor liquid.

4 With the help of a teaspoon, place 50 mounds of mixture on the baking trays. Bake, one tray at a time for 12–15 minutes. Cookies should be moist inside; they will firm up on the outside when cool. Transfer to a wire rack to cool.

5 Melt chocolate in a bowl over gently simmering water. Pour into a piping bag and drizzle in fine lines across the cookies.

Try this, too...

For Pina Colada Kisses, substitute lime juice for lemon juice. Fold 50 g (⅓ cup/2 oz) finely chopped dried pineapple into meringue mixture with the coconut.

For Dark and Light Kisses, colour half of the meringue mixture with 1 tbsp cocoa powder and drizzle dark meringues with white chocolate when baked.

Peppernuts

Make these 3 or 4 weeks before Christmas to allow the flavours to develop.
These traditional German cookies, called Pfeffernüsse, can be bought ready-made.

2 eggs

230 g (1 cup/8 oz) brown sugar

2 tablespoons marzipan paste, chilled

60 g (⅓ cup/2¼ oz) candied lemon peel, finely chopped

250 g (2 cups/9 oz) plain (all-purpose) flour

1 teaspoon baking powder

1 teaspoon ground mixed spice (allspice)

60 ml (¼ cup/2 fl oz) Kirsch

1 egg white

210 g (1⅔ cups/7½ oz) icing (confectioners') sugar

MAKES 60–70

PREPARATION TIME 30 minutes plus resting time overnight

COOKING TIME 20 minutes per baking tray plus 2 days softening

1 Use 2 large baking trays; line with baking (parchment) paper. Beat eggs and sugar for 5 minutes until pale and fluffy. Finely grate the marzipan paste; fold it into beaten egg mixture with the candied peel.

2 Mix flour, baking powder and mixed spice and sift over the egg mixture. Knead well to form a smooth dough. On a lightly floured work surface, shape the dough into 60–70 balls, each about 2.5 cm (1 in) in diameter. Place on baking trays and flatten slightly. Cover; leave in a cool place overnight.

3 Preheat oven to 160°C (315°F, gas mark 2–3). Brush the bases of the cookies with Kirsch; reserve a few drops for the icing. Bake the cookies for about 20 minutes.

4 To make the icing, beat the egg white until stiff; gradually stir in the icing sugar and remaining Kirsch. Dip cookies in the icing and replace on baking tray. Leave to dry for 3–4 minutes in a warm oven.

5 The cookies will now be very hard. Leave, covered with a cloth, in a humid, warm place to soften for 2 days. Then place in a tin with a slice of fresh bread or a small apple or orange; leave for at least 2 weeks to allow the flavours to develop.

Top Tip

To make these cookies look more festive, add a few drops of red food colouring to half the icing. Cover the iced cookies in hundreds and thousands or chocolate sprinkles.

Fruity Mince Pies

These traditional Christmas favourites are delicious served hot with cream.
This version has an unusual iced topping that is baked on.

215 g (1¾ cups/7½ oz) plain (all-purpose) flour

80 g (¾ cup/2¾ oz) ground almonds

Finely grated zest of 1 orange

2 tablespoons caster (superfine) sugar

150 g (⅔ cup/5½ oz) butter, chilled and cut into small cubes

1 egg, lightly beaten

About 550 g (1¾ cups/1 lb 4 oz) fruit mince, bought or homemade

125 g (½ cup/4½ oz) brandy butter, bought or homemade

2 tablespoons milk

1 egg white

185 g (1½ cups/6½ oz) icing (confectioners') sugar, sifted

MAKES 20

PREPARATION TIME 40 minutes plus 30 minutes chilling time

COOKING TIME 35 minutes

1 Use 20 tartlet tins. Sift the flour into a bowl; mix in the ground almonds, zest and sugar. Rub butter into flour mixture until the mixture resembles fine breadcrumbs. Use a round-bladed knife and mix in the egg until the dough comes together. Gather into a ball; knead briefly on a lightly floured work surface until smooth. Wrap in cling wrap; chill for 30 minutes.

2 Preheat oven to 200°C (400°F, gas mark 6). Roll out the dough very thinly; cut out 20 rounds 6 cm (2½ in) in diameter with a fluted cookie cutter. Gather the trimmings and roll again very thinly; cut out 20 rounds 8 cm (3 in) in diameter.

3 Place larger rounds in the tins. Fill with fruit mince; top with 1 tsp brandy butter. Brush edges of pastry with a little milk and place a smaller round on top of each pie, pressing the edges together to seal.

4 Brush the tops with the milk and make a hole in the lid of each pie. Bake in the centre of the oven for 25 minutes or until golden brown. Remove from oven, leave to cool in the tins for 5 minutes, then lift out onto a wire rack to cool for 10 minutes.

5 For the icing, whisk the egg white until frothy, then beat in the sifted icing sugar. Spread a little icing over the top of the mince pies and arrange them on a baking tray. Bake at 200°C (400°F, gas mark 6) for 5–10 minutes or until the icing has browned a little and the pies are heated through. Leave them to cool for about 5 minutes before serving.

Rich Fruit Ring Cake

Most festive fruit cakes are high in fat and added sugar, but this one is relatively low in fat and depends mainly on dried fruits soaked in apple juice for natural sweetness.

85 g (1 cup/3 oz) dried cranberries

85 g (²⁄₃ cup/3 oz) sultanas

85 g (1 cup/3 oz) dried pears

85 g (¹⁄₃ cup/3 oz) stoned prunes

85 g (¹⁄₂ cup/3 oz) dried figs

85 g (¹⁄₂ cup/3 oz) stoned dried dates

250 ml (1 cup/9 fl oz) apple juice

55 g (¹⁄₂ cup/2 oz) pecan nuts

55 g (¹⁄₄ cup/2 oz) candied ginger, chopped

Finely grated zest and juice of 1 lemon

5 tablespoons sunflower oil

1 egg

80 g (¹⁄₃ cup/2³⁄₄ oz) dark brown sugar

125 g (1 cup/4 oz) self-raising (self-rising) flour

115 g (³⁄₄ cup/4 oz) self-raising wholemeal (self-rising whole-wheat) flour

1 teaspoon baking powder

2 teaspoons ground mixed spice (allspice)

3–4 tablespoons milk, as needed

FOR DECORATION

2 tablespoons apricot jam

55 g (¹⁄₄ cup/2 oz) glacé (candied) cherries

30 g (¹⁄₄ cup/1 oz) hazelnuts (filberts)

35 g (¹⁄₃ cup/1 ¹⁄₄ oz) pecan nut halves

35 g (¹⁄₃ cup/1 ¹⁄₄ oz) walnut halves

55 g (¹⁄₄ cup/2 oz) candied ginger, sliced

Icing (confectioners') sugar

1 Use a 23-cm (9-in) ring tin and brush with a little oil. Chop all the dried fruits into small pieces and place in a saucepan with the apple juice; bring slowly to the boil over a moderate heat. Then simmer gently, covered, for about 4 minutes or until the fruit begins to absorb the liquid.

2 Remove pan from the heat and leave, covered, until completely cold. Stir in chopped pecan nuts, the ginger, lemon zest and juice.

3 Preheat oven to 150°C (300°F, gas mark 2). Beat the sunflower oil, egg and brown sugar together until smooth.

4 Sift the flours, baking powder and mixed spice into a large bowl, tipping in any bran left in the sieve. Add the soaked fruit and the egg mixture; stir well to combine. Stir in enough milk to make a fairly soft mixture.

5 Spoon mixture into prepared tin and smooth the top. Bake for 1¼–1½ hours or until risen, firm and golden brown; it should just be beginning to shrink away from the side of the tin.

6 Leave cake to cool in the tin for at least 1 hour before running a knife around the edge and turning it out. Wrap in baking (parchment) paper and foil. Store for 2–3 weeks before serving, to allow the flavours to mature.

7 To decorate the cake, heat the jam with 1 tsp water over a low heat, then press through a sieve. Brush the top of the cake with the jam. Gently press the cherries, nuts and candied ginger into the jam. Dust with sifted icing sugar.

Try this, too…

For easier slicing, bake the cake in a long loaf tin.

Soak the fruit in cherry brandy or a liqueur of your choice, instead of apple juice.

Top Tip

Dried figs are a good source of fibre. Drying the fruit concentrates its nutrients and makes it a useful source of calcium and iron.

Pecans are a source of protein and unsaturated fats. They also provide useful amounts of vitamin E, fibre and folate.

SERVES 18

PREPARATION TIME 40 minutes plus soaking and 2–3 weeks maturing

COOKING TIME 1¼–1½ hours

Christmas Cake

Covered with almond paste and iced in a simple style, this rich fruit cake looks impressive.
It should be prepared at least one month ahead to allow the flavours to develop.

FOR THE CAKE

250 g (1 cup/9 oz) butter

280 g (1½ cups/10 oz) brown sugar

6 eggs

250 g (2 cups/9 oz) plain
(all-purpose) flour, sifted

375 g (3 cups/13 oz) sultanas
(golden raisins)

300 g (2 cups/10½ oz) currants

375 g (3 cups/13 oz) seedless
raisins, roughly chopped

420 g (2 cups/15 oz) glacé
(candied) cherries, cut in halves

140 g (¾ cup/5 oz) mixed candied
peel, chopped

80 g (¾ cup/2¾ oz) ground
almonds

Finely grated zest of 1 large orange
and 1 large lemon

80 ml (⅓ cup/2½ fl oz) rum, whisky
or brandy, for sprinkling over the
cake before icing

FOR THE ALMOND PASTE

455 g (4½ cups/1 lb) ground
almonds

185 g (1½ cups/6½ oz) icing
(confectioners') sugar, sifted

345 g (1½ cups/12 oz) caster
(superfine) sugar

8 egg yolks

1 teaspoon almond essence or
vanilla essence (extract)

3 tablespoons apricot jam, heated
and sieved

FOR THE ROYAL ICING

375 g (3 cups/13 oz) icing
(confectioners') sugar, sifted

4 egg whites

2 teaspoons lemon juice

CAKE

1 Use a 23-cm (9-in) cake tin; line the base and side with a double layer of baking (parchment) paper.

2 Preheat oven to 150°C (300°F, gas mark 2). Place butter and sugar in a large mixing bowl; beat until very light and fluffy. Add eggs one at a time; beat well after each addition. (The mixture will curdle a little at this point because of the unusually high proportion of eggs to other ingredients in this recipe. It will come together when the dry ingredients are added.)

3 Fold in the flour. Stir in dried fruit, glacé cherries, chopped peel, ground almonds and zests.

4 Spoon mixture into tin; smooth the top. Bake in the centre of the oven for 3½–4 hours or until a skewer inserted in the centre of the cake comes out clean.

5 Remove the cake from the oven; leave to cool in tin for 1 hour. Carefully turn cake out onto a wire rack and leave to cool completely. Do not remove the baking paper.

6 Wrap the cold cake, still in the baking paper, in cling wrap and wrap it again in foil. Place the cake in an airtight container and store in a cool, dry, airy cupboard until ready to ice it.

SERVES 12

PREPARATION TIME 1 hour

COOKING TIME 3 1/2–4 hour

ALMOND PASTE

1 Mix the ground almonds with the sifted icing sugar and the caster sugar. Add egg yolks and the almond or vanilla essence and mix to form a soft, but not sticky, paste. Smooth by kneading very briefly on a work surface lightly sifted with icing sugar.

2 Remove cake from wrappings and place upside-down in the centre of a 30-cm (12-in) round gold or silver cake board, or on a cake stand, if preferred.

3 Using a fine skewer, make several holes in the base of the cake; insert the skewer to a depth of about 4 cm (1½ in). Spoon rum, whisky or brandy over the base of the cake and allow it to gradually seep into the holes.

4 Roll out the almond paste to a neat round about 33-cm (13-in) in diameter. Turn cake right side up and brush all over with the warm, sieved apricot jam.

5 Carefully lift the paste onto the cake; smooth it evenly over the top and down the side, pressing it gently but firmly into position. Trim off any excess paste from the base. Smooth paste with a palette knife.

6 Leave cake, uncovered, in a cool, dry place for 24 hours to allow the paste to dry completely before adding the icing.

PREPARATION AND APPLICATION TIME 1 hour

DRYING TIME 24 hours

ROYAL ICING

1 Place sifted icing sugar and the egg whites in a large mixing bowl and beat until smooth and fluffy; beat in the lemon juice.

2 Spoon 3 tbsp of icing mixture onto the cake; spread evenly over the top only. Using a metal ruler, smooth the icing by pulling the ruler across the top of the cake. Trim away any excess icing. Leave overnight to dry.

3 Put remaining icing in a clean bowl, cover the surface closely with cling wrap and refrigerate. Next day, beat the icing and coat the top of the cake again; smooth icing as before.

4 Spread remaining icing around the side of the cake; let a little come up onto the top (see picture). Use a palette knife to work icing up into attractive peaks and swirls.

5 Leave icing to dry overnight. Decorate with your choice of Christmas ornaments.

PREPARATION AND ICING TIME 1 hour

DRYING TIME 24 hours

yeast
& quick
breads

Light White Bread

This loaf is a good everyday basic. To make it more moist, finely grate a day-old cooked potato and knead it into the dough.

500 g (4 cups/1 lb 2 oz) plain (all-purpose) flour

1 teaspoon salt

1 teaspoon oil

250 ml (1 cup/9 fl oz) buttermilk

1 teaspoon sugar

1 tablespoon (14 g/½ oz) dry (powdered) yeast

MAKES 1 loaf

PREPARATION TIME 30 minutes plus 30 minutes rising time

COOKING TIME 30 minutes

1 Use a baking tray. Line tray with baking (parchment) paper. Place flour, salt and oil in a bowl. Heat the buttermilk in a pan with the sugar until lukewarm. Sprinkle yeast over to dissolve.

2 Add the yeast mixture to flour mixture. Knead to a smooth dough either with the dough hooks of an electric mixer or by hand.

3 Place dough on a lightly floured work surface; knead and punch down vigorously by hand for about 10 minutes until it is elastic and no longer sticky.

4 Shape dough into an oval and place on baking tray; sprinkle with water. Using a sharp knife, make 3 diagonal incisions in the top of the loaf.

5 Cover loaf and leave to rise in a warm place for 30 minutes until doubled in size. Preheat oven to 250°C (500°F, gas mark 9).

6 Bake for 15 minutes; reduce temperature to 200°C (400°F, gas mark 6). Brush the loaf with water; cook a further 15 minutes until golden brown.

Yeast Party Rolls

Warm, freshly baked rolls are a great accompaniment to a cheese platter and salads. It's best to bake the rolls a day ahead and briefly reheat them just before serving.

500 g (4 cups/1 lb 2 oz) plain (all-purpose) flour

1 teaspoon salt

60 ml (¼ cup/2 fl oz) oil

Pinch of pepper

Pinch of grated nutmeg

250 ml (1 cup/9 fl oz) milk

1 tablespoon (14 g/½ oz) dry (powdered) yeast

½ teaspoon sugar

1 egg

FOR DECORATION

1 egg yolk

2 tablespoons milk for brushing

Coarse salt, caraway seeds or poppy seeds for sprinkling

1 Use 2 baking trays. Line trays with baking (parchment) paper. Place the flour, salt, oil, pepper and nutmeg in a bowl. Heat milk until lukewarm, beat in yeast, sugar and egg and pour onto flour mixture.

2 Knead the mixture to a sticky dough. Cover; leave to rise in a warm place for 30 minutes.

3 Turn the dough onto a lightly floured work surface; knead and punch it down for 10 minutes. Shape dough into a cylinder and cut into 20 equal pieces. Shape into pretzels, round rolls or small rings and place on baking trays.

4 Whisk egg yolk with milk and brush over the dough. Sprinkle salt, caraway seeds or poppy seeds on the top of the rolls.

5 Make a cross-shaped incision in the top of any large rolls. Cover dough and leave to rise in a warm place for 20 minutes. Preheat oven to 200°C (400°F, gas mark 6).

6 Bake rolls, one baking tray at a time, for 15–18 minutes. Cool briefly on a wire rack. Serve warm.

MAKES 20

PREPARATION TIME 30 minutes plus 50 minutes rising time

COOKING TIME 15–18 minutes per baking tray

Classic Yeast Plait

If you want to serve this yeast plait fresh for breakfast, prepare the yeast dough
to the end of step 4 the night before. The dough can be kept in the refrigerator overnight
in a large bowl covered with cling wrap.

500 g (4 cups/1 lb 2 oz) plain
(all-purpose) flour

250 ml (1 cup/9 fl oz) milk

85 g (1/3 cup/3 oz) sugar

1 tablespoon (14 g/1/2 oz) dry
(powdered) yeast

90 g (1/3 cup/3 1/4 oz) butter,
softened and cut into small pieces

1/2 teaspoon salt

1 egg

Grated zest of 1 lemon

60 g (1/2 cup/2 1/4 oz) sultanas
(golden raisins)

60 g (1/3 cup/2 1/4 oz) slivered
almonds

1 egg yolk, for brushing

60 g (1/3 cup/2 1/4 oz) chopped
almonds, for sprinkling

MAKES 1 loaf

PREPARATION TIME 40 minutes plus
65 minutes rising time

COOKING TIME 35 minutes

1 Use a baking tray. Line the tray with baking (parchment) paper. Reserve a little flour and place the rest in a large bowl. Make a well in the centre. Heat 2 tbsp milk and 1 tsp sugar until lukewarm; sprinkle on yeast to dissolve. Pour the yeast mixture into the well; cover lightly with the reserved flour.

2 Cover bowl with a cloth; leave to rise in a warm place for 15 minutes until cracks are visible in the flour cover. Add the remaining milk and sugar, the butter and the salt and egg.

3 Knead into a smooth dough. Turn onto lightly floured work surface and knead and punch down for about 10 minutes until elastic and no longer sticky. Shape dough into a ball, place in a bowl. Cover and leave to rise in a warm place for 30 minutes.

4 Soak the sultanas in lukewarm water, then drain. Knead dough on lightly floured work surface and work in the lemon zest, sultanas and almonds.

5 Divide the dough into 3 equal pieces; roll pieces into ropes of equal length and weave into a plait. Push ends of dough together and fold just under plait. Place plait on the baking tray, cover with a cloth and let rise for 20 minutes. Preheat oven to 200°C (400°F, gas mark 6).

6 Whisk the egg yolk with 2 tbsp water. Brush over plait; sprinkle with the chopped almonds. Bake for 35 minutes. If loaf is becoming too dark, shield it with a piece of foil.

Try this, too...

For an Easter Nest, prepare dough as described in main recipe and divide into 5 equal pieces. Roll each piece into a rope and work all 5 strands together into a plait. Bend plait into a wreath and tuck in ends so that they are no longer visible. Traditionally, dyed hard-boiled eggs are placed between the woven strands of the plait and in the centre. The wreath is then baked as in the main recipe.

Top Tip

If you prefer to use fresh yeast in place of dry (powdered) yeast, remember that dry yeast is twice as concentrated as fresh.

Irish Soda Bread

Quick and simple to make, freshly baked soda bread has a delicious flavour. This version uses plain and wholemeal flour to give it a pleasing coarse texture and nutty flavour.

250 g (2 cups/9 oz) plain (all-purpose) flour

250 g (2 cups/9 oz) plain wholemeal (all-purpose whole-wheat) flour, plus a little extra for sprinkling

1 teaspoon bicarbonate of soda (baking soda)

½ teaspoon salt

310 ml (1 ¼ cups/10¾ fl oz) buttermilk

SERVES 8

PREPARATION TIME 10 minutes

COOKING TIME 30 minutes

1 Use a baking tray; grease tray. Preheat oven to 200°C (400°F, gas mark 6). Sift flours, bicarbonate of soda and salt into a bowl, tipping in any bran left in the sieve.

2 Make a well in the centre and pour in the buttermilk. Using a wooden spoon, gradually stir flour into the buttermilk to form a soft dough. Bring dough together with your hands, then turn it out onto a lightly floured work surface. Knead briefly to a smooth dough. Shape into a ball.

3 Place dough on baking tray and flatten slightly to make a round, domed loaf about 19 cm (7½ in) in diameter. Using a sharp knife, make a deep cross in the top, cutting half-way down into the dough. Sprinkle extra wholemeal flour over the top.

4 Bake for about 30 minutes or until well risen and browned and the bread sounds hollow when tapped on the base. (If it still seems to be moist and heavy, bake for a further 3–5 minutes and test again.)

5 Transfer loaf to a wire rack and leave to cool completely. Serve on the day it is baked, as it quickly becomes stale. Or, you can toast it the following day.

Try this, too...

If you can't find buttermilk, use the same quantity of semi-skimmed milk to which you have added 1 tbsp lemon juice. Alternatively, use semi-skimmed milk and sift 2 tsp cream of tartar into flours, bicarbonate of soda and salt.

Gluten-free Bread

This golden, crusty loaf has a delicious, moist, close-textured interior. The addition of bicarbonate of soda and cream of tartar helps to make the bread rise.

200 g (1 cup/7 oz) brown rice flour

200 g (1 cup/7 oz) potato flour

100 g (½ cup/3½ oz) soya flour

1 teaspoon salt

2 teaspoons (7 g/¼ oz) dry (powdered) yeast

400 ml (1½ cups/14 fl oz) lukewarm water

1 teaspoon honey

1 teaspoon olive oil

1 teaspoon bicarbonate of soda (baking soda)

2 teaspoons cream of tartar

MAKES 1 loaf

PREPARATION TIME 10 minutes plus about 30 minutes rising time

COOKING TIME 25–30 minutes

1 Use a non-stick 900-g (2-lb) loaf tin; grease well. Sift the rice, potato and soya flours into a large bowl with the salt. Remove about one-quarter of the mixture and set aside. Make a well in the centre of the dry ingredients.

2 Sprinkle the yeast onto water to dissolve. Add to the well with the honey and olive oil. Stir the dry ingredients into the liquid to make a smooth, thick batter.

3 Cover bowl with cling wrap and leave in a warm place for about 30 minutes. Preheat oven to 200°C (400°F, gas mark 6).

4 Mix bicarbonate of soda and cream of tartar with reserved flour mixture; sift mixture on top of the yeast batter. Stir gently until combined; the mixture will have a foamy appearance. Transfer to the loaf tin.

5 Bake for 25–30 minutes or until firm, crisp and golden brown. Turn onto a wire rack to cool. This loaf keeps well for up to 2 days and is very good toasted.

Try this, too…

For dark gluten-free bread, use half the amount of soya flour and in place of potato flour use 200 g (1 cup/7 oz) buckwheat flour. The loaf has a dark crust and dark, moist crumb with a close texture.

For a corn-flavoured gluten-free loaf, use 200 g (1⅓ cups/7 oz) each of cornmeal and cornflour and 100 g (3¼ cups/3½ oz) buckwheat flour instead of the brown rice, potato and soya flours. Decrease water to 360 ml (1½ cups/12 fl oz). The loaf has a paler crust and a level, slightly crackelled top.

For a ground rice gluten-free loaf, substitute 200 g (1⅓ cups/7 oz) cornmeal or polenta and 200 g (1⅓ cups/7 oz) ground rice for the brown rice, potato and soya flours. Use 360 ml (1½ cups/ 12 fl oz) lukewarm water. This loaf has a grainy texture.

Focaccia

This light Italian flat bread is prepared from a soft dough enriched with olive oil. Extra olive oil is traditionally sprinkled over the dough before baking to give a good texture and flavour.

2 teaspoons (7 g/¼ oz) dry (powdered) yeast

300 ml (1¼ cups/10¾ fl oz) lukewarm water

450 g (1⅔ cups/1 lb) strong white (bread) flour

1 teaspoon salt

4 tablespoons extra virgin olive oil

¼ teaspoon coarse sea salt

MAKES 1 loaf

PREPARATION TIME 15 minutes plus about 45 minutes rising time

COOKING TIME 15 minutes

1 Use a baking tray; grease tray. Sprinkle yeast onto water to dissolve. Place flour in a large bowl and stir in the salt. Make a well in the centre; pour in yeast mixture and 3 tbsp oil. Mix flour into liquid ingredients, using a wooden spoon first and then your hands, to make a soft, slightly sticky dough.

2 Turn dough out onto a lightly floured work surface; knead for about 10 minutes or until smooth and elastic. Keep dough moving by turning, punching and folding it to prevent it from sticking. Sprinkle a little more flour onto work surface, if necessary; be careful not to add too much or dough will become dry and loose its elasticity.

3 Shape dough into a ball and place it on the baking tray. Roll out dough (or push it out with your hands) into a round approximately 20 cm (8 in) in diameter and 2 cm (¾ in) thick. Cover tray loosely with a cloth kitchen towel; tuck ends underneath. Leave in a warm place for about 45 minutes or until dough has doubled in thickness.

4 Preheat oven to 230°C (450°F, gas mark 8). Remove the towel. Pour a little lukewarm water into a cup, then dip your fingers into the water and press them into the risen dough, making deep indents over the whole surface; wet your fingers each time so that the top of the loaf is very moist. Brush remaining oil over the bread and sprinkle on the coarse sea salt.

5 Bake focaccia for 15 minutes or until golden brown. Transfer to a wire rack; cool for 15 minutes. Wrap the bread in a clean towel to soften the crust as it continues to cool. Serve warm or cold. Focaccia can be kept in a polythene bag for up to 2 days.

Teacakes

These lightly spiced teacakes are packed with nutritious dried fruit. Simple to make, they are delicious served lightly toasted and spread with butter or jam.

225 g (1³/₄ cups/8 oz) strong white (bread) flour

225 g (1³/₄ cups/8 oz) strong wholemeal (whole-wheat bread) flour

1 teaspoon salt

2 teaspoons (7 g/¹/₄ oz) dry (powdered) yeast

300 ml (1¹/₄ cups/10³/₄ fl oz) lukewarm milk, or as needed, plus extra for brushing

60 g (¹/₄ cup/2¹/₄ oz) unsalted butter, cut into small pieces

2 tablespoons caster (superfine) sugar

85 g (²/₃ cup/3 oz) sultanas (golden raisins)

85 g (²/₃ cup/3 oz) currants

¹/₂ teaspoon ground cinnamon

MAKES 10

PREPARATION TIME 25 minutes plus 1¹/₂–3 hours rising time

COOKING TIME 10–15 minutes

1 Use 2 baking trays. Grease the trays. Sift flours and salt into a large bowl, tipping in any bran left in the sieve. Sprinkle the yeast onto the milk to dissolve.

2 Rub butter into flour mixture. Stir in sugar, sultanas, currants and cinnamon. Make a well in the centre; pour in the yeast mixture. Mix dry ingredients into the liquid, adding a little more milk, if needed, to make a soft dough.

3 Turn dough out onto a lightly floured work surface; knead for 10 minutes until smooth and elastic. Place in a lightly greased bowl, cover with a cloth and leave to rise in a warm place for 1–2 hours or until doubled in size.

4 Turn dough onto the floured work surface and knock it back. Knead for 2–3 minutes, then divide it into 10 equal pieces. Shape each piece into a round teacake.

5 Place teacakes on baking trays; cover with a cloth. Leave to rise in a warm place for 30–60 minutes or until puffy.

6 Towards the end of the rising time, preheat the oven to 220°C (425°F, gas mark 7). Uncover the teacakes and lightly brush the tops with milk. Bake for 10–15 minutes or until browned; transfer to a wire rack to cool a little. Serve warm or split them open and toast lightly. Teacakes are best eaten on the day they are made, but if they are to be toasted, they will keep for 1–2 days.

Try this, too...

Instead of making individual teacakes, shape the dough into a large round. Place on a greased baking tray. Cover; leave to rise again for 30–60 minutes. Bake for about 25 minutes.

Brioches

Sweet and buttery, these French breakfast rolls are beautiful to look at and delicious to eat.
Though they require a little bit of work, the result is spectacular.

350 g (2³/₄ cups/12 oz) plain
   (all-purpose) flour

¹/₂ teaspoon salt

100 g (¹/₃ cup/3¹/₂ oz) butter,
   softened, plus extra for greasing

80 ml (¹/₃ cup/2¹/₂ fl oz) lukewarm
   milk

1 teaspoon (3¹/₂ g/¹/₈ oz) dry
   (powdered) yeast

3 eggs

1¹/₂ tablespoon sugar

1 egg yolk, for brushing

MAKES 20

PREPARATION TIME 35 minutes plus
   3–4 hours resting time

COOKING TIME 15–20 minutes

1 Use individual fluted brioche tins. Grease generously with butter. To make the dough, place the flour, salt and butter in a bowl. Place milk in a jug, sprinkle yeast over to dissolve. Whisk in the eggs and sugar; add to the flour mixture. Knead for 5 minutes using dough hooks of an electric mixer; dough should no longer stick to the side of the bowl. (This dough is wet and sticky; an electric mixer makes the task of kneading much easier than if you try to work with your hands.)

2 Cover dough and leave to rise in a cool place for 2 hours; it must not get too warm. Knead for a further 5 minutes. Cover; leave to rise for 30–50 minutes until doubled in size.

3 Turn dough out onto a lightly floured work surface and shape into a cylinder. Slice into 25 pieces. Shape 20 pieces into balls and press them into the tins.

4 Using an index finger, make a deep hole in the centre of each of the 20 balls. Cut each remaining piece of dough into 4; shape into small balls. Pull a pointed cone of dough up from each one and push the point deep into the holes made in the large dough balls.

5 Beat egg yolk with 2 tbsp water and brush over the brioches. Cover and leave for 30–50 minutes until doubled in size. Preheat oven to 220°C (425°F, gas mark 7).

6 Bake brioches for 15–20 minutes until golden; they should slip out of the tins easily.

Try this, too...

For a Brioche Loaf, prepare dough as for the main recipe. Grease a 26-cm (10¹/₂-in) long loaf tin and place dough in it. Let dough rise; brush with egg yolk mixture. Make several diagonal incisions in the top with a sharp knife. Bake loaf for 25–30 minutes until golden.

Top Tip

If the eggs are large, 2 eggs and 1 egg yolk will be sufficient; otherwise the dough will be too liquid.

Sunflower Potato Bread

Thanks to the potato, this grain-filled loaf is lovely and moist.
It will slice best if it is left to cool completely overnight.

250 g (9 oz) floury boiling potatoes
(2 medium potatoes)

1 teaspoon salt

2 tablespoons sunflower oil

300 g (2 cups/10½ oz) wholemeal
(whole-wheat) flour

100 g (1 cup/3½ oz) each of
oatmeal and original rolled
(porridge) oats

2 tablespoons ground aniseed

1 tablespoon (14 g/½ oz) dry
(powdered) yeast

90 g (¾ cup/3¼ oz) sunflower
seeds

MAKES 1 loaf

PREPARATION TIME 40 minutes plus
35 minutes resting time

COOKING TIME 1 hour

1 Use a 30- x 11-cm (12- x 4¼-in)
loaf tin. Grease the tin. Peel the
potatoes; cut into quarters. Cook in
boiling salted water until soft; drain.
Place in a large bowl and mash well;
stir in the oil. Cool completely.

2 Add flour, oatmeal, rolled oats
and aniseed to mashed potato.
Sprinkle yeast over. Knead mixture
into a smooth dough. Cover with a
towel and leave to rise in a warm
place for about 20 minutes.

3 Lightly flour a work surface and
scatter with half the sunflower
seeds. Turn the dough out onto the
flour mixture and knead well.

4 Place dough in tin, cover and
leave to rise in a warm place
for about 15 minutes. Preheat oven
to 200°C (425°F, gas mark 7).

5 Brush dough with water and
sprinkle remaining sunflower
seeds on top. Bake the loaf on the
lowest rung of the oven for about
1 hour. Remove from oven; cool for
20 minutes. Turn onto a wire rack
to cool completely.

Fruit and Nut Loaf

This heavily fruited German-style loaf contains no added fat (the only fat present comes from the nuts), but the dried fruits give it a rich, moist texture and good keeping qualities.

400 g (3¼ cups/14 oz) strong white (bread) flour

½ teaspoon salt

Grated zest of ½ lemon

2 teaspoons (7 g/¼ oz) dry (powdered) yeast

250 ml (1 cup/9 fl oz) lukewarm water

85 g (½ cup/3 oz) each of roughly chopped dried apricots, dried pears and prunes

50 g (⅓ cup/2 oz) roughly chopped dried figs

50 g (⅓ cup/2 oz) chopped mixed nuts such as almonds, hazelnuts (filberts) and cashews

1 Use a baking tray. Grease well. Mix flour, salt and lemon zest in a large bowl. Sprinkle yeast over the water to dissolve. Add chopped fruits and nuts to the bowl and stir in the yeast mixture. Working with your hands, bring together to make a soft-textured, heavy dough.

2 Turn dough out onto a lightly floured work surface and knead for 10 minutes or until elastic. Place in a lightly greased bowl, cover with a damp cloth and leave to rise in a warm place for 1½–2 hours or until doubled in size.

3 Turn the dough out onto the floured work surface and knock it back with your knuckles to return it to its original size. Gently knead dough into a round. Place it on the baking tray and cover with a damp cloth; leave to rise in a warm place for 1 hour or until doubled in size.

4 Preheat oven to 200°C (400°F, gas mark 6). Bake the loaf for 30–40 minutes or until the surface is brown and loaf sounds hollow when tapped on the base. If it is browning too fast, cover it with a piece of foil. Transfer to a wire rack to cool. The loaf keeps well for up to 5 days.

Top Tip

Dried apricots are an excellent ingredient to have on hand. They are very nutritious, providing an excellent source of beta-carotene and a useful source of calcium. Use dried apricots in cakes, cookies and sweet yeasted breads, as well as adding them to casseroles and breakfast cereals.

SERVES 10

PREPARATION TIME 50 minutes plus 2½–3 hours rising time

COOKING TIME 30–40 minutes

197

Seed-topped Flatbread

Not only are sunflower and pumpkin seeds highly nutritious, but they give this flatbread a satisfying crisp and crunchy texture.

285 g (2¼ cups/10 oz) plain (all-purpose) flour

¼ teaspoon cayenne pepper

Pinch of salt

3 teaspoons unsalted butter

170 ml (⅔ cup/5½ fl oz) water

1 tablespoon vegetable oil

1 egg white lightly beaten with 2 teaspoons water

30 g (¼ cup/1 oz) shelled pumpkin seeds

30 g (¼ cup/1 oz) shelled, dry-roasted sunflower seeds

2 tablespoons grated Parmesan cheese

MAKES 4

PREPARATION TIME 20 minutes plus 1 hour resting

COOKING TIME 12 minutes

1 Use 2 large baking trays; spray with non-stick cooking spray. Place the flour, cayenne pepper and a pinch of salt in a bowl. Cut in the butter with 2 knives until mixture resembles coarse crumbs. Gradually add water and oil; work the mixture into a soft dough. Knead 5 minutes or until smooth and elastic. Transfer the dough to a lightly greased bowl. Cover; leave to rest for 1 hour.

2 Preheat oven to 210°C (415°F, gas mark 6–7). Cut the dough into 4 equal pieces. Roll each piece out to a 23-cm (9-in) round about 2 mm (⅟₁₆ in) thick. Transfer to the baking trays. Brush the rounds with the egg white mixture and sprinkle with pumpkin and sunflower seeds. Top with the grated cheese. Bake for 12 minutes or until the bread is lightly puffed, golden and crisp.

Sunflower Drop Rolls

The great taste of these rolls belies the simplicity of the cooking method. If you thought you'd never have the time or skills to make your own bread, start with this recipe.

185 g (1 ½ cups/6 ½ oz) plain (all-purpose) flour

2 teaspoons baking powder

½ teaspoon bicarbonate of soda (baking soda)

Pinch of salt

Pinch of cayenne pepper

1 ½ tablespoons unsalted butter

1 ½ tablespoons vegetable oil

185 ml (¾ cup/6 fl oz) buttermilk

60 g(½ cup/2 ¼ oz) dry-roasted sunflower seeds

MAKES 12

PREPARATION TIME 10 minutes

COOKING TIME 15 minutes

1 Use a large baking tray; spray with non-stick cooking spray. Preheat oven to 220°C (425°F, gas mark 7).

2 Place the flour, baking powder, bicarbonate of soda and the salt and cayenne pepper in a large bowl. Cut in butter with 2 knives until the mixture resembles coarse crumbs. Stir in the oil, buttermilk and sunflower seeds and mix to a soft dough; do not overmix.

3 Drop the dough in heaped tablespoons 5 cm (2 in) apart onto the baking tray. Bake for about 12 minutes or until golden brown and crusty.

Top Tip

As well their use in the production of polyunsaturated oil, sunflower seeds are also roasted and ground to make a flour, which is available from health food shops.

199

Mediterranean Spiral Loaf

The dough for this loaf is rolled up around a filling of roasted vegetables
so that when the loaf is sliced there is a colourful spiral running through it.

250 g (2 cups/9 oz) strong white (bread) flour

200 g (1⅔ cups/7 oz) strong wholemeal (whole-wheat bread) flour

1 teaspoon salt

Pinch of caster (superfine) sugar

1 tablespoon fennel seeds

310 ml (1¼ cups/10 fl oz) milk

2 tablespoons butter

2 teaspoons (7 g/¼ oz) dry (powdered) yeast

2 red or yellow capsicums (bell peppers), halved and seeds removed

3 tablespoons sun-dried tomato paste or basil pesto

½ small red onion, thinly sliced

3 tablespoons freshly grated Parmesan cheese

1 teaspoon extra virgin olive oil

MAKES 1 loaf

PREPARATION TIME 35 minutes plus 1½–2 hours rising time

COOKING TIME 35–40 minutes

1 Use a 900-g (2-lb) loaf tin. Lightly grease the tin. Sift flours and salt into a bowl; tip in any bran left in the sieve. Stir in sugar and fennel seeds. Make a well in the centre.

2 Gently heat the milk with the butter until the butter melts. Sprinkle yeast onto the liquid to dissolve. Pour yeast mixture into the well. Gradually draw the flour into the liquid ingredients to make a soft dough.

3 Turn dough out onto a lightly floured work surface and knead for 10 minutes or until the dough is smooth and no longer sticky. Shape into a ball, place in a greased bowl and cover with a damp cloth. Leave dough to rise in a warm place for 1–1½ hours or until doubled in size.

4 Preheat the grill to high. Grill the capsicum halves, skin side up, until slightly blackened. Place in a polythene bag and leave to cool; peel off the skins. Slice capsicum into long strips.

5 Turn out dough onto a lightly floured work surface and knock back; knead briefly until smooth. Roll out into a 20- x 33-cm (8- x 13-in) rectangle. Spread with sun-dried tomato paste, leaving a 1 cm (½ in) border all round. Cover dough with a single layer of the capsicum strips and red onion slices. Sprinkle 2 tbsp Parmesan cheese evenly on top.

6 Roll up the dough firmly from a short side, to resemble a Swiss roll. Tuck the ends under. Place in the loaf tin. Cover and leave in a warm place for 30 minutes or until risen and springy to the touch.

7 Preheat oven to 230°C (450°F, gas mark 8). Uncover the loaf and make several incisions across the top with a sharp knife. Brush with the olive oil and sprinkle with remaining Parmesan cheese. Bake for 15 minutes; reduce temperature to 200°C (400°F, gas mark 6). Bake for a further 20–25 minutes or until the loaf is risen and golden brown and sounds hollow when tapped on the base.

8 Turn loaf out onto a wire rack and leave to cool. This loaf is best eaten on the day it is made.

Top Tip

Red capsicums (bell peppers) offer an impressive arsenal of disease-fighting compounds. In addition to providing an excellent source of vitamin C and beta-carotene, they also contain two other important phytochemicals called lutein and zeaxanthin. They are thought to help provide protection against macular degeneration of the eyes.

Cinnamon Pull-apart Bread

Towering and tasty, dozens of homemade cinnamon rolls are piled high in a honeycomb formation. This bread is easy to make and spectacular to serve.

625 g (5 cups/1 lb 6 oz) plain (all-purpose) flour

110 g (½ cup/3¾ oz) white (granulated) sugar

1½ teaspoons salt

435 ml (1¾ cups/15¼ fl oz) milk

185 g (¾ cup/6½ oz) butter, softened

1 tablespoon (14 g/½ oz) dry (powdered) yeast

1 large egg, at room temperature

45 g (¼ cup/1¾ oz) firmly packed light brown sugar

1 teaspoon cinnamon

MAKES 24

PREPARATION TIME 25 minutes plus 30 minutes rising

COOKING TIME 35 minutes

1 Use a 25-cm (10-in) ring tin or tube pan. Coat pan with non-stick cooking spray. Combine 150 g (1¼ cups/5½ oz) flour, half the white sugar and all the salt in a bowl.

2 Heat milk with 4 tbsp butter until lukewarm. Sprinkle on the yeast to dissolve; stir into the flour mixture. Stir in the egg. Add enough flour (at least 425 g/3½ cups/15 oz) to work into a soft dough.

3 Turn dough out onto a lightly floured work surface; knead for about 10 minutes until elastic; add remaining flour to keep dough from sticking. Melt remaining butter. Mix remaining white sugar, the brown sugar and the cinnamon in a bowl.

4 Pull off pieces of dough the size of a golf ball, arrange in a single layer in the pan and brush with half the melted butter. Sprinkle top with half the sugar mixture. Repeat for a second layer. Cover with a damp cloth towel. Leave to rise in a warm place until doubled in size, about 30 minutes.

5 Preheat oven to 190°C (375°F, gas mark 5). Bake bread for about 35 minutes or until browned on top. Stand pan on a wire rack; cool for 10 minutes; unmould and serve rolls warm.

Top Tip

Traditional recipes for pull-apart bread call for each dough ball to be dipped in melted butter before being placed in the pan. Instead, drizzle each layer of dough with melted butter, instead of each ball; this way the saturated fat content is kept to a more acceptable level.

Banana–Walnut Quick Bread

Ripe bananas, nature's star sweetener, are the basis for this moist, tasty loaf.

50 g (½ cup/1¾ oz) original rolled (porridge) oats

40 g (⅓ cup/1½ oz) coarsely chopped walnuts

155 g (1¼ cups/5½ oz) plain (all-purpose) flour

75 g (½ cup/2½ oz) plain wholemeal (all-purpose whole-wheat) flour

2 teaspoons baking powder

¾ teaspoon bicarbonate of soda (baking soda)

¾ teaspoon salt

300 g (1¼ cups/10½ oz) mashed banana (about 3 bananas)

155 g (⅔ cup/15½ oz) dark brown sugar

125 ml (½ cup/4 fl oz) buttermilk

2 egg whites

2½ tablespoons walnut oil or extra-light olive oil

1 Use a 22- x 12-cm (8½- x 4½-in) fluted or plain loaf tin. Coat tin with cooking spray. Preheat oven to 190°C (375°F, gas mark 5).

2 Place the oats and walnuts on a baking tray; toast in the oven until the oats are golden brown and walnuts are crisp, about 7 minutes.

3 Combine flours, baking powder, bicarbonate of soda and salt in a bowl. Place the mashed banana, sugar, buttermilk, egg whites and oil in a separate large bowl. Stir to thoroughly combine. Fold in flour mixture and the oats and walnuts.

4 Spoon batter into the loaf pan. Bake 50–55 minutes or until a skewer inserted in the centre of the loaf comes out clean. Leave to cool in pan for 10 minutes; turn onto a wire rack to cool completely.

Top Tip

Store bananas in a paper bag at room temperature if they need ripening. Sliced bananas darken when exposed to air. To keep them from turning brown, toss the slices with a little citrus juice. To prevent bananas from overripening, store them in the refrigerator; the skin will turn an alarming black, but the bananas will be fine.

MAKES 12 slices

PREPARATION TIME 10 minutes

COOKING TIME 55 minutes

Maple and Walnut Bread

This healthy bread has just the right amount of sweetness, with a delicious moist crumb and the satisfying crunch of nuts. The only thing it doesn't have is lots of unwelcome fat!

340 g (2¾ cups/12 oz) self-raising (self-rising) flour

90 g (⅓ cup/3¼ oz) butter, softened

350 ml (1 cup/12 fl oz) maple syrup

1 egg, lightly beaten

170 ml (⅔ cup/5½ fl oz) low-fat evaporated fat-free milk

1 teaspoon vanilla essence (extract)

60 g (½ cup/2¼ oz) walnuts, toasted and chopped

MAKES 16 slices

PREPARATION TIME 15 minutes

COOKING TIME 50 minutes

1 Use a 23- x 13-cm (9- x 5-in) loaf tin. Coat with cooking spray. Preheat oven to 180°C (350°F, gas mark 4). Place flour in a large bowl and make a well in centre.

2 Place butter in a medium bowl; beat until creamy; mix in the syrup. Beat in the egg, then add the milk and vanilla. Pour mixture into the well; stir just until combined. Do not overbeat; a few lumps of flour should still be visible. Stir in the walnuts.

3 Scrape the batter into the loaf tin. Bake for about 50 minutes until golden brown and a skewer inserted in the centre comes out with moist crumbs attached to it. If the bread is browning too quickly, cover it loosely with foil during the last 15 minutes of baking.

4 Place pan on wire rack; leave bread to cool for 10 minutes. Turn bread out onto wire rack to cool completely.

Top Tip

Pure maple syrup, the top of the line, comes from the sap of maple trees, gathered through a process known as maple tapping. Maple-flavoured syrup is a mixture of a less expensive syrup, such as corn syrup, and contains only a small percentage of pure maple syrup. Pancake syrup is often corn syrup flavoured with artificial maple extract. For this bread recipe, buy the best syrup that you can afford. The better the syrup, the better the flavour will be.

Zesty Cheddar Scones

One of the quickest and yummiest homemade breads you'll ever bake.

125 g (1 cup/4½ oz) plain (all-purpose) flour

100 g (⅔ cup/3½ oz) plain wholemeal (all-purpose whole-wheat) flour

35 g (¼ cup/1¼ oz) oat bran

2 tablespoons sugar

2 teaspoons baking powder

¾ teaspoon cayenne pepper

¾ teaspoon salt

½ teaspoon bicarbonate of soda (baking soda)

2 tablespoons olive oil

1 tablespoon grainy mustard

30 g (¼ cup/1 oz) grated cheddar cheese

3 spring onions (scallions), thinly sliced

250 g (1 cup/9 oz) natural (plain) yogurt

MAKES 8

PREPARATION TIME 15 minutes

COOKING TIME 30 minutes

1 Use a large baking tray. Line with baking (parchment) paper. Preheat oven to 200°C (400°F, gas mark 6).

2 Combine the flours, oat bran, sugar, baking powder, cayenne, salt and bicarbonate of soda in a large bowl. Using two knives, cut in the oil and mustard until mixture is moistened and forms crumbs.

3 Add cheese and spring onions. Make a well in the centre of the mixture and stir in the yogurt until combined. Do not overmix.

4 Transfer dough to the tray; flour hands and shape into a 20-cm (8-in) round. Mark 8 even wedges with a sharp knife, cutting all the way through the dough but without separating the wedges.

5 Bake scone round until golden brown and cooked through, about 30 minutes. Cool on the tray for 10 minutes before serving.

Peaches and Cream Loaf

Fresh peaches and sour cream make this a moist loaf. You can eat it as a dessert topped with frozen yogurt and thickly sliced fresh peaches.

2–3 peaches

185 g (1½ cups/6½ oz) plain (all-purpose) flour

110 g (¾ cup/3¾ oz) plain wholemeal (all-purpose whole-wheat) flour

25 g (¼ cup/1 oz) toasted wheat germ

165 g (¾ cup/5¾ oz) sugar

1 teaspoon bicarbonate of soda (baking soda)

½ teaspoon salt

125 g (½ cup/4½ oz) sour cream

1 egg plus 2 egg whites

2 tablespoons extra-light olive oil

1 teaspoon almond essence (extract)

1 Use a 23- x 13-cm (9- x 5-in) loaf tin. Coat tin with cooking spray. Preheat oven to 180°C (350°F, gas mark 4).

2 Blanch peaches in a saucepan of boiling water for 20 seconds. Peel, pit and finely chop; you will need 185 g (1 cup/6 oz) peach flesh.

3 Combine flours, wheat germ, sugar, bicarbonate of soda and salt in a large bowl. Combine sour cream, egg, egg whites, oil and the essence in a separate bowl. Make a well in the centre of dry ingredients. Pour in sour cream mixture; stir just until combined. Fold in peaches.

4 Spoon batter into tin; level the top. Bake for about 1 hour until a skewer inserted in centre comes out clean. Place tin on a wire rack; cool loaf in tin for 10 minutes. Turn out onto rack to cool completely.

MAKES 16 slices

PREPARATION TIME 15 minutes

COOKING TIME 1 hour

Top Tip

The 'heart' of the wheat kernel, wheat germ has a nutty flavour; it contains cardioprotective nutrients which include vitamin E, folate, magnesium and zinc. It's easy to use wheat germ in your meals: add it to smoothies, pie and crumble toppings and to breadcrumbs for coating chicken or fish or burgers.

Cheese and Watercress Scones

Peppery watercress and mature cheddar flavour these nutritious savoury scones.
Serve warm with soup instead of bread or split and fill them with salad ingredients for lunch.

125 g (1 cup/4½ oz) self-raising (self-rising) flour

150 g (1 cup/5½ oz) self-raising wholemeal (self-rising whole-wheat) flour

1 teaspoon baking powder

3 tablespoons butter, cut into small pieces

50 g (⅓ cup/1½ oz) original rolled (porridge) oats

85 g (3 cups/3 oz) chopped, watercress (coarse stalks removed)

75 g (½ cup/2½ oz) grated mature cheddar cheese

125 ml (½ cup/4 fl oz) milk, plus a little extra to glaze

MAKES 8

PREPARATION TIME 20 minutes

COOKING TIME 10–15 minutes

1 Use a large baking tray; grease the tray. Preheat oven to 230°C (450°F, gas mark 8). Sift the flours and baking powder into a bowl; tip in any bran left in the sieve. Rub in butter with fingertips until mixture resembles fine breadcrumbs.

2 Add the rolled oats, watercress and about three-quarters of the cheese; season with salt and black pepper. Stir in the milk with a fork. Scrape the dough together with a spatula and turn out onto a well-floured work surface. Shape into a smooth, soft ball; it will be a little softer than a standard scone dough.

3 Pat or roll out the dough to 2 cm (¾ in) thick. Use a 7.5 cm (3 in) round cutter to stamp out scones. Press the trimmings together lightly, re-roll and stamp out more scones.

4 Place the scones on the baking tray, arranging them so they are not touching. Brush the tops lightly with milk and sprinkle with the remaining grated cheese. Bake for 10–15 minutes or until risen and golden brown. Cool on a wire rack. These scones are best eaten on the day they are made.

Try this, too…

To make a scone round, place the dough on a greased baking tray and press out into a flat round about 2.5 cm (1 in) thick. Cut the dough into 8 wedges; cut all the way through the dough but do not separate the wedges. Bake for 15 minutes until golden.

Potato Scones

This is a good recipe for young beginner cooks. Curry powder can be used
in place of mustard powder for a spicy result.

225 g (1 ¾ cups/8 oz) self-raising (self-rising) flour

½ teaspoon salt

¼ teaspoon mustard powder

1 ½ teaspoon baking powder

2 tablespoons butter, cut into small pieces

About 4 tablespoons milk

170 g (¾ cup/6 oz) cold mashed potato (without any milk or butter added)

Extra milk or beaten egg, to glaze

2 teaspoons oatmeal

MAKES 6

PREPARATION TIME 10 minutes

COOKING TIME 15–20 minutes

1 Use a baking tray; lightly grease the tray. Preheat oven to 220°C (425°F, gas mark 7). Sift flour, salt, mustard and baking powder into a bowl. Rub in butter with fingertips until the mixture resembles fine breadcrumbs.

2 In another bowl, stir the milk into the mashed potato, mixing well. Add to the dry ingredients and stir with a fork to mix; add another 1–2 tbsp milk, if needed, to make a soft dough.

3 Turn the dough onto a lightly floured work surface; knead for a few seconds until smooth; roll out to a 15-cm (6-in) round about 2 cm (¾ in) thick. Place on the baking tray. Using a sharp knife, mark the scone round into 6 wedges.

4 Brush with milk or beaten egg, then sprinkle with the oatmeal. Bake for 15–20 minutes or until well risen and golden brown.

5 Transfer to a wire rack; break into wedges. Serve warm or leave to cool. Scones can be kept in an airtight tin for up to 3 days. To reheat before serving; place on a baking tray, cover with foil and warm in a low oven for 5 minutes.

Try this, too...

For Potato and Feta Scones, instead of using butter, stir 85 g (½ cup/ 3 oz) finely crumbled feta cheese and 2 tbsp snipped fresh chives into the dry ingredients.

Blackberry and Lemon Scones

Make these scones when firm, sweet blackberries are in season.
The addition of buttermilk to the mixture ensures the result is light and flaky.

125 g (1 cup/4½ oz) self-raising
(self-rising) flour

115 g (¾ cup/4 oz) self-raising
wholemeal (self-rising whole-
wheat) flour

1 teaspoon baking powder

55 g (¼ cup/2 oz) caster
(superfine) sugar

55 g (¼ cup/2 oz) unsalted butter,
cut into small pieces

Finely grated zest of 1 lemon

85 g (½ cup/3 oz) fresh blackberries

125 ml (½ cup/4 fl oz) buttermilk,
or more as needed

MAKES 8

PREPARATION TIME 15 minutes

COOKING TIME 20–25 minutes

1 Use a baking tray; lightly grease the tray. Preheat oven to 200°C (400°F, gas mark 6). Sift flours and baking powder into a large bowl, tipping in any bran left in the sieve. Stir in sugar. Add butter; rub in with fingertips until mixture resembles fine breadcrumbs.

2 Stir in the lemon zest. Very gently stir in the blackberries. Do not overmix as the blackberries can easily become crushed.

3 Lightly stir in buttermilk using a round-bladed knife; again, be careful not to crush the fruit. Add a little more buttermilk if there are any dry bits of dough remaining in the bowl.

4 As soon as the mixture comes together in a soft dough, lift it onto a lightly floured work surface and knead gently 2 or 3 times only, just enough to form a rough ball.

5 Pat out dough carefully with your hands to make an 18-cm (7-in) round. Transfer to the baking tray. Mark into 8 wedges; sprinkle with a little extra white flour. Bake for 20–25 minutes or until risen and lightly golden. Serve warm, broken into the marked wedges. These are best eaten freshly baked, or on the day they are made, but will still be good the next day; store them in an airtight tin.

Try this, too...

To make Cinnamon Raisin Scones, use 55 g (½ cup/2 oz) raisins in place of blackberries and ½ tsp ground cinnamon in place of lemon zest. Increase buttermilk to 170 ml (⅓ cup/5 fl oz). Roll dough out to 2.5 cm (1 in) thick and stamp out rounds with a 5-cm (2-in) plain cutter. Place on a greased baking tray; brush with a mixture of 1 tbsp milk and 2 tsp caster (superfine) sugar. Bake for 12–15 minutes or until risen and light golden.

209

light bites
& lunches

Pork and Herb Pasties

Versatile recipes are a boon. These little pasties are ideal for the lunchbox and for a main course served with salad. It's a good idea to freeze a few. They can quickly be thawed and reheated.

FOR THE PASTRY

500 g (4 cups/1 lb 2 oz) plain (all-purpose) flour

3 teaspoons (10 g/¼ oz) dry (powdered) yeast

250 ml (1 cup/9 fl oz) lukewarm water

120 g (½ cup/4¼ oz) butter

1 egg

1 teaspoon salt

FOR THE FILLING

2 tablespoons sunflower oil

2 white onions, peeled and finely diced

150 g (5½ oz) raw pork schnitzel or cooked roast pork, finely diced

55 g (1½ cups/2 oz) parsley, chopped

2 tablespoons stock

2 tablespoons sour cream

1 teaspoon each of sweet paprika and dried marjoram

Salt and freshly ground black pepper

1 egg, for brushing

MAKES 20

PREPARATION TIME 50 minutes plus 10 minutes resting time

COOKING TIME 15 minutes per baking tray

1 Use 2 baking trays. Line with baking (parchment) paper. Sift flour into a bowl. Sprinkle the yeast onto water to dissolve; stir once.

2 Melt butter; cool to lukewarm. Add yeast, butter, egg and salt to flour. Knead into a sticky dough.

3 Place dough on a lightly floured work surface; knead vigorously for 10 minutes until elastic and no longer sticky. Return dough to bowl, cover and let rise in a warm place for about 30 minutes.

4 Heat oil in pan; sauté onions and schnitzel, stirring, until onions are transparent and meat is browned all over. If using cooked roast meat, add when the onions are transparent and briefly reheat.

5 Remove pan from heat; stir in the parsley, stock, sour cream, paprika, marjoram, salt and pepper.

6 Preheat oven to 200°C (350°F, gas mark 4). On a lightly floured work surface, roll out the dough to 1 cm (½ in) thick. Cut out 20 rounds about 8 cm (3 in) in diameter. Place 1 tsp filling in centre of each round.

7 Separate egg. Brush the edges of the rounds with beaten egg white; fold rounds in half to make semicircles; press edges together. Brush pasties with egg yolk; place on baking trays. Leave to rise for 10 minutes. Bake for 15 minutes until golden, one tray at a time.

Try this, too...

For Puff Pastry Pasties, in place of yeast dough, use 2 sheets ready-rolled puff pastry, thawed (about 300 g/10½ oz). For the filling, chop 3 onions finely. Finely chop 30 g (1 oz) chives and dice 250 g (9 oz) pork. Sear pork in 2 tbsp hot oil. Stir in the onion, chives, 2 tbsp butter, 2 tbsp plain (all-purpose) flour and 150 ml (½ cup/5 fl oz) cream and season with salt and pepper; bring briefly to the boil. Place the pastry sheets on top of one another and roll out. Cut into rounds, fill and continue as for the main recipe.

Feta Cheese Pastries

Big on flavour, these delicious pastries are quick and easy to make. If fresh herbs are unavailable, use 2 teaspoons of shop-bought pesto in the filling.

2 sheets ready-rolled puff pastry, thawed (about 300 g/10½ oz)

FOR THE FILLING AND GLAZE

110 g (¾ cup/4 oz) feta cheese

40 g (1 cup/1½ oz) each of dill and flat-leafed parsley

A few sprigs of basil

Black pepper, to taste

1 egg yolk

1 tablespoon milk

MAKES 12

PREPARATION TIME 20 minutes plus 20 minutes cooling time

COOKING TIME 15–20 minutes per baking tray

1 Use 2 baking trays; line with baking (parchment) paper. Preheat oven to 220°C (425°F, gas mark 7).

2 For the filling, crumble the feta finely with a fork. Finely chop the dill and parsley and cut basil leaves into strips. Stir herbs through cheese; season with pepper to taste.

3 Roll out pastry thinly and cut into 12 x 12-cm (4½-in) squares. Place a teaspoon of cheese mixture in the centre of each square.

4 Brush edges of squares with a little combined beaten egg yolk and milk. Fold the squares into triangles; press edges together and decorate with the tines of a fork.

5 Place pasties on baking trays, brush with the remaining egg mixture; chill for about 20 minutes. Bake for 15–20 minutes until golden brown. Serve pasties hot or warm.

Spicy Vegetable Triangles

Serve these mildly spicy pastries as an appetiser or as a light meal with salad.
Mango chutney or yogurt flavoured with garlic and mint go well with them.

FOR THE PASTRY

350 g (2¾ cups/12 oz) plain
   (all-purpose) flour

1 egg

60 ml (¼ cup/2 fl oz) oil

1 tablespoon vinegar

FOR THE FILLING

2 cloves garlic

2 tablespoons oil

4 spring onions (scallions), chopped

150 g (1 cup/5½ oz) grated
   pumpkin (acorn squash)

150 g (1 cup/5½ oz) grated potato

100 g (1½ cups/3½ oz) chopped
   broccoli

1 tablespoon mild curry powder

2 teaspoons lemon juice

1 egg yolk

60 ml (¼ cup/2 fl oz) cream

Oil and 1 egg white, for brushing

Sesame seeds, for sprinkling

1 Line a baking tray with baking (parchment) paper. Place flour, egg, oil and vinegar in a bowl; knead briefly to combine. Place on a lightly floured work surface and knead for 10 minutes; shape into a ball. Heat a ceramic bowl, invert it over dough. Leave dough to rest for 30 minutes.

2 For the filling, peel and chop the garlic. Heat oil in a large saucepan. Add all the vegetables and cook for 5 minutes. Add curry powder, lemon juice, egg yolk and cream; season with salt and pepper.

3 Preheat oven to 220°C (425°F, gas mark 7). Flatten pastry ball a little and cut into 12 equal pieces; stretch each piece into a rectangle approximately 8 x 30 cm (3¼ x 12 in). Brush with oil.

4 Place 1 tbsp filling on a narrow end of a rectangle; fold over the opposite end and wrap pastry a few times diagonally around the filling to make a triangle. Make sure edges are sealed. Repeat with remaining pastry. Brush triangles generously with oil; place on baking tray. Bake for 20 minutes. Brush with beaten egg white and sprinkle with sesame seeds; bake for a further 5 minutes.

MAKES 12

PREPARATION TIME 50 minutes

COOKING TIME 25 minutes

Tomato and Basil Galettes

Galette is the French term for a flat, round pastry or cake. In this recipe,
the galettes are made from wholemeal scone dough flavoured with a little Parmesan cheese.
Serve as a snack or starter, or as a light lunch with a mixed leaf salad.

FOR THE PASTRY

125 g (1 cup/4½ oz) self-raising (self-rising) flour

60 g (½ cup/2¼ oz) self-raising wholemeal (self-rising whole-wheat) flour

1 teaspoon baking powder

Pinch of salt

2 tablespoons butter, chilled and diced

2 tablespoons finely grated Parmesan cheese

120 ml (½ cup/4 fl oz) milk

FOR THE TOPPING

3 teaspoons extra virgin olive oil

1 clove garlic, crushed

3 tablespoons sun-dried tomato paste or basil pesto

3 tablespoons shredded fresh basil leaves

3 large plum tomatoes, thinly sliced

40 g (¼ cup/1½ oz) pine nuts

Basil leaves to garnish

SERVES 6

PREPARATION TIME 20 minutes

COOKING TIME 10–12 minutes

1 Use a non-stick baking sheet. Preheat oven to 220°C (425°F, gas mark 7). Sift the flours, baking powder and salt into a bowl; tip in any bran left in sieve. Rub in butter until mixture resembles fine breadcrumbs. Stir in Parmesan cheese.

2 Make a well in the centre and pour in the milk. Mix together to make a fairly soft dough. Knead briefly until smooth.

3 Roll out the dough on a lightly floured work surface to 5 mm (¼ in) thickness. Cut out 6 rounds about 10 cm (4 in) in diameter. You will need to re-roll the trimmings to cut out the last round. Transfer rounds to baking sheet; space them well apart. Mark edges with a fork.

4 Brush tops with 2 tsp olive oil. Mix the remaining oil with the garlic, tomato paste and basil and spread thinly over rounds, leaving a clear border of about 5 mm (¼ in). Arrange tomato slices on top, overlapping them slightly and covering all of the basil topping.

5 Bake for 7 minutes, then scatter the pine nuts over the tomatoes. Return to the oven and bake for 3–5 minutes or until the galettes are risen and the edges are golden brown. Serve hot, garnished with basil leaves.

Try this, too...

For Caramelised Onion Galettes, thinly slice 4 red onions. Cook in 2 tbsp olive oil over low heat, partly covered, for 10 minutes, stirring occasionally. Add 2 tsp balsamic vinegar and 1 tsp light brown sugar. Cook for a further 4 minutes, stirring, until mixture is soft. Remove from heat; stir in 1 tbsp chopped dry-packed sun-dried tomatoes and season with black pepper. Make galette bases, following the main recipe; add 2 tsp chopped fresh thyme to the dry ingredients and rub in only 1 tbsp butter and 55 g (¼ cup/ 2 oz) crumbled feta cheese. Omit the Parmesan cheese. Spoon the onion mixture onto the galettes. Bake in a preheated 220°C (425°F, gas mark 7) oven for 10 minutes or until risen and golden brown.

Top Tip

Wholemeal (whole-wheat) flour contains more B vitamins, iron, selenium and zinc than white flour, but used on its own makes heavy pastry and scone mixtures. Mixing wholemeal and white flour together produces a lighter result.

In addition to its culinary uses, basil is prescribed by herbalists as a natural tranquilliser and to help relieve upset stomachs and cramps.

Souffléd Salmon Tartlets

Individual tartlets served with a salad garnish make an attractive starter.
The fish filling used here is very light; whisked egg whites are folded into the sauce
producing an airy soufflé-like texture. Serve straight from the oven.

FOR THE PASTRY

125 g (1 cup/4½ oz) plain (all-purpose) flour

55 g (¼ cup/2 oz) butter, chilled and diced

FOR THE FILLING

25 g (scant 1 oz) cornflour (cornstarch)

170 ml (⅔ cup/5½ fl oz) milk

About 180 g (⅔ cup/6 oz) tinned skinless, boneless pink salmon, drained and flaked

2 tablespoons each of chopped fresh dill and chives

2 eggs, separated

TO SERVE

175 g (4 cups/6 oz) mixed salad leaves, such as frisée and rocket (arugula)

1 red capsicum (bell pepper), seeds removed, cut into thin strips

SERVES 6

PREPARATION TIME 40 minutes plus at least 30 minutes chilling

COOKING TIME 15 minutes

1 Use 6 individual 9-cm (3½-in) non-stick tartlet tins with loose bases. Sift flour into a large bowl. Add butter, rub in until the mixture resembles fine breadcrumbs, then sprinkle over 2 tbsp cold water. Mix with a round-bladed knife to form a dough. Gather into a smooth ball, wrap in cling wrap and chill for at least 30 minutes.

2 Blend cornflour with 2 tbsp milk to make a smooth paste. Heat the remaining milk to boiling point; pour a little into cornflour mixture, stirring. Add the mixture to the milk in the pan. Bring to the boil and stir until sauce thickens. Reduce heat and leave to simmer gently for 2 minutes.

3 Remove the pan from the heat. Stir in salmon, dill and chives; add salt and black pepper to taste. Mix in the egg yolks. Set aside.

4 Preheat oven to 200°C (400°F, gas mark 6). Divide pastry into 6 equal pieces. Roll out each piece thinly to line the tartlet tins.

5 Prick the pastry cases several times with a fork. Place tins on a baking sheet. Line the tins with baking (parchment) paper; fill with dried beans. Cook for 10 minutes. Remove paper and beans; bake for a further 5 minutes or until pastry is lightly golden. Allow to cool, then carefully remove the tartlet cases from tins and replace them on the baking sheet.

6 Whisk the egg whites until stiff and fold into salmon mixture. Spoon mixture into cases and bake for 15 minutes or until well risen and golden. Serve immediately on individual plates, garnished with the salad leaves and capsicum strips.

Try this, too...

Instead of salmon, use tinned tuna in spring water, well drained.

Serve the tartlets cold for an easy picnic dish. Although they will not have a soufflé appearance, they will still taste delicious.

To make Souffléd Spinach and Parmesan Tartlets, heat 125 g (4½ oz) frozen spinach over low heat until thawed. Squeeze out excess moisture, add spinach to sauce with ½ tsp grated nutmeg; omit salmon, dill and chives. Stir in egg yolks and 2 tbsp freshly grated Parmesan cheese. Fold in egg whites; bake as for the main recipe. Serve with salad leaves and cherry tomatoes.

Ricotta Herb Scones

These savoury rolls are made with soft cheese and plenty of fresh herbs.
A mixture of flat-leafed parsley, chives, thyme and rosemary tastes good, although any favourite combination will do. The scones are eaten warm from the oven, with soup or salad.

450 g (3²/₃ cups/1 lb) self-raising (self-rising) flour

¹/₂ teaspoon salt

Black pepper, to taste

225 g (1 cup/8 oz) ricotta cheese

1 egg

3 tablespoons chopped mixed fresh herbs

250 ml (1 cup/9 fl oz) milk, or as needed, plus extra to glaze

1 tablespoon sesame seeds

MAKES 8

PREPARATION TIME 20 minutes

COOKING TIME 20–25 minutes

1 Use a large baking tray; grease the tray. Preheat oven to 190°C (375°F, gas mark 5). Sift flour into a large bowl; stir in salt and freshly ground black pepper.

2 Place ricotta, egg and herbs in another bowl; stir until smooth. Add to the flour; mix with a round-bladed knife. Work in enough of the milk to make a slightly soft but not sticky dough.

3 Turn dough out onto a lightly floured work surface; knead briefly until smooth. Divide dough into 8 equal portions; shape each one into a rough-looking ball.

4 Place scones on baking tray; they should not be touching. Glaze lightly with milk; top with a sprinkling of sesame seeds. Bake for 20–25 minutes or until lightly browned. When tapped on the base, they should make a hollow sound.

5 Transfer to a wire rack to cool slightly. Serve scones straight away or store in an airtight tin for up to 24 hours.

Try this, too...

Instead of a mixture of herbs, use just one kind such as chopped parsley or finely shredded fresh basil leaves.

For Goat's Cheese, Olive and Thyme Scones, replace ricotta with the same quantity of soft fresh goat's cheese and the mixed fresh herbs with 2 tbsp sliced black olives and 1 tbsp chopped fresh thyme.

Top Tip

Ricotta, which is made from the whey drained off when making cheeses such as mozzarella, has a high moisture content. This makes it lower in fat and calories than most other soft, creamy cheeses.

Using fresh herbs in cooking helps reduce the need for salt, which is an acquired taste. If you gradually reduce the amount you use, your palate will adapt over a period of about 4 weeks.

Mediterranean Herb Muffins

Serve with grilled vegetables, soups and salads. Eat them plain or spread with ricotta.

225 g (1¾ cups/8 oz) plain (all-purpose) flour

1 tablespoon baking powder

Pinch of salt

1 tablespoon chopped fresh thyme

Small handful of fresh basil leaves, torn into small pieces

75 g (½ cup/2½ oz) fine cornmeal or instant polenta, plus extra for sprinkling

3 spring onions (scallions), thinly sliced

2 tablespoons finely grated Parmesan cheese

60 ml (¼ cup/2 fl oz) extra virgin olive oil

140 g (⅔ cup/5 oz) natural (plain) yogurt

170 ml (⅔ cup/6 fl oz) milk

2 eggs

MAKES 12

PREPARATION TIME 15 minutes

COOKING TIME 20 minutes

1 Use a 12-hole deep muffin pan. Line with paper cases. Preheat oven to 190°C (375°F, gas mark 5).

2 Sift the flour, baking powder and salt into a large bowl. Stir in thyme, basil, cornmeal, spring onions and Parmesan until evenly combined.

3 Beat the oil, yogurt, milk and eggs together in another bowl. Pour the egg mixture over the dry ingredients; mix only until just combined; a little dry flour should still be visible.

4 Spoon mixture into cases and sprinkle with a little extra cornmeal. Bake for 20 minutes or until muffins are well risen, pale golden and just firm to the touch.

5 Transfer to a wire rack to cool. Serve fresh, preferably slightly warm from the oven. These muffins are best eaten within 24 hours.

Try this, too...

For Parmesan and Leek Muffins, replace spring onions and herbs with 1 finely chopped small leek (about 150 g/5½ oz). Cook the leek in a little butter for 3 minutes or until softened but not coloured. Cool; add to the dry ingredients.

Top Tip

Parmesan is a high-fat cheese, but it offers plenty of flavour so can be used in modest quantities and still have a big impact.

Onions are a flavouring ingredient in numerous savoury recipes, but that's not the only reason to use them. Research suggests that they can help to lower blood cholesterol levels and lessen the risk of blood clots forming, so reducing the risk of coronary heart disease.

Ham and Wild Rice Parcels

The flavours of smoky ham, mushrooms and zucchini work well with wild rice in the filling for these filo pastries. The ideal accompaniment is a simple side salad.

5 sheets filo pastry, 30 x 50 cm (12 x 20 in) each (about 150 g/ 5½ oz in total)

2 tablespoons butter, melted

2 teaspoons poppy seeds

FOR THE FILLING

100 g (½ cup/3½ oz) mixed basmati and wild rice

310 ml (1¼ cups/10¾ fl oz) chicken stock

1 tablespoon extra virgin olive oil

1 red onion, finely chopped

About 100 g (1 cup/4 oz) shiitake mushrooms, sliced

About 100 g (1 cup/4 oz) chestnut mushrooms, sliced

2 small zucchini (courgettes), diced

150 g (1 cup/5½ oz) ham, trimmed of fat and snipped into strips

2 teaspoons chopped fresh tarragon (optional)

SERVES 4

PREPARATION TIME 40 minutes

COOKING TIME 10 minutes

1 Use a non-stick baking tray. Preheat oven to 190°C (375°F, gas mark 5). For the filling, put rice and stock in a saucepan and bring to the boil. Reduce heat to low, then cover and simmer gently for about 20 minutes or until rice is tender.

2 Heat oil in a large frying pan. Add onion, mushrooms and zucchini, cover and cook for 6–8 minutes, stirring occasionally, until softened. Leave to cool.

3 Lay out 4 filo pastry sheets, one on top of the other. (Keep fifth sheet covered so it doesn't dry out.) Trim filo stack into a 30- x 45-cm (12- x 18-in) rectangle. Cut in half lengthwise and then crosswise into 3, making 24 x 15 cm (6 in) squares.

4 Lay out 4 squares on a work surface and brush very lightly with butter. Place another 4 squares on top at a slight angle and butter them. Repeat the layering to make 4 rough piles, each with 6 buttered squares of pastry.

5 Add the rice and ham to the mushroom mixture. Stir in the tarragon, if using, and season with salt and pepper to taste. Divide the mushroom mixture among the filo stacks, spooning it into the centre. Lift up pastry edges to contain but not completely enclose filling; the parcels should be slightly open at the top. Place on the baking tray.

6 Cut the remaining sheet of filo pastry in half lengthwise and then across into thin strips. Brush strips with remaining butter, then scrunch them up and place on top of the parcels to cover the filling.

7 Scatter poppy seeds over the parcels. Bake for 10 minutes or until pastry is crisp and golden brown. Serve hot.

Try this, too...

For Spicy Chorizo, Rice and Olive Parcels, cook 100 g (½ cup/3 oz) white long-grain rice in a covered pan with 6 sliced dry-packed, sun-dried tomatoes and 250 ml (1 cup/9 fl oz) chicken stock for 10–15 minutes or until the rice is tender and the stock has been absorbed. Heat 1 tbsp oil in a pan. Add 100 g (3 oz) chorizo sausage, chopped, 1 finely sliced red onion and 1 diced red capsicum (bell pepper); cover and cook for 6–8 minutes or until onion is tender. Stir in the rice mixture with 45 g (¼ cup/2 oz) sliced black olives, about 200 g (1 cup/7 oz) tinned sweetcorn kernels, drained and 20 roughly torn fresh basil leaves. Season with salt and black pepper to taste. Use to fill filo pastries. Scatter sesame seeds on the top; cook as for the main recipe.

Cheese and Cranberry Tartlets

The little pastry cases have a tart/sweet filling of cranberry sauce, goat's cheese and a yogurt custard. They make a sophisticated lunch.

3 sheets ready-rolled shortcrust pastry, thawed

FOR THE FILLING

3 large eggs

125 ml (½ cup/4 fl oz) low-fat natural (plain) yogurt

310 ml (1 ¼ cups/10 fl oz) milk

4 tablespoons (⅓ cup) cranberry sauce

3 tablespoons snipped fresh chives

85 g (⅔ cup/3 oz) goat's cheese, crumbled

SERVES 6

PREPARATION TIME 45 minutes

COOKING TIME 25–30 minutes

1 Use 6 individual 12.5-cm (5-in) non-stick tartlet tins with loose bases. Preheat oven to 190°C (375°F, gas mark 5). Cut pastry into 6 equal pieces. Roll out each piece thinly on a lightly floured work surface and use to line the tins.

2 Prick pastry several times with a fork. Place tins on a baking sheet. Line with baking (parchment) paper; fill with dried beans. Bake for 12 minutes; remove paper and beans. Return to oven for a further 8–10 minutes or until light golden brown. Remove from oven. Lower oven temperature to 180°C (350°F, gas mark 4).

3 Beat eggs in a small bowl. Add yogurt and milk and season with salt and pepper; mix well.

4 Spread 2 tsp cranberry sauce in the bottom of each pastry case. Top with chives and goat's cheese. Pour egg mixture into cases. Bake for 25–30 minutes or until filling is slightly puffed and golden brown. Serve warm.

Try this, too...

Add texture to the pastry by rolling it out on a sprinkling of original rolled (porridge) oats. This makes the pastry more nutritious. too.

Prawn Tartlets

Filled with stir-fried prawns (large shrimp) and a mixture of crisp, colourful vegetables, these tartlets make a good light snack or starter. The pastry cases can be made ahead.

1 tablespoon sunflower oil

1 teaspoon toasted sesame oil

3 sheets filo pastry, 30 x 50 cm (12 x 20 in) each (about 90 g/ 3¼ oz in total)

1 clove garlic, crushed

3 spring onions (scallions), sliced

1 tablespoon finely chopped fresh root ginger

1 carrot, cut into fine strips

300 g (10½ oz) peeled raw tiger prawns (large shrimp)

75 g (2½ oz) snow peas (mange-tout) sliced diagonally

85 g (3 oz) pak choy, sliced

65 g (¾ cup/2½ oz) bean sprouts

1 tablespoon light soy sauce

Sprigs of fresh coriander (cilantro), to garnish

SERVES 4

PREPARATION TIME 30 minutes

COOKING TIME 15 minutes

1 Use a 12-hole non-stick muffin pan. Preheat oven to 200°C (400°F, gas mark 6). Combine the sunflower and sesame oils. Lay the filo pastry sheets out, one on top of the other. Trim the stacked pastry to 30 x 40 cm (12 x 16 in). Cut stack lengthwise into 3 and then across into 4, making 10 cm (4 in) squares. You will have 36 squares of filo.

2 Place a filo square in each hole in the muffin pan. Brush very lightly with the oil mixture. Place another filo square on top, putting it at an angle to the first one. Brush with oil; place a third filo square on top, again with the corners offset. Bake pastry cases for 5–7 minutes or until golden brown and crisp.

3 Meanwhile, heat the remaining oil mixture in a wok or a large frying pan. Add the garlic, spring onions and ginger and stir-fry over moderate heat for 30 seconds. Add

carrot; stir-fry for 2 minutes. Add the prawns; stir-fry for 2 minutes or until they turn pink.

4 Add snow peas with the pak choy and bean sprouts. Stir-fry over high heat for 2–3 minutes or until vegetables are just tender and the mixture is piping hot. Sprinkle with the soy sauce and toss to mix.

5 Spoon the prawn and vegetable mixture into the pastry cases and serve immediately, garnished with sprigs of coriander.

Try this, too...

For vegetarians, replace the prawns with 300 g (2 cups/10½ oz) cubed, chilled tofu. Add at the end of step 3; stir-fry for 2–3 minutes.

Replace the pak choy with other leafy greens such as shredded Chinese leaves or baby spinach.

Turkey Empanadas

There are many versions of these savoury Mexican pastries. The filling here is
a mixture of lean turkey and vegetables, subtly flavoured with spices, nuts and dried fruit.

175 ml ($^2/_3$ cup/6 fl oz) warm water

1 packet white bread or pizza dough mix (about 250 g/9 oz)

1 small egg, beaten

$^1/_4$ teaspoon paprika

FOR THE FILLING

1 tablespoon sunflower oil

1 onion, thinly sliced

1 clove garlic, crushed

1 fresh green or red chilli, seeds removed, finely chopped

About 250 g (2$^1/_2$ cups/9 oz) turkey mince (ground turkey)

300 g (10$^1/_2$ oz) potatoes, peeled and cut into 1 cm ($^1/_2$ in) dice

$^1/_2$ teaspoon each ground cinnamon, coriander and cumin

80 ml ($^1/_3$ cup/2$^1/_4$ fl oz) dry sherry or white wine

1 large carrot, coarsely grated

45 g ($^1/_3$ cup/$^1/_2$ oz) raisins

40 g ($^1/_4$ cup/1$^1/_2$ oz) blanched almonds, toasted and roughly chopped

2 tablespoons chopped fresh coriander (cilantro)

2 tablespoons tomato paste (concentrated purée)

SERVES 5

PREPARATION TIME about 30 minutes, plus 10–15 minutes rising

COOKING TIME 25 minutes

1 Use a non-stick baking tray. To make the filling, heat the oil in a frying pan; cook onion, garlic and chilli on medium–high heat for 2–3 minutes, stirring, until softened and lightly browned. Add turkey mince; stir for a further 5 minutes.

2 Part-cook the diced potatoes in a saucepan of boiling water for 5 minutes. Drain well.

3 Stir ground spices into turkey mixture; cook for 30 seconds. Add the sherry or wine; simmer for 2–3 minutes or until the liquid has almost evaporated.

4 Stir in potato, carrot, raisins, almonds, coriander and tomato paste; season with salt and pepper. Remove from the heat.

5 Stir the water into the bread or pizza mix; knead for 2 minutes or until smooth. Cover and leave to rest for 5 minutes, then divide into 5 equal pieces. On a lightly floured work surface, roll out each piece to a 20-cm (8-in) round.

6 Spoon the filling into centre of rounds. Brush the edge of each round with beaten egg, then fold over into a half-moon shape. Press edges together and roll over to seal. Place on baking sheet, cover with oiled cling wrap. Leave pastries in a warm place for 10–15 minutes or until slightly risen. Preheat oven to 220°C (425°F, gas mark 7).

7 Uncover the empanadas, glaze with the rest of the beaten egg and sprinkle with paprika. Bake for 10 minutes. Reduce temperature to 180°C (350°F, gas mark 4) and bake for a further 15 minutes.

Try this, too...

Sprinkle the empanadas with poppyseeds instead of paprika.

Make a large pie instead of pasties. Roll out two-thirds of the dough and use to line a greased 23-cm (9-in) shallow pie dish. Add the filling, smoothing surface evenly. Moisten edges with beaten egg. Roll out the remaining dough and cover the pie, sealing the edges firmly. Make a steam hole in the centre of the lid. Leave to rise in a warm place for 10–15 minutes, then glaze with beaten egg. Bake for 10 minutes. Reduce heat and bake for a further 20–25 minutes.

Top Tip

Minced (ground) turkey contains less fat than beef, lamb or chicken mince, making it one of the lowest fat meats available.

White bread and pizza dough are both good sources of carbohydrate. It is recommended that at least half the calories in a healthy diet should come from starchy foods.

Raisins, like other dried fruits, are very good sources of dietary fibre. They are also virtually fat-free and provide useful amounts of iron.

Sesame Cheese Twists

These crisp cheese sticks are delicious served fresh and still warm from the oven. Enriched with egg yolks and well-flavoured with freshly grated Parmesan cheese, they are made with a combination of wholemeal and plain flour so that they are substantial without being at all heavy.

85 g (²/₃ cup/3 oz) plain wholemeal (all-purpose whole-wheat) flour

85 g (²/₃ cup/3 oz) plain (all-purpose) flour

3 tablespoons butter, softened

3 tablespoons freshly grated Parmesan cheese

1 large egg

2 tablespoons milk

1 teaspoon paprika

1 tablespoon sesame seeds

MAKES 40

PREPARATION TIME 10–15 minutes

COOKING TIME 15 minutes

1 Use 2 large baking sheets lined with baking (parchment) paper. Preheat oven to 180°C (350°F, gas mark 4). Sift flours and a pinch of salt into a bowl; tip in any bran left in sieve. Rub in butter until mixture resembles fine breadcrumbs. Stir in the Parmesan cheese.

2 Whisk egg and milk together. Reserve 1 tsp; stir the rest into the dry ingredients to make a firm dough. Knead briefly on a lightly floured work surface until smooth.

3 Sprinkle paprika over floured surface; roll out the dough on it to form a square slightly larger than 20 cm (8 in). Trim edges neatly.

4 Brush dough with reserved egg mixture; sprinkle the sesame seeds over the top. Cut the dough in half, then cut into 10-cm (4-in) sticks about 1 cm (½ in) wide.

5 Twist sticks; place on baking sheets. Lightly press the ends of the sticks down so that they do not untwist during baking.

6 Bake for 15 minutes or until lightly browned and crisp. Cool briefly on baking sheets, then serve warm. Or, transfer to a wire rack to cool completely. Twists can be kept in an airtight container for 5 days.

Top Tip

Sesame seeds are a good source of calcium as well as providing iron and zinc.

Wholemeal flour has a lot to offer in a healthy diet: dietary fibre, B vitamins and vitamin E, as well as iron, selenium and magnesium.

Italian Pizza Crackers

Simple, stylish snack food is a boon for the busy cook.

FOR THE PASTRY

400 g (14 oz) ready-made frozen pizza dough, thawed at room temperature

1 egg yolk

FOR THE TOPPING

Caraway seeds

Chopped almonds

Poppyseeds

Sunflower seeds

MAKES 36

PREPARATION TIME 15 minutes

COOKING TIME 10–15 minutes per baking tray

1 Use large baking trays and line with baking (parchment) paper. Preheat oven to 200°C (400°F, gas mark 6).

2 Roll out pizza dough on lightly floured work surface to 5 mm (½ in) thick. Whisk egg yolk with 2 tbsp water; brush over dough. Cut dough into 6 cm (2½ in) squares to make 36 in total.

3 Combine topping ingredients; sprinkle over the squares. Place on baking trays and cook, one tray at a time, for 10–15 minutes or until pastry is golden. Remove from the trays, cool briefly and serve warm.

Try this, too...

For Turkish Feta Pastries, roll out 400 g (14 oz) pizza dough into a thin sheet. Sprinkle crumbled feta over one half of the dough. Fold over the other side; press to seal. Bake in a preheated 200°C (400°F, gas mark 6) oven for 20–25 minutes. Remove from oven, cut into pieces and serve.

229

Spicy Filo Triangles

This version of Indian samosas is baked rather than deep-fried for a healthy, light result. The crisp filo parcels contain curry-spiced vegetables and can be served hot from the oven with a fresh mango and ginger salsa as a starter or light snack.

2 sheets filo pastry, 30 x 50 cm (12 x 20 in) each (60 g/2 oz in total)

1 tablespoon sunflower oil

1/2 tsp coriander seeds, coarsely crushed

FOR THE FILLING

1 potato, about 170 g (6 oz), peeled and diced

1 small carrot, peeled and diced

65 g (1/2 cup/2 1/2 oz) frozen peas

1 tablespoon mild curry powder

1 tablespoon chopped fresh coriander

Pinch of salt

MANGO AND GINGER SALSA

1 large ripe but firm mango

1/2 teaspoon grated fresh root ginger

1 teaspoon lemon juice

1 teaspoon caster (superfine) sugar

1/4 teaspoon crushed dried chillies

1 teaspoon sunflower oil

MAKES 12

PREPARATION TIME 35 minutes

COOKING TIME 10–15 minutes

1 Use 2 non-stick baking sheets. Preheat oven to 200°C (400°F, gas mark 6). For the filling, cook potato and carrot in boiling water for 5 minutes. Add peas and cook for a further 2 minutes. Drain well; tip the vegetables into a bowl. Stir in curry paste, coriander and salt; mash the mixture very slightly to combine. Leave to cool.

2 Take 1 sheet of pastry (keep the other one covered to prevent it drying out) and cut it crosswise into 6 x 30-cm (12-in) long strips. Brush them with a little of the oil.

3 Lay a pastry strip lengthwise in front of you; place 1 rounded tbsp filling in the middle of the end nearest to you. Lift one end corner and fold it diagonally over filling to make a triangular shape, flattening the filling slightly. Continue folding the strip over in a triangular shape until you come almost to the end. Trim off any excess pastry. Repeat with the remaining filo pastry and filling to make 12 triangles.

4 Place filo triangles on baking sheets, brush with remaining oil and scatter crushed coriander seeds over the top. Bake for 10–15 minutes or until golden.

5 To make the salsa, cut mango cheeks from both sides of the stone, then peel and cut the flesh into small dice. In a serving bowl, combine with ginger, lemon juice, sugar, chillies and oil. Serve with hot filo triangles.

Top Tip

Using vegetables in imaginative, flavoursome ways, such as in this filling, can help to boost intake so that the recommended 5 portions of fruit and vegetables a day can be achieved.

Fresh mangoes are an excellent source of beta-carotene, which the body can convert into vitamin A. Beta-carotene acts as a powerful antioxidant, helping to protect against heart disease and cancer.

Frozen peas are likely to be more nutritious than fresh, as they are frozen straight after picking and shelling. In particular, the vitamin C content is higher.

Tunisian Tuna and Egg Briks

Traditionally made with a special pastry called malsouka and deep-fried,
this version uses baked filo pastry and is much lower in fat but still great on taste.

2½ tablespoons extra virgin olive oil

8 spring onions (scallions), thinly
sliced

200 g (7 oz) baby spinach leaves,
roughly torn

4 sheets filo pastry, 30 x 50 cm
(12 x 20 in) each (120 g/4 oz
in total)

About 200 g (7 oz) tinned tuna in
spring water, drained and flaked

2 eggs, hard-boiled and finely
chopped

Dash of chilli sauce

TO SERVE

4 ripe tomatoes, chopped

1 small cucumber, chopped

1 tablespoon lemon juice

4 tablespoons mango or apricot
chutney

SERVES 4

PREPARATION TIME 30 minutes

COOKING TIME 12–15 minutes

Top Tip

Using tuna in spring water, rather
than in oil, helps to keep the fat
content of the dish low.

1 Use a large non-stick baking
tray. Heat 2 tsp oil in a large
saucepan. Add spring onions; cook
over low heat for 3 minutes until
beginning to soften. Add spinach,
cover with a tight-fitting lid and
cook a further 2–3 minutes or until
tender and wilted; stir a few times.
Tip into a colander and leave to
drain and cool.

2 Using a saucer as a guide, cut
out 24 filo pastry rounds about
12.5 cm (5 in) in diameter, 6 rounds
from each sheet. Stack filo rounds;
cover with cling wrap to stop them
drying out.

3 When cool, squeeze as much
excess liquid out of the spinach
as possible; transfer spinach to a
bowl. Add tuna, eggs and sauce and
salt and pepper to taste. Mix well.

4 Preheat oven to 200°C (400°F,
gas mark 6). Take 1 filo round
and brush very lightly with some of
the remaining oil. Place a second
round on top; brush with a little oil.
Repeat with a third round.

5 Place 1 heaped tbsp filling in
the middle of the round, then
fold the pastry over to make a half-
moon shape. Fold in edges, twisting
them to seal; place on baking tray.
Repeat with the remaining pastry
and filling to make 8 briks.

6 Lightly brush the briks with the
remaining oil. Bake for 12–15
minutes or until the pastry is crisp
and golden brown.

7 Place tomatoes and cucumber
in a bowl; sprinkle with lemon
juice and season to taste. Serve the
briks hot with salad and chutney.

Try this, too...

**Serve with natural (plain) low-fat
yogurt** rather than fruit chutney.

**For Turkish Boreks with Feta and
Tomato,** cut filo pastry into 24 x
12.5-cm (5-in) squares. Crumble
200 g (1⅓ cups/7 oz) feta cheese;
mix with 3 chopped tomatoes
(seeds removed), 30 g (⅓ cup/1 oz)
toasted flaked almonds, 2 tbsp
each of chopped fresh coriander
(cilantro) and mint. Season with
salt and black pepper. For each
borek, layer 3 pastry squares,
brushing each square with oil.
Add a spoonful of filling; bring
the 4 corners together over the
top, pinching to seal. Brush with
remaining oil and bake as in the
main recipe.

Ham Croissants

These croissants are very versatile. They can be filled with meat, seafood or vegetables.
Try a mixture of fine strips of smoked salmon and diced ham.

2 sheets ready-rolled puff pastry,
thawed (about 300 g/10½ oz)

FOR THE FILLING

110 g (⅔ cup/4 oz) mixed cured
meats such as Parma ham,
pancetta and salami

1 small gherkin

FOR THE GLAZE

2 tablespoons cream

MAKES 12

PREPARATION TIME 30 minutes plus
20 minutes cooling time

COOKING TIME 10–15 minutes

1 Use a large baking tray. Line with baking (parchment) paper.

2 Roll the pastry out on a floured work surface into 3-mm (⅛-in) thick round. Cut the round up like a cake into 12 triangular slices.

3 Make an incision in the tips of the slices about 2.5 cm (1 in) towards the centre, then pull apart slightly. To make the filling, slice the meats and gherkin into small pieces or fine strips; combine.

4 Spread a little filling on wide end of each slice and then roll up into mini croissants. Bend tips gently to form crescents, then place on baking tray. Chill for 20 minutes. Preheat oven to 220°C (425°F, gas mark 7).

5 Mix cream with 2 tbsp water and brush over the croissants. Bake for 10–15 minutes until golden brown. Cool briefly on baking tray; serve lukewarm.

Olive Snails

Brushed with an aromatic paste, puff pastry turns into a delicious snack in a flash.

2 sheets ready-rolled puff pastry, thawed (about 300 g/10½ oz)

FOR THE FILLING

2 marinated anchovy fillets

4 cloves garlic, peeled

About 150 g (1 cup/5 oz) pitted black olives

1 dried chilli

6 sage leaves

1 tablespoon capers

1 teaspoon lemon juice

½ teaspoon each of dried thyme and rosemary

120 ml (½ cup/4 fl oz) olive oil

MAKES 24

PREPARATION TIME 15 minutes plus 70 minutes cooling time

COOKING TIME 10–15 minutes per baking tray

1 Use 2 baking trays. Line with baking (parchment) paper. On a lightly floured work surface, roll out the pastry into a rectangle.

2 For the filling, rinse anchovy fillets in cold water and drain. Chop anchovies, garlic, olives, chilli, sage and capers very finely and mix together. Add lemon juice, thyme, rosemary and olive oil into a paste-like mixture; add salt and pepper.

3 Spread the paste over pastry, leaving a margin of 2 cm (¾ in) along one long side. Loosely roll up pastry sheet, starting from the long side. Wrap in cling wrap and place in freezer for 40–50 minutes; turn pastry twice during this time.

4 Cut pastry roll into slices 4 mm (1½ in) thick. Place on baking trays allowing room for the snails to spread. Chill for 20 minutes.

5 Preheat oven to 220°C (425°F, gas mark 7). Brush a little water over the snails and bake, one tray at a time, for 10–15 minutes until golden. Reduce heat to 140°C (275°F, gas mark 1). Leave the snails in the oven for a further 5–10 minutes to dry. Remove and cool on the trays.

Onion and Thyme Pastries

Red onions and shallots are particularly well suited to rapid baking as they
will not lose any of their flavour or crispness.

2 small red onions

4 large shallots (golden shallots)

2 sheets ready-rolled puff pastry,
  thawed (about 300 g/10½ oz)

1 egg

12 sprigs thyme

4 tablespoons olive oil

FOR THE SALAD

115 g (4 oz) baby spinach leaves

115 g (4 oz) watercress

30 g (¼ cup/1 oz) chopped walnuts

50 g (⅓ cup/2 oz) stilton cheese

2 tablespoons cream

3 teaspoons walnut oil

1 teaspoon sherry vinegar

MAKES 4

PREPARATION TIME 30 minutes

COOKING TIME 20 minutes

1 Use a large baking tray. Preheat oven to 220°C (425°F, gas mark 7). Peel and thinly slice red onions. Peel shallots and cut into quarters.

2 On a floured work surface, roll out each piece of pastry to a rectangle of about 30 x 15 cm (12 x 6 in). Cut 2 large rounds from each, using a 13–15 cm (5–6 in) saucer as a guide; place on the baking tray.

3 Beat egg lightly and brush over the pastry, taking care not to let any trickle over the edges.

4 Divide the onions and shallots between the rounds, placing a mound in the centre of each one; leave a border of about 2 cm (¾ in) all round. Place 3 sprigs thyme on top of each mound.

5 Brush the onion mixture with a little olive oil; season to taste with salt and black pepper. Bake for 20 minutes or until pastries have puffed up and are golden brown.

6 Place salad greens and walnuts in a serving bowl. Remove rind from stilton. Place cheese in a small bowl, add the cream and mash well. Beat in the walnut oil and sherry vinegar until smooth. Season with a good grinding of black pepper. Pour dressing over the salad; toss gently. Serve hot pastries with the salad.

Try this, too...

For a milder, sweeter blue cheese dressing, try blue brie, dolcelatte or creamy Blue Castello.

Top Tip

Using a stout wooden spoon and a sturdy bowl makes it an easy job to mash the cheese and cream together when you are preparing the salad dressing.

Guacamole Choux Buns

Choux buns look spectacular, yet are easy to make. Here they are filled with a creamy mixture of avocado, tomato, cucumber and cannellini beans flavoured with lime juice and garlic.

1 quantity choux pastry
(see basic recipe on page 298 of the Better Baking section)

2 small, crisp lettuces, separated into leaves

FOR THE FILLING

About 410 g (14½ oz) tinned cannellini beans, drained and rinsed

2 small avocados

Juice of 1 lime

1 large tomato, seeds removed, finely diced

1 small red onion, finely chopped

12.5 cm (5 in) piece of cucumber, finely diced

1 clove garlic, crushed

2 tablespoons chopped fresh coriander (cilantro)

Salt and cayenne pepper, to taste

SERVES 5

PREPARATION TIME 40 minutes

COOKING TIME 25 minutes

1 Use a large baking tray; grease the tray. Preheat oven to 220°C (425°F, gas mark 7). Spoon choux pastry onto tray in 5 equal mounds, spacing them well apart. Make the mounds about 7.5 cm (3 in) across and 3 cm (1¼ in) high. Bake buns for 18–20 minutes or until they are well risen and golden brown.

2 Remove tray from oven. With a skewer or the point of a small knife, make a small hole in the side of each bun. Return tray to the oven and cook for a further 5 minutes. Transfer buns to a wire rack to cool.

3 For the filling, tip beans into a bowl and mash with a potato masher until quite smooth. Cut the avocados in half; remove stones and scoop flesh into another bowl; mash roughly with a fork. Stir into beans with the lime juice.

4 Add tomato, onion, cucumber, garlic and coriander; season with salt and cayenne pepper to taste. Mix well.

5 Just before serving, split open buns and fill with guacamole mixture. Serve buns garnished with lettuce leaves.

Try this, too...

To make Crunchy Hummus Choux Buns, drain and rinse a can of chickpeas, about 410 g (14½ oz). Purée beans with 1 tbsp tahini paste, 1 crushed clove of garlic and the juice of 1 lemon. Stir in 10-cm (4-in) piece of cucumber, diced, 1 grated carrot, 2 chopped spring onions (scallions) and 1 capsicum (bell pepper), seeds removed and flesh finely diced. Add ½ tsp ground cumin and salt and pepper to taste. Spoon into the cooked choux buns. Garnish with radicchio leaves. Serve with a tomato salad.

Top Tip

Cannellini beans, like other pulses or legumes, are a very good source of protein and carbohydrate, while being low in fat.

Avocados are unusual in that they are fruits that contain a lot of fat. The fat is predominantly mono-unsaturated, however, particularly in the form of oleic acid. This can help to lower levels of the harmful LDL cholesterol while raising levels of the beneficial HDL cholesterol.

Lime juice contains vitamin C; it helps to improve the absorption of iron from the cannellini beans.

239

pizzas & tarts

Spicy Potato and Leek Quiche

A creamy potato, leek and cheese filling is complemented by a crisp pastry case speckled with hot chilli and fragrant thyme.

FOR THE PASTRY

170 g (1⅓ cups/6 oz) plain (all-purpose) flour

2 fresh red chillies, seeds removed, finely chopped

2 teaspoons chopped fresh thyme

1 egg

80 ml (⅓ cup/2½ fl oz) sunflower oil

1 tablespoon lukewarm water

FOR THE FILLING

350 g (12 oz) waxy new potatoes

250 g (9 oz) leeks, cut into 1 cm (½ in) slices

65 g (½ cup/2¼ oz) grated gruyère cheese

2 tablespoons chopped chives

55 g (1¼ cups/2 oz) rocket (arugula), roughly chopped

2 eggs

150 ml (½ cup/5 fl oz) milk

SERVES 4

PREPARATION TIME 30 minutes plus 30 minutes resting

COOKING TIME 40–45 minutes

1 Use a baking tray and a 20-cm (8-in) round, fluted loose-based quiche tin. Sift flour and a pinch of salt into a large bowl. Add the chilli and thyme, then make a well in the centre. Whisk the egg, oil and water and add to the dry ingredients; mix quickly with a fork to make a dough.

2 Place dough on a lightly floured work surface; knead briefly just until smooth. Place in a dry bowl, cover with a damp cloth towel and leave to rest for about 30 minutes before rolling out.

3 For the filling, cook potatoes in boiling water for 10–12 minutes or until almost tender. Steam leeks over the potatoes for 6–7 minutes, until tender. Drain thoroughly and leave until cool enough to handle.

4 Preheat oven to 200°C (400°F, gas mark 6) and put the baking tray in to heat. On a lightly floured work surface, roll out pastry thinly to line the flan tin. Scatter half the cheese in the case.

5 Thickly slice the potatoes and toss with the leeks, remaining cheese and chives. Season with salt and pepper. Arrange half the potato and leek mixture in the pastry case. Scatter rocket on top, then add the rest of the potato and leek mixture.

6 Lightly beat eggs in a jug. Heat milk to just below boiling point, then add to the eggs; whisk gently to combine.

7 Place tin on the hot baking tray. Pour the warm egg custard into the case. Bake for 10 minutes, then reduce oven temperature to 180°C (350°F, gas mark 4). Bake a further 30–35 minutes or until the filling is lightly set. Leave quiche in the tin for 5 minutes. Serve warm.

Top Tip

Chillies contain more vitamin C weight for weight than citrus fruit. But the quantity of chillies usually eaten means the overall intake of this vitamin is not huge.

Rocket (arugula), like other dark green leafy vegetables, is a good source of folate, a vitamin involved in the production of red blood cells.

Like many other cheeses, gruyère has a high saturated-fat content: this makes it a good source of fat-soluble vitamins such as A and D.

Leek Tart with Pine Nuts

Leeks give this tart a pleasant, mild flavour. A combination of red onions and leeks could also be used. Try adding chopped, sautéed bacon to the filling, too.

100 g (⅓ cup/3½ oz) low-fat sour cream for pastry; 2 tablespoons extra for filling

4 eggs

100 ml (8 tbsp/3½ fl oz) olive oil

180 g (1½ cups/6 oz) plain (all-purpose) flour

2 teaspoons baking powder

2 tablespoons butter

1 kilo (2 lb 4 oz) leeks, cut into fine strips

100 ml (8 tbsp/3½ fl oz) milk

185 g (¾ cup/6½ oz) ricotta cheese

2 tablespoons finely chopped parsley

55 g (⅓ cup/2 oz) pine nuts

Pinch of grated nutmeg

1 Use a 26-cm (10½-in) spring-form tin. Grease tin. Mix sour cream, 1 egg, a pinch of salt and 3 tbsp oil in a bowl. Reserve 1 tbsp flour. Sift the remaining flour and baking powder over cream mixture; knead into a dough. Roll into a ball, cover and leave in a cool place.

2 Preheat oven to 200°C (350°F, gas mark 4). Heat 2 tbsp oil and the butter in a wide saucepan. Add leeks and sauté until transparent. Sprinkle in reserved flour, add milk and stir to combine.

3 Bring mixture to a boil. Remove pan from heat; leave to cool. Stir in ricotta, 3 eggs, extra 2 tbsp sour cream, the parsley and two-thirds of the pine nuts. Season with the nutmeg and salt and pepper.

4 Roll out the pastry thinly on a lightly floured work surface to line the tin. Pour leek mixture into pastry case and sprinkle with the remaining pine nuts.

5 Bake tart for 40 minutes until lightly browned. Serve warm.

SERVES 8

PREPARATION TIME 50 minutes

COOKING TIME 40 minutes

243

Broccoli Quiche with Salmon

Make an extra quantity of dough and keep it in the freezer for those times
when you need to prepare a meal in a hurry.

FOR THE DOUGH

100 g (⅓ cup/3½ oz) low-fat
   sour cream

2 eggs

1 teaspoon sunflower oil

Pinch of salt

220 g (1¾ cups/8 oz) plain
   (all-purpose) flour

1 teaspoon (3 g/⅛ oz) dry
   (powdered) yeast

FOR THE FILLING

600 g (10 cups/1 lb 5 oz) broccoli

200 g (7 oz) sliced smoked salmon

200 g (¾ cup/7 oz) low-fat
   sour cream

3 eggs

1 tablespoon cornflour (cornstarch)

20 g (⅓ cup/¾ oz) finely
   chopped dill

Pinch of grated nutmeg

1 teaspoon grated horseradish

1–2 teaspoons lemon juice

SERVES 8

PREPARATION TIME 45 minutes

COOKING TIME 35–45 minutes

1 Use a 28-cm (11¼-in) ceramic fluted quiche dish. Mix the sour cream, eggs, oil and salt in a bowl until smooth. Combine the flour and dry yeast; add to sour cream mixture. Knead into a sticky dough. Cover the bowl; leave dough to rise in a warm place for 30 minutes.

2 Separate florets from broccoli stems. Peel thick stems thinly and cut into large pieces.

3 Place the florets and stems in a steamer. Pour 250 ml (1 cup/9 fl oz) water into a saucepan. Place the steamer in the pan. Bring water to a boil. Cover steamer; steam broccoli for about 8 minutes. Remove florets from steamer and set aside. Mash stems finely in a mixing bowl with the cooking water. Leave to cool.

4 Cut salmon slices into narrow strips. Whisk sour cream, eggs and cornflour; stir in the dill. Stir the mixture into the broccoli purée. Add the nutmeg, horseradish and lemon juice and season with salt and pepper.

5 Preheat oven to 200°C (400°F, gas mark 6); grease flan dish. On a lightly floured work surface, roll out pastry to line dish. Spread broccoli florets and strips of salmon over the pastry base. Pour broccoli mixture over the top.

6 Bake the flan for 35–45 minutes until the pastry is crisp and the filling slightly browned. Serve warm.

Try this, too...

For Asparagus Quiche with Salmon, make pastry as described in main recipe and use to line the dish. In place of the broccoli, use 500 g (1 lb 2 oz) green asparagus; peel ends thinly, if necessary. Cut the asparagus into 5 cm (2 in) pieces; steam over 250 ml (1 cup/9 fl oz) water for 5–8 minutes until crisp/tender. Peel and dice 2 shallots. Heat 1 tbsp butter; sauté shallots until transparent. Sprinkle 1 tbsp flour over the top; sweat shallots for a few minutes over low heat. Add the asparagus cooking water, mixing it in quickly with a whisk; make sure the flour doesn't form lumps. Bring to a boil; cook until mixture starts to thicken. Remove from heat. Whisk in 3 eggs and 100 g (⅓ cup/3½ oz) sour cream. Season sauce with lemon juice, nutmeg and salt and pepper. Add 2 tbsp finely chopped parsley. Cut 200 g (7 oz) sliced smoked salmon into narrow strips; scatter over the pastry base with the steamed asparagus; pour the sauce over the top. Bake quiche as described in main recipe and serve warm.

Potato and Zucchini Quiche

This is a versatile pastry-free quiche that works well with different vegetables and cheeses. Keep the potato as a constant, but try grated carrots or thinly sliced leeks in place of zucchini. Replace the emmentaler with gouda or cheddar cheese.

60 ml (¼ cup/2 fl oz) olive oil

1 onion, chopped

1 clove garlic, chopped

200 g (7 oz) waxy potatoes

2 firm zucchini (courgettes)

1 teaspoon grated lemon zest

20 g (⅓ cup/¾ oz) finely chopped parsley

2 teaspoons each of finely chopped fresh marjoram, lemon thyme and thyme

1 teaspoon dried oregano

2 eggs

3 tablespoons cornflour (cornstarch)

2 tablespoons sour cream

40 g (⅓ cup/1 ½ oz) grated emmentaler cheese

2 tablespoons freshly grated Parmesan

2 tablespoons ground hazelnuts (filberts)

SERVES 8

PREPARATION TIME 40 minutes

COOKING TIME 35 minutes

1 Use a 24-cm (9½-in) ceramic fluted quiche dish; grease the dish. Preheat oven to 210°C (415°F, gas mark 6). Heat 2 tbsp olive oil in a frying pan. Sauté the onion and garlic and cook until they are both transparent. Remove from heat and let mixture cool.

2 Peel potatoes and grate finely. Discard ends of zucchini, grate the flesh coarsely. Combine onion mixture, grated vegetables and the lemon zest in a bowl. Add chopped herbs and dried oregano.

3 Stir the eggs, cornflour, 1 tbsp olive oil, the sour cream and cheese into the vegetable mixture. Season well with salt and pepper.

4 Pour vegetable mixture into the flan dish; smooth top. Sprinkle with Parmesan and hazelnuts. Bake for 35 minutes until golden brown. Serve warm.

Try this, too…

For Potato and Zucchini Tart with Bacon, cut 175 g (6 oz) bacon into thin strips; fry until crisp. Add the onion and garlic and cook until transparent. Prepare mixture as for the main recipe, adding the bacon and onion mixture. Line dish with about 115 g (4 oz) bacon slices, then pour over vegetable mixture. Bake as for main recipe. Note: Use very little salt as the bacon is quite salty.

Top Tip

The quiche will be especially light if you separate the eggs and mix in the egg yolks first. Beat egg whites until stiff; carefully fold into the vegetable mixture, using a whisk.

Onion Tart

For an inexpensive yet stylish meal, an onion tart fresh from the oven
is always a hit. A young white wine goes particularly well with this tart.

250 g (2 cups/9 oz) plain
   (all-purpose) flour

2 teaspoons (7 g/¼ oz) dried
   (powdered) yeast

125 ml (½ cup/4 fl oz) lukewarm
   milk

125 g (½ cup/4½ oz) butter

¼ teaspoon salt

2 kilos (4 lb 8 oz) red onions,
   thinly sliced

2 eggs

55 g (2 oz) bacon, finely diced

¼ teaspoon caraway seeds

3 egg yolks

185 ml (¾ cup/6 fl oz) cream

1 Use a 28-cm (11¼-in) springform tin; grease the tin. Place
flour in a bowl and make a well in
the centre. Sprinkle yeast onto the
milk. Pour into well; sprinkle with
flour from the sides. Cover and let
rise in a warm place for 15 minutes.

2 Add 1 tbsp butter and the salt
to yeast mixture. Knead into a
dough. Cover and leave to rise in a
warm place for 30 minutes. Knead
vigorously for 10 minutes; leave to
rise for a further 30 minutes.

3 Preheat oven to 220°C (425°F,
gas mark 7). In a frying pan,
heat remaining butter and fry the
onion until transparent. Whisk the
eggs in a bowl; stir in onions.

4 Roll out dough to line the tin.
Pour in onion mixture; sprinkle
with the bacon and caraway seeds.
Bake for 10 minutes. Reduce oven
temperature to 180°C (350°F, gas
mark 4). Combine egg yolks, a pinch
of salt and the cream. Pour mixture
over tart; bake a further 50 minutes.

SERVES 8

PREPARATION TIME 45 minutes plus
   1¼ hours resting

COOKING TIME 1 hour

Spinach Quiche

The base of this quiche can be baked ahead of time.
Place spinach and cream mixture on top 30 minutes before serving and bake until done.

FOR THE PASTRY

200 g (1⅔ cups/7 oz) plain (all-purpose) flour

½ teaspoon salt

1 egg yolk

115 g (⅔ cup/4 oz) butter

FOR THE FILLING

90 g (⅓ cup/3¼ oz) sour cream

125 ml (½ cup/4 fl oz) cream

3 eggs and 1 egg white

55 g (½ cup/2 oz) grated Parmesan

Pinch of grated nutmeg

600 g (1 lb 5 oz) frozen leaf spinach, thawed

1 onion, finely chopped

1 clove garlic, finely chopped

2 tablespoons flaked almonds

1 Use a 26-cm (10½-in) spring-form tin. Grease tin. Preheat oven to 180°C (350°F, gas mark 4). Place flour, salt, egg yolk, butter and 2 tbsp water in a bowl. Knead well; gather into a smooth dough. Shape into a ball, wrap in cling wrap and chill for 30 minutes.

2 Combine sour cream, cream, eggs, ½ egg white, Parmesan and nutmeg. Squeeze spinach out well and chop coarsely.

3 Roll the dough out on a lightly floured work surface to line tin. Prick pastry base with a fork; line with baking (parchment) paper and dried beans. Bake for 12 minutes. Remove baking paper and beans.

4 Brush remaining egg white over the pastry base. Spread chopped spinach, onions and garlic over the base. Pour in the cream mixture and sprinkle with flaked almonds. Bake quiche for 30–35 minutes. Serve hot.

SERVES 6

PREPARATION TIME 45 minutes plus 30 minutes chilling

COOKING TIME 12 minutes plus 30–35 minutes

Quiche Lorraine

This classic is simply unbeatable. If you are planning to stock up your freezer, take the quiche out of the oven 5 minutes before the end of the baking time, allow to cool, cut into pieces and freeze in individual servings.

FOR THE PASTRY

200 g (1⅔ cups/7 oz) plain (all-purpose) flour

120 g (½ cup/4¼ oz) butter, chopped

½ teaspoon salt

1 egg yolk

FOR THE FILLING

160 g (⅔ cup/5¾ oz) sour cream

3 eggs and 1 egg yolk

Pinch of grated nutmeg

150 g (1 cup/5½ oz) sliced ham or bacon

200 g (1½ cups/7 oz) grated emmentaler or Swiss cheese

SERVES 6

PREPARATION TIME 35 minutes plus 30 minutes chilling

COOKING TIME 1 hour 20 minutes

1 Use a 26-cm (10½-in) spring-form tin. Grease the base. Place the flour, butter, salt, egg yolk and 2 tbsp water in a bowl. Knead into a smooth dough. Shape into a ball, wrap in cling wrap and chill for 30 minutes.

2 Preheat oven to 180°C (350°F, gas mark 4). Roll dough out on a lightly floured work surface to line the tin; side of pastry case should be about 5 cm (2 in) high.

3 Prick pastry base several times with a fork, cover with baking (parchment) paper and dried beans and bake for 12 minutes. Remove baking paper and dried beans and cook base for a further 45 minutes. Remove from oven; cool slightly.

4 To make the filling, combine sour cream with eggs, egg yolk, nutmeg, pepper and a little salt.

5 Cut ham into strips and spread over the pastry base with the cheese. Pour in egg mixture.

6 Bake for 25–35 minutes. Cover the top with foil if it looks as though it is browning too quickly. Allow quiche to cool in the tin for 5 minutes before serving.

Try this, too...

This quiche can be made very quickly if frozen pizza dough is used instead of making your own pastry.

Top Tale

Both France and Germany have had a part to play in the story of this classic quiche. Lorraine is a province of northern France, but was also under the sovereignty of Germany several times in the past. It is thought that the word quiche (or kiche) may have come from the German word kuchen, which means cake or pastry.

Alsatian Tarte Flambé

This tart is traditionally baked by Alsatian bakers on the bottom of their bread ovens. As the bacon fat drips onto the oven floor, it catches fire—hence the name—producing a deep, smoky flavour.

FOR THE DOUGH

2 tablespoons sunflower oil

½ teaspoon salt

350 g (2¾ cups/12 oz) plain (all-purpose) flour

About 185 ml (¾ cup/6 fl oz) lukewarm milk

½ teaspoon sugar

2 teaspoons (7 g/¼ oz) dry (powdered) yeast

FOR THE TOPPING

80 g (½ cup/3 oz) diced smoked bacon or speck

3–4 large onions, diced

310 g (1¼ cups/11 oz) sour cream

2 egg yolks

1 tablespoon sunflower oil

Pinch of grated nutmeg

1 Use a baking tray. Brush with oil. Place sunflower oil, salt and flour in a bowl. Combine milk and sugar and sprinkle yeast on top to dissolve. Pour into the flour mixture. Knead with dough hooks of a hand mixer for 5 minutes until dough no longer sticks to the side of the bowl. Alternatively, knead vigorously by hand. Cover dough and leave to rise in a warm place for 30 minutes.

2 Place bacon in a frying pan and heat gently until fat becomes transparent (a process known as rendering). Add the onion; fry until transparent. Whisk the sour cream, egg yolks, oil and nutmeg in a jug.

3 Knead the dough on a lightly floured work surface for about 5 minutes. With wet hands, stretch dough out on tray. Shape a narrow edge; prick surface with a fork.

4 Leave the dough to rise for a further 30 minutes until it is roughly doubled in size. Preheat oven to 220°C (425°F, gas mark 7).

5 Spread onion mixture, then the cream mixture over the pastry. Bake 15–18 minutes. Cut into slices and serve straightaway.

SERVES 6–8

PREPARATION TIME 35 minutes plus 1 hour resting

COOKING TIME 15–18 minutes

Deluxe Asparagus Tart

The light, yeasted pastry case is surprisingly low in fat.
Small minted new potatoes would make a perfect accompaniment.

FOR THE DOUGH

155 g (1 ¼ cups/5 ½ oz) plain (all-purpose) flour

45 g (1 ½ oz) butter, chilled and diced

1 teaspoon (3 g/⅛ oz) dry (powdered) yeast

1 egg

2 tablespoons lukewarm water

FOR THE FILLING

4 cloves garlic, unpeeled

20 slender asparagus spears, cut in half

1 tablespoon finely grated pecorino cheese

55 g (⅓ cup/2 oz) prosciutto or parma ham, trimmed of excess fat and cut into thin strips

55 g (⅓ cup/2 oz) frozen peas, thawed

2 eggs

1 egg yolk

250 ml (1 cup/9 fl oz) milk

1 Use a 25-cm (10-in) shallow tart tin with a loose base. Sift the flour and a pinch of salt into a large bowl; rub in the butter until the mixture resembles fine bread-crumbs. Dissolve yeast in a little warm water; add to mixture. Mix egg and water; sprinkle onto flour mixture. Work ingredients together to make a dough.

2 Turn the dough onto a lightly floured work surface; knead briefly until smooth. Place in bowl, cover with cling wrap and leave at room temperature for 45 minutes.

3 Place garlic in the bottom of a steamer with about 5 cm (2 in) of hot water. Place asparagus stalks in top part of steamer and steam for 1 minute over a moderate heat. Add asparagus tips; steam a further 1–1½ minutes or until just starting to soften. (Thicker spears may need a little longer.) Remove garlic and asparagus from steamer; set aside.

4 Preheat oven to 200°C (400°F, gas mark 6) and put a baking tray in to heat. Roll out the dough thinly (there is no need to knead it again) on a lightly floured work surface to line the flan tin.

5 Scatter pecorino cheese over the base of the pastry case, then arrange the asparagus and Parma ham on top, filling the gaps with peas.

6 Squeeze the softened garlic from the skins and mash to a paste. Whisk in the eggs, egg yolk, and season with salt and pepper. Heat milk to boiling point; add to egg mixture, whisking to combine.

7 Place the flan tin on the hot baking tray. Pour egg mixture into pastry case. Bake 5 minutes, then reduce oven temperature to 180°C (350°F, gas mark 4). Bake for a further 25–30 minutes or until filling is lightly set and the pastry is golden brown.

8 Leave tart in tin for 5 minutes. Serve hot or warm.

SERVES 4

PREPARATION TIME 30 minutes plus 45 minutes resting

COOKING TIME 30–35 minutes

Chicken and Ham Pie

Pies like this look attractive decorated with pastry leaves or with patterns
cut into the edge of the pie.

FOR THE PASTRY

250 g (2 cups/9 oz) plain
  (all-purpose) flour

120 g (½ cup/4½ oz) butter,
  chopped

1 egg, beaten

Milk, for brushing

FOR THE FILLING

About 500 g (3 cups/1 lb 2 oz)
  boneless chicken, skinned and cut
  into large cubes

30 g (1 cup/1 oz) chopped fresh
  parsley

1 small onion, peeled and chopped

About 250 g (3 cups/1 lb 2 oz)
  ham steak, rind removed, cut into
  cubes the size of the chicken cubes

¼ teaspoon ground mace

170 ml (⅔ cup/5½ fl oz) cream
  (thick cream suitable for whipping)

1 Use a deep 20-cm (8-in) pie
  plate. Sift flour and a pinch of
salt into a mixing bowl and rub in
butter until mixture resembles fine
breadcrumbs. Add the beaten egg
and sufficient cold water to mix to
a firm dough. Wrap dough in cling
wrap; chill for 30 minutes.

2 Preheat oven to 220°C (425°F,
  gas mark 7). Roll out just over
half the dough into a round large
enough to line the base and sides
of the pie plate. Place a pie funnel
in the centre and arrange chicken
around it. Season with pepper and
sprinkle on parsley and onion. Add
the ham; then sprinkle with mace
and more black pepper.

3 Brush edges of the dough with
  cold water. Roll out remaining
dough into a round large enough to
cover pie. Cut a cross in the centre
to accommodate pie funnel. Firmly
press edges of the dough together
to seal, then trim and decorate the
edge with a fork or spoon. Decorate
the top of the pie with leaves made
from the trimmings, if desired.

4 Brush pie all over with milk;
  bake in the centre of the oven
for 15 minutes. Reduce temperature
to 190°C (375°F, gas mark 5); bake
a further 1 hour. Cover loosely with
foil if pastry browns too quickly.

5 Remove pie from oven. Put the
  cream in a saucepan and bring
it almost to the boil. Carefully pour
it into the pie through the funnel.
Serve at once.

SERVES 4–6

PREPARATION TIME 30 minutes plus
  30 minutes chilling

COOKING TIME 1¼ hours

Mushroom Pie

Use a mixture of mushrooms such as oyster mushrooms, chanterelles and shiitake.

FOR THE PASTRY

500 g (4 cups/1 1b 2 oz) plain (all-purpose) flour

2 teaspoons (7 g/¼ oz) dry (powdered) yeast

250 ml (1 cup/9 fl oz) lukewarm water

115 g (⅔ cup/4 oz) butter, softened

1 egg

FOR THE FILLING

500 g (5½ cups/1 lb 2 oz) mixed mushrooms

1 tablespoon butter

500 g (1 lb 2 oz) onions, diced

2 cloves garlic, finely chopped

250 ml (1 cup/9 fl oz) cream

30 g (1 cup/1 oz) chopped parsley

1 teaspoon chopped fresh thyme

1 tablespoon lemon juice

1 egg and 1 egg yolk

2 tablespoons milk

1 Use a deep 28-cm (11¼-in) fluted quiche dish. Grease dish. Place flour in a bowl. Sprinkle yeast on 250 ml (1 cup/9 fl oz) lukewarm water to dissolve. Add to flour with the butter, egg and 1 tsp salt. Knead with the dough hooks of an electric mixer or by hand. Place the dough in a bowl; cover and leave to rise in a warm place for 30 minutes.

2 For the filling, wipe mushrooms with a paper towel and chop coarsely. Heat butter in a pan and sauté the onion until transparent. Add the mushrooms and garlic and sauté for 5 minutes. Stir in cream and allow to reduce for 2 minutes.

3 Stir the parsley and thyme into the mushroom mixture. Season with lemon juice, salt and pepper. Remove from heat and stir in egg.

4 Preheat oven to 200°C (425°F, gas mark 7). Knead dough on a lightly floured work surface for 10 minutes. Roll out to 5 mm (¼ in) thick. Invert the quiche dish on the dough and cut out a circle for a lid that is a little larger than the dish; make a hole in the middle. Roll out the rest of the dough to line the dish. Place mushroom mixture in pastry base and top with pastry lid; press it down onto the side of dish to seal. Beat the egg yolk and milk together; brush over the top of the pie. Bake for 60–70 minutes.

SERVES 8

PREPARATION TIME 1¼ hours

COOKING TIME 60–70 minutes

Festive Meat Pie

The meat filling can be baked on its own in a loaf tin, then sliced thinly and served with salad.

FOR THE PASTRY

200 g (1 ⅔ cups/7 oz) plain (all-purpose) flour

115 g (½ cup/4 oz) butter, chilled

1 egg

2 sheets frozen puff pastry, thawed

1 egg yolk

1 tablespoon milk

FOR THE FILLING

600 g (1 lb 5 oz) minced (ground) pork

2 bay leaves

125 ml (½ cup/4 fl oz) white wine

125 ml (½ cup/4 fl oz) chicken stock

1 carrot, finely diced

2 sticks celery, finely diced

2 onions, finely chopped

1 clove garlic, crushed

85 g (½ cup/3 oz) smoked bacon or speck, finely diced

30 g (1 cup/1 oz) chopped parsley

Leaves of 4 sprigs each of fresh marjoram and oregano, chopped

2 eggs, lightly beaten

55 g (⅔ cup/2 oz) soft white (fresh) breadcrumbs

1 tablespoon flour

2 teaspoons marinated green peppercorns

Pinch of grated nutmeg

Pinch of allspice

2 teaspoons dried thyme

½ teaspoon sweet paprika

SERVES 6

PREPARATION TIME 2 hours plus overnight chilling

COOKING TIME 65–70 minutes

1 Use a 26-cm (10½-in) springform tin. For the filling, place half the pork and the bay leaves in a ceramic or glass dish and pour wine over the top. Cover and refrigerate overnight.

2 To make pastry, place flour in a large bowl and make a well in the centre. Dot the flour with butter. Place egg, a pinch of salt and 2 tbsp water in the well. Starting from the centre, knead into a smooth dough. Shape into a ball, wrap in cling wrap and chill for 1 hour.

3 Bring wine and stock to a boil, add carrot and celery; simmer 6–8 minutes until soft. Mash into the liquid to make a fine purée.

4 In a bowl, combine marinated minced meat (discarding bay leaves), the remaining minced meat, the vegetable purée, onion, garlic, bacon, chopped herbs, eggs, breadcrumbs, flour and peppercorns. Add remaining spices and herbs; season with salt and pepper.

5 Roll out the puff pastry sheets thinly on a lightly floured work surface. Grease tin. Preheat oven to 200°C (400°F, gas mark 6).

6 Roll out the chilled pastry on a floured work surface to line tin. Fill with meat mixture; cover with 1 sheet puff pastry. Make a hole in the middle; insert a piece of rolled-up foil so that steam can escape during baking.

7 Cut stars or other shapes out of the second puff pastry sheet and use to decorate the pie. Whisk combined egg yolk and milk; brush over pie. Bake for 65–70 minutes until golden brown. Serve warm.

Top Tip

Minced (ground) beef or freshly minced turkey meat may be used instead of minced pork.

Steak and Kidney Pie

This great British classic is both an excellent family dish and a winner when entertaining, particularly during cold weather. Although it involves quite a lot of work, it can be made ahead and popped in the oven to reheat when needed.

60 ml (¼ cup/2 fl oz) olive oil

1 onion, peeled and chopped

1 kilo (2 lb 4 oz) braising steak (such as round, flank or skirt), trimmed of excess fat and cut into 5 cm (2 in) cubes

250 g (9 oz) ox kidney, skinned, cored and sliced

30 g (¼ cup/1 oz) plain (all-purpose) flour, seasoned with salt and freshly ground black pepper

625 ml (2½ cups/21½ fl oz) beef stock

500 ml (2 cups/17 fl oz) Guinness or other dark full-flavoured beer

Bouquet garni

125 g (1⅓ cups/4½ oz) field, flat or open-cup mushrooms, wiped and quartered

625 g (1 lb 6 oz) frozen puff pastry (thawed)

1 egg, beaten

SERVES 6

PREPARATION TIME
 Day 1: 25 minutes
 Day 2: 30 minutes plus overnight chilling

COOKING TIME
 Day 1: about 3 hours
 Day 2: 1 hour

1 Use a pie dish with a 1.25-litre (5-cup/44-fl oz) capacity. Heat 1 tbsp olive oil in a heavy-based saucepan, add onion and fry on low heat until softened, not browned; then transfer to a plate.

2 Heat remaining oil in pan and fry steak and kidney in batches until evenly browned. Remove the meat as it browns and put it with the onion.

3 Stir the flour into the pan, then gradually stir in the stock and Guinness. Bring to the boil, stirring and scraping any brown residue off the bottom of the pan. Return the meat and onion to the pan, adding any juices left on the plate. Bring to the boil; add bouquet garni. Reduce heat to as low as possible, cover pan and cook for 2 hours, or until meat is tender. Add mushrooms; cook for a further 10 minutes. Remove from heat, cool and refrigerate overnight.

4 The next day, remove bouquet garni, season meat with salt and pepper and transfer it to the pie dish. Add sufficient meat juices to cover the meat, reserving the remainder.

5 On a floured work surface, roll out puff pastry to 5 cm (2 in) larger than the top of the pie dish. Trim off a strip 2–3 cm (1 in) wide from around the edge.

6 Brush the edge of the pie dish with water, press the pastry strip onto it and brush strip with water. Cover pie with the remaining pastry, pressing the edges together to seal. Trim and decorate the edge. Brush with beaten egg and make a small hole in the centre of the lid. Chill pie while heating the oven to 220°C (425°F, gas mark 7).

7 Bake pie for 25–30 minutes, then cover loosely with foil to prevent further browning. Reduce oven temperature to 160°C (315°F, gas mark 2–3); cook for a further 20–25 minutes or until the pastry is cooked. Reheat the reserved meat juices and serve separately with the pie. When reheating the pie, place a sheet of foil loosely over the top to prevent pastry from overbrowning.

Onion, Apple and Sage Pie

This attractive savoury pastry-wrapped envelope is ideal picnic fare.

FOR THE PASTRY

250 g (2 cups/9 oz) plain (all-purpose) flour

Pinch of salt

125 g (½ cup/4¼ oz) butter

60 ml (¼ cup/2 fl oz) cold water

1 small egg, beaten, or milk, to glaze

FOR THE FILLING

4 small onions, peeled, halved and thinly sliced

3 small cooking apples, peeled, cored and thinly sliced

2 teaspoons finely chopped fresh sage or 1 teaspoon dried sage

¼ teaspoon each of salt and freshly ground black pepper

80 g (⅓ cup/3 oz) sour cream

Sage leaves, to garnish

SERVES 4

PREPARATION TIME 1 hour plus 1 hour chilling

COOKING TIME 40 minutes

1 Use a large baking tray. For the pastry, sift flour and salt into a bowl. Rub in butter until mixture resembles fine breadcrumbs. Add the water and mix to a firm dough. Turn it onto a lightly floured work surface; knead gently until smooth. Shape into a ball, cover in cling wrap and chill for 30 minutes.

2 Roll out the dough on a lightly floured work surface to make a square a little larger than 30 cm (12 in). Trim to that size; place on the baking tray. Put half the sliced onions, followed by half the apples, in the centre of the dough square and sprinkle with half the sage, salt and pepper. Add remaining onion, apple and seasonings and spread the sour cream on top.

3 Brush the beaten egg or milk around the edges of the dough and fold the two opposite corners over the filling so that they meet and overlap slightly in the centre. Repeat with the other two corners to make an envelope. Press joins together gently to seal. Decorate the pie with the pastry trimmings. Chill for at least 30 minutes.

4 Preheat oven to 220°C (425°F, mark 7). Brush the chilled pie all over with the remaining beaten egg or milk and bake in the centre of the oven for 40 minutes or until pastry is crisp and golden brown. If the pastry is overbrowning, cover it loosely with a piece of foil.

5 Carefully transfer the pie to a serving plate or board; garnish with the sage leaves. Serve hot or cold, on its own or with cold meats, sausages and cheese.

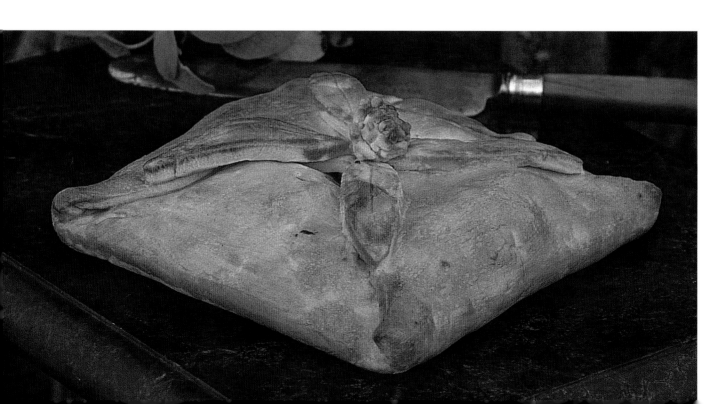

Pizza with Mushrooms

It's well worth making pizza dough for the freezer. When you're
in a hurry it'll help in making a quick and easy meal.

1 quantity frozen pizza dough,
   thawed (see page 262)

FOR THE TOPPING

About 125 ml (½ cup/4 fl oz)
   olive oil

1 white onion, diced

2 cloves garlic, finely sliced

400 g (1⅔ cups/14 oz) can
   chopped tomatoes

2 tablespoons tomato paste
   (concentrated purée)

1 teaspoon oregano leaves

300 g (3⅓ cups/10½ oz) mixed
   mushrooms

100 g (3½ oz) ham

110 g (4 oz) each of gouda and
   mozzarella cheese

2 tablespoons chopped parsley

1 Use a large baking tray. Grease
with oil. Roll out dough to fit
baking tray. Place dough on tray.

2 Heat 2 tbsp olive oil in a pan;
fry the onion and garlic until
transparent. Add tomatoes; cook,
uncovered, for 5 minutes to reduce.
Stir in the tomato paste and season
with oregano and salt and pepper.

3 Preheat oven to 250°C (500°F,
gas mark 9). Clean mushrooms
with a paper towel, if needed; slice
finely. Cut ham into strips. Remove
rind from gouda and grate coarsely;
slice the mozzarella.

4 Spread the tomato mixture over
dough. Scatter the mushrooms,
ham, both cheeses and the parsley
over the top. Season with salt and
pepper and drizzle with remaining
olive oil. Bake for 12–15 minutes
until the edges of the dough are
light brown.

SERVES 12

PREPARATION TIME 20 minutes

COOKING TIME 12–15 minutes

261

Pizza with Four Cheeses

The types of soft cheese used here melt to a delicious consistency. You can also try grating some of the harder cheeses such as gouda, pecorino or emmentaler.

FOR THE DOUGH

310 g (2½ cups/11 oz) plain (all-purpose) flour

2 tablespoons olive oil

½ teaspoon salt

2 teaspoons (7 g/¼ oz) dry (powdered) yeast

FOR THE TOPPING

60 ml (¼ cup/2 fl oz) olive oil

2 cloves garlic, finely chopped

400 g (1⅔ cups/14 oz) can chopped tomatoes

2 tablespoons tomato paste (concentrated purée)

1 teaspoon fresh oregano leaves

85 g (3 oz) each of fresh mozzarella, Bel Paese, gorgonzola and firm ricotta cheese

100 g (¾ cup/3½ oz) black olives

1 Use a large baking tray. Grease with oil. Place flour, 2 tbsp olive oil and salt in a bowl. Sprinkle yeast over 160 ml (⅔ cup/5½ fl oz) luke-warm water to dissolve; add to the flour mixture.

2 Knead ingredients together in the bowl, then turn out onto a lightly floured work surface. Knead vigorously for at least 5 minutes. Roll out dough to fit the baking tray. Place on the tray, cover and leave to rise in a warm place for 30 minutes.

3 For the topping, heat 1 tbsp oil in a pan and fry the garlic until transparent. Add tomatoes; cook, uncovered, for 5 minutes to reduce. Stir in tomato paste and season with oregano and salt and pepper.

4 Preheat oven to 250°C (500°F, gas mark 9). Cut the cheeses into small slices, barely 1 cm (½ in) thick. Spread tomato sauce over the dough and cover with cheese slices. Dot olives on the top. Drizzle pizza with the remaining oil and leave to rise again for a few minutes. Bake for 10–12 minutes.

SERVES 10

PREPARATION TIME 40 minutes plus 30 minutes resting

COOKING TIME 10–12 minutes

Pizza with Artichokes

Bake this pizza as soon as you put the topping on so that the dough does not become soggy from the anchovies and artichokes.

FOR THE DOUGH

310 g (2½ cups/11 oz) plain (all-purpose) flour

60 ml (¼ cup/2 fl oz) olive oil

½ teaspoon salt

2 teaspoons (7 g/¼ oz) dry (powdered) yeast

160 ml (⅔ cup/5½ fl oz) lukewarm water

FOR THE TOPPING

60 ml (¼ cup/2 fl oz) olive oil

2 cloves garlic, finely chopped

2 x 400 g (1⅔ cups/14 oz) cans chopped tomatoes

2 tablespoons tomato paste (concentrated purée)

1 teaspoon fresh oregano leaves

250 g (9 oz) ham

6 anchovy filets

220 g (1 cup/8 oz) artichoke hearts marinated in oil

100 g (¾ cup/3½ oz) black olives

SERVES 10

PREPARATION TIME 40 minutes

COOKING TIME 12–15 minutes

1 Use a baking tray. Grease tray with oil. Place flour, olive oil and the salt in a bowl. Sprinkle the yeast over the lukewarm water to dissolve; add to the flour mixture.

2 Knead ingredients together in the bowl, then turn out onto a lightly floured work surface. Knead vigorously for at least 5 minutes. Roll out dough to fit the baking tray. Place on the tray, cover and leave to rise in a warm place for 30 minutes.

3 For the topping, heat 1 tbsp olive oil in a pan and fry garlic until transparent. Add tomatoes; cook, uncovered, for 5 minutes to reduce. Stir in the tomato paste and season with oregano and salt and pepper.

4 Preheat oven to 250°C (500°F, gas mark 9). Cut the ham into strips. Drain the anchovies and cut into strips. Drain the artichokes and cut into quarters.

5 Spread the pizza base with the tomato sauce. Cover with ham, anchovies, artichokes and olives and drizzle on 2 tbsp olive oil. Bake pizza tart for 12–15 minutes until the edge of the dough is slightly browned. Cut into slices on baking tray while still hot. Serve at once.

Pissaladière

This French version of a pizza is traditionally made with yeast dough
but can also be made with shop-bought frozen puff pastry.

1 quantity yeast dough (use recipe
on page 263)

FOR THE TOPPING

3–4 large red onions

2 tablespoons olive oil

60 ml (¼ cup/2 fl oz) white wine

6–8 plum tomatoes

½ teaspoon fresh thyme leaves

1 teaspoon fresh oregano leaves

150 g (1¼ cups/5½ oz) grated
gruyère or emmentaler cheese

16 anchovy fillets

150 g (1 cup/5½ oz) black olives

1 egg

SERVES 10

PREPARATION TIME 20 minutes plus
30 minutes resting

COOKING TIME 10–15 minutes

1 Use a baking tray. Grease tray with oil. Roll out the dough to fit the tray. Place on tray, cover and leave to rise in a warm place for 30 minutes. Preheat oven to 250°C (500°F, gas mark 9).

2 For the topping, peel onions and slice into thin rings. Heat oil in a large pan and cook onions over medium heat until transparent and soft. Add the wine and salt and pepper. Spread mixture over dough, leaving an edge 2.5 cm (1 in) wide.

3 Slice tomatoes; spread evenly on top of onions. Sprinkle with herbs and cheese. Rinse anchovy fillets, pat dry and slice into 2 or 3 pieces lengthwise. Arrange strips in a diamond pattern over the top of the pissaladière. Place an olive in the centre of the diamonds.

4 Whisk egg with 1 tbsp water and brush over edges of the dough. Briefly leave pissaladière to rise in a cool place, then bake for 10–15 minutes. Cut into slices while hot and serve.

Gruyère Gougère

There is something very satisfying about making choux pastry and it definitely impresses.
It's not hard to make, though it does need a strong arm for the wooden spoon!

FOR THE PASTRY

60 g (¼ cup/2 oz) butter

85 g (⅔ cup/3 oz) plain
  (all-purpose) flour

2 eggs, beaten

55 g (½ cup/2 oz) finely grated
  gruyère cheese

½ teaspoon cayenne pepper

FOR THE FILLING

2 tablespoons extra virgin olive oil

1 large eggplant (aubergine), cut
  into 2 cm (¾ in) chunks

2 zucchini (courgettes), cut into
  2 cm (¾ in) chunks

1 red and 1 green capsicum (bell
  pepper), seeds removed, diced

1 onion, chopped

3 cloves garlic, finely chopped

About 420 g (15 oz) tinned pinto or
  kidney beans, drained and rinsed

About 400g (1⅔ cups/15 oz)
  chopped tomatoes

3 tablespoons chopped fresh parsley

2 tablespoons chopped fresh thyme

SERVES 6

PREPARATION TIME 40 minutes

COOKING TIME About 1 hour

1 Use a large roasting tin for the filling and a greased 1.25-litre (5-cup/44-fl oz) round or oval oven-proof dish for the gougère. Preheat oven to 220°C (425°F, gas mark 7). First make the filling. Drizzle the oil over the bottom of the roasting tin. Add eggplant, zucchini, capsicum, onion and garlic; toss them in the oil. Cook for 35–40 minutes or until golden brown and tender; toss the vegetables again after 20 minutes.

2 For the pastry, place butter and 125 ml (½ cup/4 fl oz) water in a saucepan. Heat gently until butter has melted, then bring to the boil. As soon as mixture boils, remove pan from heat; quickly tip in all the flour. Beat very vigorously with a wooden spoon until mixture forms a ball and the base of the pan is coated with a white film. Cool for 2 minutes. Beat in the eggs one at a time to make a stiff, smooth paste. Beat in cheese and cayenne pepper.

3 Spoon pastry evenly around the edge of the greased dish. Place in the oven (the same temperature as before) and bake for 25 minutes until well risen and golden brown. (Do not open the oven door while choux pastry is cooking.)

4 When the gougère is almost done, put the borlotti beans in a saucepan. Add the tomatoes with their juice, the parsley and thyme and salt and pepper to taste. Cook over a low heat, stirring from time to time, until heated through.

5 Add roasted vegetables to the bean mixture and stir gently to combine. Spoon into the centre of the freshly baked gougère to serve.

Cherry Tomato Pizza Tart

A Parmesan-flavoured pizza dough makes a delicious case for a filling of ricotta
cheese and herbs, all topped with sweet cherry tomatoes and black olives.

FOR THE DOUGH

170 g (1⅓ cups/6 oz) plain
(all-purpose) flour

½ teaspoon salt

30 g (⅓ cup/1 oz) freshly grated
Parmesan cheese

2 teaspoons (7 g/¼ oz) dry
(powdered) yeast

125 ml (½ cup/4 fl oz) lukewarm
water

1 tablespoon extra virgin olive oil

FOR THE FILLING

170 g (⅔ cup/6 oz) ricotta cheese

2 tablespoons each of chopped fresh
oregano and parsley

250 g (1⅔ cups/9 oz) cherry
tomatoes, cut in halves

60 g (½ cup/2¼ oz) black olives,
pitted

2 tablespoons balsamic vinegar

1 tablespoon olive oil

1 small sprig of fresh rosemary

1 clove garlic, crushed

FOR THE SALAD

55 g (⅓ cup/2 oz) each of pumpkin
seeds and sunflower seeds

2 teaspoons poppyseeds

1 teaspoon soy sauce

2 teaspoons sunflower oil

1 teaspoon each of walnut oil
and cider vinegar

150 g (3 cups/5½ oz) mixed salad
leaves of your choice

SERVES 4

PREPARATION TIME 35–40 minutes
plus 1 hour rising

COOKING TIME 15–20 minutes

1 Use a baking tray and a 25-cm
(10-in) shallow tart tin with a
loose base. Grease tin with oil. To
make the dough, sift flour and salt
into a bowl. Add Parmesan cheese.
Make a well in the centre. Sprinkle
yeast onto the water to dissolve;
pour into the well with the oil. Mix
to form a dough; add more water
if needed.

2 Turn out onto a lightly floured
work surface; knead 10 minutes
or until smooth and elastic. Return
to the bowl, cover with cling wrap
and leave in a warm place to rise for
1 hour or until doubled in size.

3 Preheat oven to 220°C (425°F,
gas mark 7); place the baking
tray inside to heat. Knock down the
dough, turn it out onto the floured
work surface and knead briefly. Roll
out a 30-cm (12-in) round 5 mm
(¼ in) thick. Use to line the tart tin;
leave the edges ragged and slightly
overhanging the tin.

4 For the filling, combine ricotta,
oregano and parsley; season
with salt and pepper. Spread evenly
in dough case. Arrange tomatoes
cut side up and place olives on top.

5 In a small pan, heat the vinegar
gently with olive oil, rosemary
and garlic. Bring to a rolling boil for
1–2 minutes or until the mixture
has reduced a little, then drizzle it
over tomatoes and olives.

6 Place tart tin on the preheated
baking tray. Bake for 15–20
minutes or until the case is crisp
and golden brown and tomatoes
are slightly caramelised.

7 In a small non-stick frying pan,
toast pumpkin, sunflower and
poppy seeds over a medium heat
for 2–3 minutes, turning frequently.
Sprinkle on the soy sauce and toss
the seeds to coat; they will stick
together initially, separating as the
mixture dries. Remove from heat.

8 Whisk the oils and vinegar in
a small jug and season to taste.
Place salad leaves in a serving bowl
and sprinkle in the toasted seeds.
Add dressing and toss salad to coat.

9 Remove tart from the tin and
cut into 4 wedges. Serve hot
with the salad.

Top Tip

Tomatoes are an excellent source
of vitamin C. This important
nutrient is found mainly in the
jellylike substance surrounding
the tomato seeds.

Pizza alla Napoletana

If you're building up a repertoire of pizzas, this classic from Naples with its topping of tomatoes, mozzarella, anchovies and olives is a must.

FOR THE DOUGH

2 teaspoons (7 g/¼ oz) dried (powdered) yeast

200 ml (¾ cup/7 fl oz) lukewarm water

340 g (2¾ cups/12 oz) strong white (bread) flour

½ teaspoon salt

2 tablespoons extra virgin olive oil

FOR THE TOPPING

2 tablespoons extra virgin olive oil

1 small onion, finely chopped

2 cloves garlic, crushed

800 g (3¼ cups/1 lb 12 oz) tinned chopped tomatoes

½ teaspoon caster (superfine) sugar

Small handful of fresh basil leaves, torn into pieces

150 g (1 cup/5½ oz) mozzarella cheese, thinly sliced

8 anchovy fillets, halved lengthwise

8 black olives, stoned and halved

SERVES 4

PREPARATION TIME 45 minutes plus 1–1½ hours for rising

COOKING TIME 20–25 minutes

1 Use a 30-cm (12-in) round pizza tray. Grease the tray. Sprinkle yeast onto water to dissolve. Place flour in a bowl and stir in the salt. Make a well in the centre; add the yeast mixture and the olive oil. Mix with a round-bladed knife to make a soft dough; if needed, add a little more water.

2 Turn dough out onto a lightly floured work surface and knead for 10 minutes or until smooth and elastic. Place the dough in a lightly greased bowl, cover with cling wrap and leave to rise in a warm place for 1–1½ hours until doubled in size.

3 For the topping, heat the oil in a saucepan, add the onion and garlic and cook until softened. Add tomatoes with their juice and the sugar; season with salt and pepper. Bring the mixture to the boil. Cook, uncovered, until reduced by about half to a thick sauce, stirring frequently. Remove from the heat and leave to cool.

4 Turn out the risen dough onto the lightly floured work surface and knock it down, then knead very lightly. Roll or press out to a round to fit the pizza tray; place on tray.

5 Stir basil into the sauce. Spread sauce over pizza base to within 1 cm (½ in) of the edge. Arrange the mozzarella, anchovies and olives over the top; leave pizza in a warm place for about 15 minutes. Preheat oven to 220°C (425°F, gas mark 7).

6 Bake pizza for 20–25 minutes or until the crust has risen and is golden and the cheese has melted. Cut into wedges and serve warm.

Try this, too...

For a Spinach and Chorizo Pizza, place 200 g (2 cups/7 oz) baby spinach leaves in a pan, cover and cook for 1–2 minutes until just wilted. Fry 200 g (2 cups/7 oz) sliced mushrooms in 2 tbsp butter until liquid evaporates and they are starting to colour. Place spinach and mushrooms over tomato sauce. Scatter 30 g (1 oz) chorizo sausage and 2 tbsp pine nuts on top. Leave to rise; then cook as for the main recipe.

Top Tip

Tinned tomatoes are a rich source of the phytochemical lycopene (other good sources include pink grapefruit, watermelon and guava). Lycopene can help protect against several types of cancer and also heart disease.

Allicin, the compound that gives garlic its characteristic smell and taste, acts as a powerful antibiotic. It also has antiviral and antifungal properties. Recent studies suggest that garlic may also help to protect against cancer of the stomach.

Pizza Margherita

The colours of Italy are much in evidence here. The topping is made of green basil, white mozzarella and red tomatoes. For the best flavour, use vine-ripened tomatoes.

FOR THE DOUGH

1 teaspoon (3 g/⅛ oz) dry (powdered) yeast

155 g (1¼ cups/5½ oz) plain (all-purpose) flour

½ teaspoon salt

60 ml (¼ cup/2 fl oz) olive oil

FOR THE TOPPING

500 g (1 lb 2 oz) vine-ripened, aromatic tomatoes

60 ml (¼ cup/2 fl oz) olive oil

1 clove garlic, finely diced

80 ml (⅓ cup/2½ fl oz) red wine

150 g (1 cup/5½ oz) fresh mozzarella, drained and diced

3 tablespoons coarsely chopped fresh basil leaves

1 tablespoon grated Parmesan cheese

SERVES 4–6

PREPARATION TIME 30 minutes plus 1½ hours rising

COOKING TIME 10–18 minutes

1 Use a 30-cm (12-in) round pizza tray. Grease tray. Sprinkle yeast over a little lukewarm water. Mix the flour and salt in a bowl; add oil and the yeast mixture. With floured hands, knead to a sticky dough; add a little more water if needed.

2 Place dough on a lightly floured work surface. Knead vigorously for about 10 minutes until dough is very elastic and no longer sticky.

3 Shape into a ball, place in the bowl, cover and leave to rise in a warm place for about 1½ hours or until doubled in size.

4 For topping, mark a cross on the base of each tomato with a small knife. Immerse tomatoes in a saucepan of boiling water until skin curls back from the crosses (about 15 seconds depending on ripeness). Transfer the tomatoes to a bowl of cold water, using a slotted spoon; cool. Peel off the skins. Cut tomatoes into halves. Cut out the stalk ends, scrape out the seeds and discard; dice flesh.

5 Heat 2 tbsp olive oil in a pan and fry garlic until transparent. Add tomatoes and wine and cook for about 5 minutes to reduce; stir occasionally. Season sauce with salt and pepper, remove from heat and leave to cool.

6 Preheat oven to 250°C (500°F, gas mark 9). Roll out dough on a lightly floured work surface into a round to fit the tray; place on tray.

7 Bake the pizza base for about 3 minutes. Remove from oven. Spread the tomato sauce and then the mozzarella over the pizza base. Sprinkle the basil and Parmesan on top; season with salt and pepper. Drizzle the remaining olive oil over the top. Bake 10–15 minutes until the mozzarella has melted and the edge of the pizza is golden.

Top Tip

Try adding the basil leaves whole to the top of the pizza 3–4 minutes before the end of the baking time. Baking the leaves briefly makes them particularly aromatic.

Picnic Roll

Picnics require portable food that stays intact during the journey to the picnic site.
This meat roll is ideal. Bake it a day ahead and leave, wrapped in foil, for the flavours to develop.
The ricotta dough is a quick alternative to yeast dough.

FOR THE DOUGH

200 g (³⁄₄ cup/7 oz) low-fat ricotta cheese

250 g (2 cups/9 oz) plain (all-purpose) flour

2 teaspoons baking powder

½ teaspoon salt

1 egg

80 ml (¹⁄₃ cup/2½ fl oz) sunflower oil

FOR THE FILLING

1 soft bread roll

2 tablespoons canola oil

150 g (1 cup/5½ oz) diced bacon

2 onions, finely diced

1 clove garlic, finely chopped

400 g (14 oz) mixed minced (ground) meat such as pork and chicken or beef and lamb

1 egg

1 teaspoon each of fresh basil, oregano and thyme leaves

Pinch of cayenne pepper

200 g (1¹⁄₃ cups/7 oz) pickled red capsicum (bell pepper) strips

1 egg yolk and 2 tablespoons milk, for brushing

SERVES 10

PREPARATION TIME 40 minutes

COOKING TIME 40–45 minutes

1 Use a large baking tray. Line with baking (parchment) paper. Place all the dough ingredients in a bowl and work into a smooth dough either by hand or using the dough hooks of an electric mixer. Preheat oven to 200°C (400°F, gas mark 6).

2 For the filling, soak the bread roll in water and then squeeze to remove the liquid. Heat oil in a pan; fry bacon until transparent. Add onion and garlic and fry until transparent. Place bacon, onion and garlic in a bowl and cool briefly.

3 Tear the bread roll into small pieces; add to onion mixture with the minced meat, egg, herbs and cayenne pepper; season with salt and pepper. Use your hands to combine ingredients thoroughly.

4 Roll out the dough on a lightly floured work surface into a rectangle 35 x 40 cm (14 x 15½ in). Spread filling evenly over the top, leaving 1 cm (½ in) strip across one long edge uncovered. Remove any excess moisture from the capsicum strips and place strips over filling.

5 Starting from the covered end, roll up dough and filling like a Swiss roll and place on baking tray with the join facing downward. Brush the surface with egg mixture, fold ends over and press together.

6 Bake picnic roll 40–45 minutes until golden brown.

Top Tip

To squeeze the moisture out of soaked, softened bread rolls and crush them into small pieces at the same time, use 2 small bread boards. Wedge the bread between them, angle them over the sink and push the boards to and fro against one another.

Italian Meat Strudel

This strudel makes a substantial main course. Serve hot with a crunchy mixed salad.

FOR THE PASTRY

3 sheets frozen shortcrust (tart) pastry, thawed

150 g (2/3 cup/5 1/2 oz) butter, melted

170 ml (2/3 cup/5 1/2 fl oz) milk or cream, for basting

FOR THE FILLING

2 tablespoons olive oil

1 onion, finely chopped

1 clove garlic, crushed

400 g (14 oz) lean minced (ground) beef

400 g (1 2/3 cups/14 oz) tinned chopped tomatoes

1 tablespoon chopped fresh basil leaves

1 teaspoon fresh oregano leaves

1 teaspoon sweet paprika

1 red onion, finely sliced

1 yellow, 1 green and 2 red capsicum (bell peppers), cut into strips

65 g (1/2 cup/2 1/2 oz) grated emmentaler cheese

SERVES 6–8

PREPARATION TIME 1 hour

COOKING TIME 35–45 minutes

1 Use a large baking dish. Grease with butter. To make the filling, heat oil in a pan and lightly fry the onion until transparent; add garlic and cook until transparent. Add the beef and, stirring occasionally, fry over high heat until it has coloured slightly and is crumbly.

2 Add tomatoes with their juices, the herbs and the paprika to the meat mixture. Cook, uncovered, for 5 minutes; stirring occasionally. Season well with salt and pepper.

3 Preheat oven to 220°C (425°F, gas mark 7); place a bowl of hot water on the oven floor to keep the air in the oven moist. Brush pastry sheets with melted butter. Divide meat mixture between the sheets; top with capsicum strips.

4 Roll up sheets and, with the join facing downward, place beside one another in the baking dish. Prick each roll several times with a fork and brush with melted butter. Bake for 35–45 minutes; baste with the milk or cream every 10 minutes. Sprinkle with grated cheese 10 minutes before the end of the baking time. When done, remove from oven and cool in the dish for 5 minutes before serving.

Bacon and Cabbage Strudel

The salty–sour taste of sauerkraut marries well with the smoked bacon.
This hearty dish is ideal for the cooler months.

FOR THE PASTRY

350 g (2¾ cups/12 oz) plain
  (all-purpose) flour

Pinch of salt

1 egg

1 tablespoon vinegar

60 ml (¼ cup/2 fl oz) sunflower oil

125 g (½ cup/4½ oz) butter,
  melted, plus extra for brushing

125 ml (½ cup/4 fl oz) lukewarm
  water

125 ml (½ cup/4 fl oz) stock or
  white wine, for basting

FOR THE FILLING

250 g (1⅔ cups/9 oz) lean smoked
  bacon or speck

600 g (2 cups/1 lb 5 oz) sauerkraut

1 tablespoon caraway seeds

125 ml (½ cup/4 fl oz) stock or dry
  white wine

MAKES 15 pieces

PREPARATION TIME 1 hour

COOKING TIME 40 minutes

1 Use a large baking dish. Grease dish with butter. Place flour, salt, egg, vinegar, oil, butter and water in a large bowl; knead with dough hooks of an electric mixer for 5 minutes, or by hand. Cover; leave to rest for 30 minutes. Preheat oven to 220°C (425°F, gas mark 7). Place an ovenproof dish of hot water on the floor of the oven.

2 For the filling, fry bacon in a large pan. Chop sauerkraut, add to bacon and season with caraway seeds. Pour in the stock, cover and braise the cabbage over low heat for 10 minutes. Season with salt and pepper; drain in a sieve.

3 Knead dough briefly on a lightly floured work surface. Divide the dough into 4 portions; brush with melted butter. Roll out each portion on a lightly floured cloth towel and, using the backs of your hands, stretch the dough into paper-thin rectangles. Brush the dough with melted butter. Spread filling over sheets keeping side and back edges free. Moisten edges with stock.

4 Roll up strudel using the cloth to help. Slice into 6-cm (2¼-in) pieces. Place pieces a little apart in baking dish. Brush with remaining melted butter. Bake for 40 minutes: basting with stock or white wine every 10 minutes. Serve hot.

275

better
baking

Better Baking

A step-by-step, how-to guide to basic baking skills, this section
will help build confidence and pave the way to success.

Baking has its rules just like any other creative process, but the more you learn, the easier and more pleasurable it becomes. Dip into the following pages for advice on ways to prepare cake batters, tart pastries and bread and pizza doughs. Here, also, are suggestions for variations to the basic recipes. Step-by-step photographs illustrate techniques clearly and simply. Tips for Success panels helps streamline the baking process and a Baking Q&A trouble-shooting section covers information on ingredients and techniques and addresses general questions on how to avoid and solve problems.

Temperatures and cooking times given in this book will need to be varied depending on the type of oven that you have and you may need to experiment a little to find out how your oven performs.

For cooking equipment, start with the basics: a range of different-sized baking tins, a measuring jug, some good-quality knives, a few bowls and a wooden spoon and a rolling pin. Happy baking!

Conversions

The conversions given in this book are approximate only and adjustments may need to be made depending on which system of measurement you choose to use. Australian measures have been used for this book. 1 cup is the equivalent of 250 ml or 250 g. A tablespoon measure is 20 ml. In North America, UK and New Zealand, the cup measure is 235 ml and 235 g and the tablespoon measure is 15 ml. A teaspoon has a 5 ml capacity and is the same for all markets. All cup and spoon measures are level.

Glossary of terms

Allspice A member of the myrtle family, this dried berry is used whole and ground. Its aroma and flavour are a combination of clove, cinnamon and nutmeg. If you do not have allspice, mixed spice can be used (see below).

Baking blind This process is used to partially or fully bake a pastry shell before a filling is added. Partial baking is done before a filling is added that needs to be cooked and which would make the base soggy. A fully baked shell is usually used for fruit and creamy fillings that do not need to be cooked. Baking blind ensures that the base remains flat and the sides do not collapse. Roll out the dough to line tart tin/s and line the base and sides with baking (parchment) paper. Place a thick layer of dried beans or uncooked rice on top. Pre-bake the pastry as the recipe requires, then remove the dried beans and baking paper. Cool the beans and store them in an airtight jar for reuse. Once baked, the beans are unsuitable for cooking.

Baking powder is a raising (rising) agent comprised of bicarbonate of soda, (baking soda) and acid (usually cream of tartar) and starch. The bicarbonate of soda and the acid react, producing carbon dioxide which makes the mixture rise.

Buttermilk Once a by-product of churning cream to make butter, nowadays buttermilk is made by thickening skimmed milk with a bacterial culture. It is used in cheesemaking and in baking.

Cake tins Using the right size and type of tin is important for a successful result. If the tin is too large for the mixture, the cake will be flat and shrunken. If it is too small, the cake mixture will bubble up and over the sides of the tin. However, the mixture for a round tin will fit a square tin that is about 2 cm (¾ in) smaller; for instance, a mixture designed to fill a 20-cm (8-in) round tin can be used to fill an 18-cm (7-in) square tin.

Cocoa powder is the product of dried, unsweetened, roasted and then ground cocoa beans.

Cornmeal is a flour made from finely ground dried corn kernels. It is used to make muffins and cornbread.

Gelatine is a setting agent made from collagen extracted from the bones and cartilage of animals. It is available in powdered and leaf or sheet form. Powdered gelatine is used in the recipes in this book. It must be reconstituted before use. Measure lukewarm liquid into a bowl and sprinkle gelatine over the surface. The gelatine will absorb the liquid and become spongy, then turning runny and clear. Make sure the water is not too hot before use.

Gougère is a choux pastry flavoured with cheese such as emmentaler and baked in a ring shape.

Icing (confectioners') sugar is a fine powder of white (granulated) sugar mixed with a small amount of cornflour (cornstarch), which prevents it forming lumps and drying out.

Mixed spice A traditional English mixture of spices which usually includes nutmeg, cinnamon and cloves and sometimes ginger. If unavailable, allspice can be substituted. Mixed spice is used in rich fruit cakes, cookies and baked puddings.

Self-raising (rising) flour is plain (all-purpose) flour sifted with baking powder usually in the proportion of 125 g (1 cup/4½ oz) flour to 2 tsp baking powder.

Speck is the upper, fatty part of a leg of bacon. Smoked and salted, it is usually sold in pieces rather than slices. It is used in Austrian cooking. Rashers of bacon can be substituted, if necesssary.

Stollen is a traditional German yeast pastry that is eaten over the Christmas period. It contains dried fruits and ground almonds.

Strudel is characterised by a wafer-thin, feather-light pastry dough. The dough is stretched out with the backs of the hands until it is possible to see through it. It is used as a wrapping for savoury and sweet fillings.

Torte is a rich dessert cake often layered with fruit, cream, a custard-type filling and nuts.

Cake Batter Basics

Chocolate Ring

160 g (²⁄₃ cup/5½ oz) white
  (granulated) sugar

250 g (1 cup/9 oz) butter

4 eggs

500 g (4 cups/1 lb 2 oz) flour

2 teaspoons baking powder

125 ml (½ cup/4 fl oz) milk

55g (⅓ cup/2 oz) choc chips
  or finely chopped chocolate

55 g (⅓ cup/2 oz) melted dark
  (semisweet) chocolate, for icing

SERVES 12

PREPARATION TIME 15 minutes

COOKING TIME See Cooking Times

● Use a 24-cm (9½-in) fluted ring tin. Preheat oven to 180°C (350°F, gas mark 4).

● Follow steps 1 to 6.

● Place mixture in tin; bake for 65 minutes (see Cooking Times). Test to see if cooked (see page 286).

● Remove cake from oven; leave in tin for 10 minutes to cool. Turn out onto a wire rack and leave to cool completely.

● When the cake has cooled, cover with melted chocolate.

Cooking Times

Flat cakes baked on baking tray
  Oven temperature 180°C (350°F, gas mark 4); middle rack; cooking time 15–20 minutes

Medium–high pastries baked on baking tray or in a loaf tin
  Oven temperature 180°C (350°F, gas mark 4); middle rack; cooking time 20–40 minutes

Tall cakes in a ring tin
  Oven temperature 180°C (350°F, gas mark 4); middle rack; cooking time 50–70 minutes

1 Weigh and measure all the ingredients. Remove any cold ingredients from the refrigerator 1 hour before beginning so that they will be at room temperature.

2 Grease cake tin; sprinkle with flour. Turn the tin and shake it gently to distribute flour evenly. Remove excess flour.

3 Beat butter and sugar until light and fluffy and sugar has dissolved. Separate eggs and stir egg yolks into mix.

4 Sift flour and baking powder; add to the mixture in batches, alternating with the milk. Mix until all ingredients are combined.

5 Beat egg whites until stiff and fold into mixture with spatula. Depending on the recipe, fold other ingredients such as chocolate chips, chopped nuts or dried fruit into the mixture at this point.

6 Pour mixture into tin; it should come about three-quarters of the way up the tin, allowing room for it to rise during baking. Smooth the top with a spatula.

Try this, too...

For a Fruit and Nut Ring, mix 50 g (⅓ cup/2 oz) chopped blanched almonds, 50 g (¼ cup/2 oz) each of chopped candied lemon and orange peel and 90 g (¾ cup/ 3¼ oz) sultanas (golden raisins). Add 2 tbsp flour. Fold ingredients into the basic mixture with the egg whites. Mix 90 g (¾ cup/3¼ oz) icing (confectioners') sugar with 2 tbsp lemon juice or rum and ice the cooled cake.

For a Chocolate Walnut Cake, chop 100 g (⅔ cup/3½ oz) chocolate and 50 g (½ cup/2 oz) walnuts and fold them into the basic mixture with the egg whites. Cover cooked and cooled cake with melted dark (semisweet) chocolate.

281

Tips for Success

Preparing baking trays and tins

● Grease baking trays and tins very carefully with butter, making sure the smallest grooves and edges are greased to prevent mixture sticking during baking. Dust inside evenly with flour; remove excess. Finely chopped nuts, breadcrumbs or cake crumbs can be used instead of flour.

● Baking trays, springform tins and loaf tins can be lined with baking (parchment) paper cut to fit. In this case it is usually not necessary to grease and dust them.

● Remove the baking paper from a cooked cake just before cutting and serving; it will stay fresh longer.

Dusting the tin with breadcrumbs or flour after greasing makes it very easy to remove the cake from the tin when cooked. Cake tins with smooth sides can be sprinkled with flaked almonds or whole pine nuts to add texture.

Turning a cake out

● Remove cake from the oven when done and leave it in the tin for 10 minutes. Then loosen cake carefully from the edge of the tin with a knife and turn out onto a wire rack. To remove a cake from a loaf tin, slide it out onto the rack sideways to prevent it breaking.

Icing the cake

● Do not try to ice a cake until it has cooled completely. For a more moist cake, first brush the surface lightly with melted, finely sieved apricot jam; then apply the icing.

Keeping qualities

● Bake cake mixture as soon as it is ready. If there is an unavoidable delay, cover bowl with cling wrap and place it in the refrigerator. Do not leave the raw mixture at room temperature; heat will prematurely activate any baking powder present in the ingredients.

● Some baked cakes (see recipes for guidance) will remain fresh for 3–5 days if placed in a cool place in a plastic bag or a tin, or under an inverted cake tin. Many cakes freeze well, keeping for up to 6 months.

Overbrowning

If a cake rises quite high during baking, its surface can quickly become overbrowned. If possible, move the cake down a rack in the oven and/or cover with a sheet of foil to protect it from burning.

If a corner of a cake breaks off, it is easily reattached with apricot jam.

● To freeze portions, cut the cake into slices and place them beside one another on a baking tray. Cover with cling wrap; freeze for several hours. Place the frozen slices in a freezer bag; seal carefully to make airtight. Slices can be removed as they're needed and thawed quickly at room temperature.

When freezing slices of cake, first pre-freeze on a tray, then wrap in portions.

Using leftover cake

● To make a trifle, cut slightly dry leftover cake into slices and drizzle with fruit juice or a mixture of fruit juice and liqueur. Layer cake slices in a bowl, alternating with layers of custard and berries or stewed fruit. Cover with cling wrap. Place in the refrigerator for at least 5 hours or preferably overnight; the cake will soften and the flavours will develop. Cover with thickly whipped cream, decorate with berries or slices of fresh fruit and serve as a dessert.

● For a quick and easy ice-cream dessert, crumble slightly dry left-over cake coarsely and stir through shop-bought ice cream. Return the mixture to the freezer to harden slightly before serving. Serve with fresh fruit or chocolate sauce.

● Crumble leftover cake and mix with melted butter. Use for dessert cakes which require a crumb base. Also use for toppings.

Quick Mix Fruit Muffins

The rule of thumb with muffins is not to overmix the batter. It is best to stir the ingredients with a wooden spoon only until just combined; that way, the muffins will be light and well risen.

200 g (1 ²/₃ cups/7 oz) plain (all-purpose) flour

2 teaspoons baking powder

110 g (¹/₂ cup/4 oz) white (granulated) sugar

2 tablespoons grated lemon zest

2 tablespoons butter, melted and cooled

1 egg

250 ml (1 cup/9 fl oz) milk or buttermilk or 250 g (1 cup/9 oz) sour cream

200 g (1 cup/7 oz) mixed fresh berries or apricots or plums cut into pieces

2 tablespoons icing (confectioners') sugar, for dusting

MAKES 12

PREPARATION TIME 15 minutes

COOKING TIME 20–25 minutes

1 Use 1 x 12-hole (80 ml/¹/₃ cup/ 2½ fl oz) muffin pan; line with paper cases. Preheat oven to 180°C (350°F, gas mark 4).

2 Mix flour, baking powder, sugar, and zest in a bowl. In another bowl, whisk butter, egg and milk.

3 Add dry ingredients with the fruit to the liquid ingredients one tablespoon at a time. Mix only until all ingredients are just moist.

4 Pour mixture into paper cases until two-thirds full. Sprinkle with sugar; bake for 20–25 minutes.

Sponge Cake Basics

Yogurt Cake

FOR THE CAKE

4 eggs

120 g (½ cup/4½ oz) caster (superfine) sugar

1 teaspoon grated lemon zest

120 g (1 cup/4½ oz) plain (all-purpose) flour

1 teaspoon baking powder

FOR THE FILLING

500 g (2 cups/1 lb 2 oz) natural (plain) yogurt

250 g (1 cup/9 oz) low-fat ricotta

Juice and grated zest of 1 lemon

150 g (⅔ cup/5½ oz) sugar

3 teaspoons (14 g/½ oz) powdered gelatine

250 ml (1 cup/9 fl oz) stiffly whipped cream

● Use a 26-cm (10½-in) springform tin. The mixing of the ingredients is crucial to the finished texture of the sponge. Using electric beaters, beat at medium speed for 1 minute and then high speed for 1–2 minutes until light and fluffy. The mixture should be very pale, almost white.

● Spread mixture into the tin and smooth the top. Bang the tin on a work surface a few times to remove any air bubbles. For tortes, spread mixture a little higher at the sides.

● Do not open the oven door during the first half of the baking time.

● If making a torte (as shown here), it is recommended that you make the sponge cake a day ahead. Slice and fill the next day.

● To make the filling, mix yogurt, ricotta, lemon juice and zest and sugar. Dissolve gelatine in a little warm water. Stir into the yogurt mixture. Finally, fold in the cream and use to fill the cake.

SERVES 16

PREPARATION TIME 30 minutes

COOKING TIME See Cooking Times

Cooking Times

Flat cakes and cookies
Oven temperature 200°C (400°F, gas mark 6); middle rack; cooking time 10–15 minutes

High cakes
Oven temperature 200°C (400°F, gas mark 6); middle rack; cooking time 18–35 minutes

1 Moisten base of tin and cover with baking (parchment) paper. Preheat oven.

2 Beat the eggs with sugar and lemon zest until a light, almost white, creamy mixture forms. Use a hand whisk or electric beaters.

Try this, too...

For a Vienna Sponge, fold 2 tbsp cooled, melted butter into the sponge mixture after adding the flour and baking powder.

For a Munich Sponge, fold 60 ml (¼ cup/2 fl oz) stiffly whipped cream into the sponge mixture.

For a Golden Sponge, substitute 8 egg yolks and 3–4 tbsp water for the 4 eggs.

For a Silver Sponge, substitute 8 egg whites for 4 eggs.

3 Sift flour and baking powder over egg mixture and fold in carefully to retain the air that has been beaten into it. Pour mixture into tin so that it is four-fifths full at the most. Level the surface.

4 Remove cake from oven. After 5 minutes, separate it from the side of the tin with a knife. Turn out onto a work surface covered with baking paper, put a weight on the cake and leave cake to cool.

5 Remove the base of the tin from the cooled cake and peel off the baking paper. The cake will be soft and elastic because of the condensed water and the sugar in the mixture.

6 Using a large knife, cut through sponge base horizontally 1–3 times, depending on the recipe. Fill according to the recipe. If the filling will need support while it sets, use a cake ring.

Tips for Success

Ingredients

● Eggs: If you are beating sponge mixture by hand, separate the eggs. Beat egg whites until stiff and fold into mixture at the end of step 2.

● Flour: Sift flour onto the sponge mixture. Sponge mixtures that use wholemeal (whole-wheat) flour are not as light. Add 1 tbsp water per 30 g (1 oz) wholemeal flour.

Preparing tins for sponge

Moisten the base with water and line with baking (parchment) paper. Do not cover or grease the sides because the mixture will shrink.

Baking

Put the mixture into a preheated oven so that the cooking time is as short as possible and the cake does not dry out. Bake cake mixture as soon as it is ready so that the air sealed in it does not escape.

A high sponge cake base is easy to divide horizontally. Make an incision 1 cm (½ in) deep all round, then place a tearproof thread in the indentation and slowly pull the two ends of the thread together crosswise.

Testing for doneness

For high cakes, insert a small metal or wooden skewer into the centre. None of the mixture should stick to it. When done, the sponge cake has a light, evenly porous texture and is golden brown and not dry. Also, the surface should bounce back quickly to the touch.

Leaving to cool

● For sponge rolls, turn out the cooked sponge cake onto a work surface covered with baking (parchment) paper. Remove neither the baking tray nor the paper lining the tray; this way, the mixture will stay moist and elastic. When the cake is completely cool, remove the top sheet of baking paper and cut off any hard edges. Fill sponge as per recipe. To roll up cake, lift the sheet of baking paper underneath to help roll straight; the roll should not be too loose.

● For tortes, turn cooked sponge out onto baking (parchment) paper; do not remove the base of the tin. Weigh it down with a heavy cup so that the cake remains flat.

Keeping and freezing

● Raw mixture: Leftover mixture collapses quickly, so it is unsuitable to freeze. Discard.

● Unfilled sponge bases: Keep in a cool place in a sealed tin or under an inverted baking tin for 3–4 days (if the weather is not too hot). Bases freeze well, wrapped securely, for up to 6 months.

It is best to place a cake ring around the sponge base to contain the torte filling until it is set.

● Filled cakes: Rolls or tortes that have jam, fruit topping or creamy fillings become soft and quickly go off. They should be eaten quickly. Keep any leftovers covered in the refrigerator.

● Cakes that are filled with fresh cream, creamy mixtures or nuts should not be kept in the freezer for more than 4 months.

● Pre-freeze unwrapped whole sponge rolls or filled cakes on a firm base such as a baking tray. Once frozen, wrap. While it is still frozen, the cakes can easily be cut with an electric or serrated knife.

● Pre-freeze pieces of prepared rolls or tortes on a tray and then tightly seal in freezer bags.

Walnut and Apple Sponge

The walnut flavour is more pronounced if the nuts are toasted in a dry pan before they're ground.

FOR THE SPONGE

2 eggs

80 g (¹⁄₃ cup/3 oz) caster (superfine) sugar

Pinch of salt

60 g (¹⁄₂ cup/2 oz) plain (all-purpose) flour

¹⁄₂ teaspoon baking powder

115 g (1 cup/4 oz) ground walnuts

FOR THE TOPPING AND DECORATION

500 g (1 lb 2 oz) soft apples such as Jonathans

16–20 halved walnuts

2–3 tablespoons apricot jam or orange marmalade

1 tablespoon apricot or orange liqueur

Icing (confectioners') sugar, for dusting

SERVES 12

PREPARATION TIME 20 minutes

COOKING TIME 20–30 minutes

1 Use a 26-cm (10½-in) springform tin. Moisten the base of the tin; line with baking (parchment) paper. Preheat oven to 200°C (400°F, gas mark 6).

2 Prepare the sponge mixture as described on page 280, adding ½ tbsp water and mix the walnuts with salt, flour and baking powder. Place mixture in tin and smooth the top.

3 Quarter, peel and core apples and make incisions on the round sides. Place the apple pieces close together on the sponge. Place walnut halves in spaces in between them. Bake for about 25 minutes.

4 Strain the jam into a small pan, mix with liqueur and melt over low heat. Brush over cake while still hot. Dust with icing sugar.

Yeast Dough Basics

Breakfast Rolls

80 ml (⅓ cup/2½ fl oz) sunflower or canola oil or 2 tablespoons softened butter

½–1 teaspoon salt

500 g (4 cups/1 lb 2 oz) strong white (bread) flour

2 teaspoons (7 g/¼ oz) dry (powdered) yeast

1 teaspoon sugar

250 ml (1 cup/9 fl oz) buttermilk, milk or water

1 egg

MAKES 10 rolls or 1 loaf

PREPARATION TIME 40 minutes plus 1–1½ hours resting time

COOKING TIME See Cooking Times

● All the ingredients should be at room temperature except for the buttermilk, milk or water. Heat this liquid until lukewarm. Test the temperature with the back of your hand. If it is too hot, the yeast will 'die' and the dough will not rise.

● Knead and punch down dough, preferably by hand, for 5–10 minutes until it is elastic. Only add enough flour or other liquid to make dough soft and no longer sticky.

● Place dough in a bowl, cover with a kitchen towel and leave to prove (rise) in a warm place away from draughts. When risen sufficiently, it will be soft and silken to the touch.

Cooking Times

Buns or rolls
Oven temperature 220°C (425°F, gas mark 7); middle rack; cooking time 10–15 minutes

Flat breads
Oven temperature 220°C (425°F, gas mark 7); middle rack; cooking time 20–35 minutes

Loaves of bread and cakes cooked in deep tins
Oven temperature 200°C (400°F, gas mark 6); second-lowest rack; cooking time 40–60 minutes

1 Place oil or softened butter and the salt in a mixing bowl. Add the flour; make a well in the centre.

2 In a jug, sprinkle yeast over lukewarm buttermilk, milk or water; leave for about 5 minutes to dissolve and froth up. Add to the well, stir in the egg.

Try this, too...

For Focaccia with Herbs and Olives, knead 500 g (4 cups/1 lb 2 oz) strong white (bread) flour, 2 tsp salt, 100 ml (3½ fl oz) olive oil, 2 tsp (7g/¼ oz) dry (powdered) yeast and 250 ml (1 cup/9 fl oz) lukewarm water into a dough. Cover and leave to prove for 30 minutes. Knead 2 tsp each of chopped rosemary, thyme and oregano and 150 g (1 cup/5½ oz) finely chopped olives into the dough. Shape dough into an oval loaf, allow to prove and bake.

For Sweet Rolls, prepare the basic dough with the butter, 1 tsp grated lemon zest, 1 tsp ground cinnamon and 3 tbsp sugar. Knead the following into the dough as desired: 90 g (¾ cup/ 3 oz) well-drained rum-soaked sultanas (golden raisins), halved toasted hazelnuts (filberts), diced candied fruit, coarsely chopped walnuts or pieces of chocolate. Shape rolls, allow to prove; brush with a mixture of 2 tbsp milk and 2 tbsp sugar before baking.

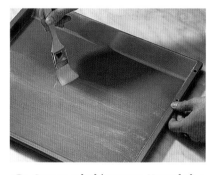

3 Grease a baking tray. Knead the 'sponge' (yeast mixture), flour, liquid and egg by hand for several minutes into a dough. Cover and allow to prove for 30 minutes in a warm place until doubled in size.

4 Quick method: Whisk liquid, sugar and egg, stir in yeast to dissolve; pour into well. Knead with an electric mixer fitted with dough hooks for 4–5 minutes. Cover and leave to prove for 30 minutes.

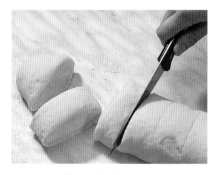

5 To make rolls, before proving, shape the dough into a long cylinder like a Swiss roll. Leave in a warm place, covered, until doubled in size. Knock back dough, kneading thoroughly. Cut into 10 pieces.

6 Shape rolls and place on the baking tray. If they are placed close together they will be soft on the sides; if there is 2.5 cm (1 in) between them they will be crusty. Leave to prove, then bake.

Tips for Success

Knead a yeasted dough by pushing and stretching it to develop the gluten; as you knead, the dough will gradually change in texture, becoming elastic, smooth and almost glossy.

Kneading the dough

● Once the yeast, flour and liquid (plus any other ingredients used) have been mixed together to make a dough that comes cleanly away from the side of the bowl, it is time to knead. Kneading gives the dough elasticity, develops and strengthens the gluten and ensures that the bread will rise evenly.

● Turn the dough out onto a lightly floured work surface. With the heel of your hand, push the dough away from you to stretch it out, then fold the side farthest away back towards you, rolling the dough into a loose ball. Turn the dough slightly, then stretch it out again. Continue this process. (Otherwise, you can use an electric mixer with a dough hook.)

Doubling in size

Shape kneaded dough into a smooth ball; place in a lightly oiled bowl and cover to prevent a dry crust forming;

leave to rise until doubled in size. This can be done in a warm place (30°C/86°F), which is the quickest way, or at room temperature. Or, the dough can even be left overnight in the refrigerator.

Shaping the loaf

● Turn the risen dough out onto a lightly floured work surface. 'Knock it back'—this is the term used for punching dough down with your fist to flatten it and expel excess air. Knead for 2–3 minutes to get it back to its original smooth texture, after which it is ready for shaping into loaves or rolls.

Cover dough with cling wrap; leave to rise in the refrigerator overnight.

● The simplest shapes are rounds and ovals for loaves and balls for rolls, all of which are baked on a greased baking tray. To shape the dough to fit a loaf tin, flatten it to an oblong, making the short sides the same length as the tin, then roll up from a short side. Turn the roll so it is seam-side down and tuck the ends under. For a plait, divide

To test if dough is properly risen, stick a finger into the centre; the indentation should remain visible after you remove your finger.

the dough into 3 equal pieces and shape each one into a long, thin sausage. Firmly press the top ends together, then plait quite loosely.

'Proving' and baking

● Once shaped, most yeast doughs are left to rise again, or to 'prove', before being baked in a preheated oven. To test if a loaf is done, tap the base with your knuckle. If the bread sounds hollow, it is cooked. If it isn't ready, just return it to the oven (without the tin) and bake for a few more minutes; test it again.

Freezing bread

● Yeasted breads and quick breads both freeze well as long as they are tightly wrapped to prevent them from drying out. Plain loaves can be frozen for 6 months and enriched breads for 3 months. Thaw in their packaging at room temperature. Flat breads (pitta and naan) should be warmed after thawing. Loosely wrap in foil; heat briefly in oven.

Rye Rolls

Rye dough needs more than just yeast to rise. Sourdough extract must also be kneaded in.

1 tablespoon sunflower or canola oil

1 teaspoon salt

250 g (2 cups/9 oz) rye flour

250 g (2 cups/9 oz) plain (all-purpose) flour

25 g sourdough extract

2 teaspoons (7 g/¼ oz) dry (powdered) yeast

1 teaspoon sugar

250 ml (1 cup/9 fl oz) lukewarm water

Coriander seeds or sesame seeds, for sprinkling

MAKES 12 rolls

PREPARATION TIME 45 minutes plus 1½ hours resting time

COOKING TIME 20–25 minutes

1 Line a baking tray with baking (parchment) paper. Put oil, salt and flours in a bowl. Beat the sourdough extract, yeast and sugar into lukewarm water to combine; add to bowl. Knead until dough does not stick to the bowl. Cover; leave in a warm place for 30 minutes.

2 Knead the dough for a further 10 minutes, then shape into a cylinder 6 cm (2½ in) in diameter. Cut into 12 even pieces and shape into rolls. Place on the baking tray 2.5 cm (1 in) apart. Brush rolls with water, then sprinkle with coriander or sesame seeds.

3 Cover rolls; leave to prove at room temperature for 1 hour. Preheat oven to 220°C (425°F, gas mark 7). Bake the rolls for 20–25 minutes until golden.

Try this, too...

For Cheese Rolls, combine 2 tbsp finely grated Parmesan cheese and 4 tbsp each of emmentaler and cheddar cheese. Knead into the dough with 1 tsp freshly ground black pepper. Shape into a cylinder; divide into 10 equal pieces and shape into rolls. Brush with milk and sprinkle with sesame seeds and poppyseeds. See Cooking Times.

For Plaited Herb Bread, prepare a dough using sunflower oil. Knead 60 g (½ cup/2 oz) sunflower seeds and 2 tbsp each of chopped dill, chervil, chives and parsley into the dough. Cut dough in 3 pieces, form into long sausage shapes and plait. Brush with cream and bake. See Cooking Times.

Sour Cream Dough Basics

Streusel Slice

185 g (³/₄ cup/6½ oz) sour cream
  or ricotta

400 g (3¼ cups/14 oz) plain
  (all-purpose) flour, plus extra for
  kneading

2 teaspoons baking powder

5–6 tablespoons sugar

1 teaspoon grated lemon zest

1 egg

2 tablespoons sunflower oil

4–5 tablespoons milk

Streusel topping (see below)

MAKES 12–16 pieces

PREPARATION TIME 15 minutes

COOKING TIME See Cooking Times

● Bake the dough as soon as it is
ready; otherwise baking powder
loses its potency. For this reason,
always prepare topping or filling
before starting to make the dough.

● For streusel topping, knead 200 g
(1⅔ cups/7 oz) flour, 115 g (½ cup/
4 oz) sugar, 100 g (⅓ cup/3½ oz)
softened butter and a large pinch
of cinnamon into a crumbly dough;
add a little more flour, if needed.

Cooking Times

Flat and small pastries
Oven temperature 180°C (350°F,
gas mark 4); middle rack; cooking
time 15–20 minutes

High cakes
Oven temperature 200°C (350°F,
gas mark 4); second lowest rack;
cooking time 25–30 minutes

1 Press ricotta through a sieve. Line a baking tray with baking (parchment) paper or grease well with butter.

2 Put flour, baking powder, sugar and zest in a bowl. Add sour cream, egg, oil and milk; knead into a crumbly dough with dough hooks of an electric mixer or by hand.

3 Place dough on a lightly floured work surface and knead into a ball; work in only a small amount of flour, or the slice will be dry.

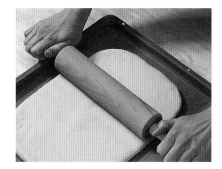

4 Roll dough out on the floured work surface or the baking tray. (For rolls and pastries, shape dough into a cylinder, divide into pieces and shape.)

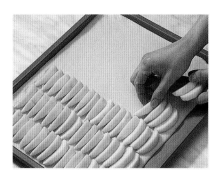

5 Spread a topping on the dough such as slices of apple; overlap like roof tiles.

6 Preheat oven to 180°C (350°F, gas mark 4). Spread streusel topping evenly over fruit. Bake for 15–20 minutes. Cool on a wire rack.

Shortcrust Pastry Basics

Fruit Tartlets

250 g (2 cups/9 oz) plain
(all-purpose) flour

Pinch of salt

2–4 tablespoons caster (superfine)
sugar or icing (confectioners')
sugar

125 g (½ cup/4½ oz) butter, chilled
and diced

1 egg or 2 egg yolks

1 teaspoon grated lemon zest

2–3 tablespoons white wine
or water

MAKES 8

PREPARATION TIME 15 minutes plus
30 minutes chilling time

COOKING TIME See Cooking Times

● For shortcrust pastry, the fat and liquid content should be cool.

● Cool hands under running water and then dry before kneading. Press mixture together quickly.

● Before filling is added, the raw pastry case is baked 'blind'. To do this, cover pastry base with baking (parchment) paper and half-fill with dried beans or uncooked rice. Heat oven to required temperature (see Cooking Times) and bake for 12–15 minutes. Remove beans and baking paper. Cool in tin on a wire rack.

● Make a filling such as that used for Mixed Berry Flan (see page 88). Spread filling into tart cases; fill with fruit of your choice.

Cooking Times

Flat pastries
Oven temperature 180°C (350°F, gas mark 4); middle rack; cooking time 7–20 minutes

Taller pastries
Oven temperature 180°C (350°F, gas mark 4); second-lowest rack; cooking time 35–40 minutes

1 To make the shortcrust pastry, place flour, salt, sugar, butter, egg or egg yolks and lemon zest in a mixing bowl. Add wine or water.

2 Using the dough hooks of an electric mixer, blend 1 minute, first on a low setting, then on high, to make a fine, crumbly mass. Then knead lightly by hand. Alternatively, rub in with fingertips.

3 Shape dough into a round or divide into small balls. Flatten a little, cover with cling wrap and place in the refrigerator for at least 30 minutes or, preferably, overnight.

4 Roll out dough on a lightly floured work surface to about 5 mm (¼ in) thick. Lift from work surface with a palette knife and line the tin or tartlet tins.

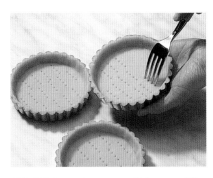

5 Prick pastry several times with a fork. Chill for 30 minutes; the pastry becomes 'shorter' and does not shrink.

6 If you want the edge to be high at the sides of the tin and the base to remain flat, bake cases blind (including dried beans or uncooked rice). See page 279 for instructions.

Try this, too...

For Salty Shortcrust Pastry, knead 300 g (2½ cups/10½ oz) plain (all-purpose) flour, 1 tsp salt, 185 g (¾ cup/6½ oz) butter, 1 egg and 4–5 tbsp water with 4 tbsp grated Parmesan cheese or 1 tsp mixed dried herbs and a pinch each of paprika and pepper.

For Nutty Shortcrust Pastry, toast 100 g (¾ cup/3½ oz) hazelnuts (filberts) in a dry pan. Allow to cool; rub off the thin skins. Grind nuts finely. Replace 90 g (¾ cup/ 3 oz) flour with the ground nuts and add 2–3 tbsp nut liqueur to pastry instead of wine or water.

Tips for Success

Rubbing in by hand

● This method is used to combine the fat and flour for shortcrust and scone pastries. While the fat should be chilled when working by hand, it should be removed from the fridge a little before time; if it is too cold, it will be very difficult to rub in.

● Use just your fingertips to blend the diced fat with the sifted flour. Lift the mixture from the bowl as you rub in, to incorporate air. When the mixture resembles fine crumbs (like breadcrumbs), bind it with a little cold water or other liquid. Add liquid slowly; too much will result in a sticky dough that will shrink during baking and toughen. On the other hand, if the dough is too dry, it will crack when rolled out and be difficult to handle. Further, it will crumble after baking and be dry.

When rubbing in, use your fingertips only to prevent the heat of your hands softening the fat. Add liquid gradually; mix it in with a flat-bladed knife. Add just enough liquid to bind the rubbed-in mixture into a dough.

To line a flan tin, drape the rolled-out dough over the tin, gently ease it in and then neatly trim off the excess dough.

● Rubbed-in pastries can be made very successfully in a food processor fitted with a metal blade. In this case, the fat should be used straight from the refrigerator and be very cold and firm. Cut the fat into small pieces and add it to the sifted flour in the processor bowl. Mix or pulse for about 3 seconds or until mixture resembles breadcrumbs. With the motor running, gradually pour in about two-thirds of the cold liquid through the feed tube; whizz for a few seconds, just until the mixture forms a ball. Turn off the machine straight away or the pastry will be difficult to handle. Add the rest of the liquid only if the dough doesn't bind. With a food processor, slightly less liquid is needed as the blade action makes the dough more sticky.

Lining a flan tin

● When making a tart case, use either a metal flan tin, preferably one with a loose base so that it will

Getting Ahead

Having pastry on hand is a boon for a busy cook, so it's a good idea to make a batch when you have some spare time. The rubbed-in mixture can be kept in an airtight container in the refrigerator for up to 2 weeks and needs only a little liquid to be added to bind it. Pastry dough, wrapped tightly in cling wrap, will keep for 2–3 days in the refrigerator, or it can be frozen for up to 3 months. Another idea for the time-poor is to freeze pastry cases in the tin. Bake from frozen, allowing an extra 5–10 minutes; you don't need baking (parchment) paper and dried beans.

be easy to remove the baked pastry case, or a flan ring placed on a baking tray. Ceramic flan dishes do not conduct the heat effectively, so the pastry base can turn out soggy.

● Roll out the pastry dough to a shape about 5 cm (2 in) larger than the flan tin. Lift dough carefully by draping it over the rolling pin and

Crimp for a decorative edge.

lay it centrally over the tin; it's less likely to tear and easier to position this way. Starting in the centre and working out to the edge, carefully ease the dough into the tin without pulling or stretching, then press it gently against the base and sides of the tin. When the dough is in place, fold the excess back over the rim of the tin and roll the rolling pin across to trim it off. Prick the base all over with a fork to release trapped air which could make the pastry rise during baking.

Baking blind

● Tart cases are often baked before the filling is added, either partially, just to set and dry the pastry, or completely. When baking unfilled, or 'blind', first line the pastry case with a sheet of baking (parchment) paper or foil, pressing it neatly into the corners. Weigh the paper down with dried beans or uncooked rice to prevent the pastry from rising and losing its shape during baking. Bake in a hot oven for 15 minutes, or according to the recipe; remove paper and beans. Bake for a further 5 minutes to dry out, or 15 minutes to cook completely.

Marzipan Rounds

Dough takes many different forms. This version is made with marzipan paste. The almond flavour is accentuated by the addition of almond liqueur and bitter almond oil.

200 g (¾ cup/7 oz) butter

150 g (5½ oz) marzipan paste

55 g (¼ cup/2 oz) sugar

Pinch of salt

2–3 drops bitter almond oil

1 egg

90 g (1 cup/3 oz) flaked almonds

200 g (1⅔ cups/7 oz) plain (all-purpose) flour

200 g (1⅔ cups/7 oz) icing (confectioners') sugar

1 egg white

1–2 tablespoons almond liqueur

Glacé (candied) cherries and pistachio nuts, to decorate

MAKES 70

PREPARATION TIME 30 minutes plus 2 hours cooling time.

COOKING TIME 20–30 minutes

1 Use 2 baking trays; line with baking (parchment) paper. Knead the butter and marzipan paste together until smooth. Add sugar, salt, bitter almond oil, egg and flaked almonds and stir in.

2 Sift flour over the mixture and knead ingredients into a dough. Shape into 2 cylinders each about 4 cm (1½ in) in diameter; wrap in cling wrap and chill for 2 hours.

3 Preheat oven to 180°C (350°F, gas mark 4). Cut cylinders into slices 5 mm (¼ in) thick and place on trays. Bake 10–15 minutes per tray. Mix icing sugar, egg white and liqueur to a thick icing. Ice cookies and decorate with glacé cherries and pistachio nuts.

Choux Pastry Basics

Profiteroles

150 g (1¼ cups/5½ oz) plain
(all-purpose) flour

250 ml (1 cup/9 fl oz) milk, water
or white wine

Large pinch of salt

65 g (¼ cup/2½ oz) butter or
4 tablespoons olive, canola or
sunflower oil

4–5 eggs

MAKES 12 large/20 small profiteroles

PREPARATION TIME 25 minutes

COOKING TIME See Cooking Times

● Line a baking tray with baking
(parchment) paper or grease and
lightly dust with flour.

● Do not open oven door during
first part of the baking time (*oven
temperature* 1) or profiteroles will
collapse. Reduce temperature (*oven
temperature* 2); bake until done.

● Cut cooled profiteroles in two
horizontally using kitchen scissors;
fill with cream.

Cooking Times

Large pastries
Oven temperature 1: 220°C (425°F,
gas mark 7); middle rack; cooking
time 20 minutes, then *oven
temperature* 2: 180°C (350°F, gas
mark 4); time 5–10 minutes

Small pastries
Oven temperature 1: 220°C (425°F,
gas mark 7); middle rack; cooking
time 8–10 minutes, then *oven
temperature* 2: 180°C (350°F, gas
mark 4); cooking time 2–5 minutes

1 Sift flour onto a piece of baking (parchment) paper. Put the milk, water or wine into a saucepan and add the salt and butter or oil. Bring to the boil and cover.

2 Turn off heat as soon as liquid begins to boil. Tip in flour all at once and stir vigorously while heating again until a thick mixture, then a lump, is formed.

3 Remove pan from heat as soon as a white film has formed on the pan base (after about 2 minutes). Place the mixture in a bowl; let cool until lukewarm.

4 Using a wooden spoon or the dough hooks of a hand mixer, beat 1 egg into lukewarm mixture. Then add 3 more eggs one at a time and beat thoroughly into mixture.

5 As soon as the pastry is very shiny and falls off the spoon or dough hooks in fairly solid peaks, it is ready. The fifth egg will not be needed in this case.

6 Using 2 spoons, place small ovals of pastry on baking tray by the spoonful, leaving about 3 cm (1¼ in) distance between them. Use tablespoons for large profiteroles and teaspoons for small ones.

Try this, too...

For Spicy Salmon and Crab Filling, mix about 50 g (2 oz) smoked salmon cut into fine strips, 115 g (4 oz) crabmeat, 1 tbsp lemon juice, 1 tbsp each of chopped dill and chives, 140 g (⅔ cup/5 oz) mascarpone cheese, 90 g (⅓ cup/ 3 oz) natural (plain) yogurt and 125 ml (½ cup/4 fl oz) thick cream. Season with salt and cayenne pepper. Fill the cooled profiteroles with the mixture.

Strudel Pastry Basics

Fruit Strudel

350 g (2¾ cups/12 oz) plain (all-purpose) flour

1 large egg

80 ml (⅓ cup/2½ fl oz) sunflower or canola oil

¼ teaspoon salt

1 tablespoon vinegar or lemon juice

About 160 g (⅔ cup/5½ oz) butter, melted, for brushing

About 185 ml (¾ cup/6 fl oz) milk or cream, for basting

MAKES 1 large/2 small strudels

PREPARATION TIME 50 minutes

COOKING TIME See Cooking Times

● Fill a ceramic or glass dish with boiling water; set aside. After the dough has been kneaded the first time, discard water and invert the dish over dough. Stand 30 minutes. The warmth of the bowl will help ensure that the dough stays soft and elastic.

● Remove rings from your fingers as well as your wrist watch; these can snag and tear the wafer-thin pastry during stretching.

● Trim thick edges from stretched, pastry; cut pastry into a rectangle. Brush with melted butter; spread half the filling over the top (refer to Apricot Strudel on page 301 or use fruit of your choice).

● Bake the strudel in preheated oven (see Cooking Times), brushing with butter every 10 minutes and also basting with the milk or cream every 20 minutes. When cooked, let strudel cool in the dish for about 5 minutes.

Cooking Times

1–3 strudels in the dish
Oven temperature: 220°C (425°F, gas mark 7); middle rack; cooking time 35–40 minutes

Individual-serve strudels
Oven temperature: 180°C (350°F, gas mark 4); middle rack; cooking time 15–20 minutes

1 Place all pastry ingredients and a scant 125 ml (½ cup/4 fl oz) lukewarm water in a mixing bowl. Knead for 5 minutes using dough hooks of an electric mixer or a food processor.

2 Knead dough, then rest under a warmed bowl for 30 minutes. Knead again for 5 minutes on a floured work surface. Shape into 1–3 balls. Brush with 1 tbsp butter to prevent dough from drying out.

Try this, too...

For an Apricot Strudel, halve and stone 500 g (1 lb 2 oz) apricots. Cut halves into slices and mix with 60 g (⅓ cup/2¼ oz) sugar. Spread fruit on one half of the pastry and sprinkle with 100g (⅔ cup/ 3½ oz) finely chopped hazelnuts (filberts), pistachio nuts or almonds.

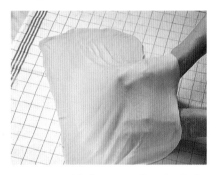

3 Dust a kitchen towel and a ball of pastry with flour. Quickly roll out into a rectangle. Then, holding dough over towel with the backs of your hands, stretch it out working from the centre.

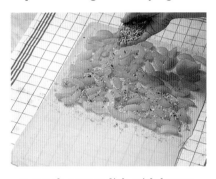

4 Brush pastry dish with butter. Spread your chosen filling over half the pastry, leaving about 2 cm (¾ in) free on both long sides. Brush the edges lightly with water.

5 Lift the edge of the towel from the narrow edge of the pastry and, using the cloth, loosely roll up the pastry. Fold pastry ends under the strudel; press firmly to seal.

6 Place strudel in the baking container, seam-side down. Brush with butter and baste with milk or cream. Slash surface several times with the tip of a knife.

301

Meringue Basics

Meringues

4 egg whites

Pinch of salt

1 tablespoon lemon juice or
   1 teaspoon white vinegar

115 g (½ cup/4 oz) caster
   (superfine) sugar

115 g (1 cup/4 oz) icing
   (confectioners') sugar

1 tablespoon cornflour (cornstarch)

Extra caster (superfine) sugar for
   sprinkling, if desired

MAKES   12 large/32 small meringues

PREPARATION TIME   20 minutes

COOKING (DRYING) TIME   See
   Cooking Times

● Only use cold egg whites straight from the refrigerator. It also helps to chill the bowl beforehand. Even the smallest trace of fat in the bowl or trace of yolk in the egg white will stop the egg white from becoming stiff, so take care not to damage the eggs when separating them.

● When piping the mixture onto the baking tray, avoid making long peaks as these quickly go brown during the drying process.

● Place meringues on a wire rack when done. They're easy to remove from the baking (parchment) paper. They should be crisp to the touch, dry inside and not browned.

● Remove meringues that are to be filled with cream 1 hour early from the oven. Gently make an indent in the bottom, then return meringues to the oven to finish drying. To serve, pipe cream into a meringue shell; place a second one on top.

Cooking Times

Slow-drying method
Oven temperature 200°C (400°F, gas mark 6); middle rack; cooking time 2–3 minutes, then switch off oven and dry for 8–12 hours

Quick-drying method
Oven temperature 100–120°C (235°F, gas mark ½–1); middle rack; drying time 2–3 hours

1 Beat egg whites and salt until stiff peaks form. Use an electric whisk first at low speed, then at a higher speed.

2 Gradually add lemon juice and the caster sugar. Keep beating egg white mixture until it is very shiny and sugar has dissolved.

3 Mix icing sugar and cornflour; sift onto egg white mixture. Fold in using a spatula. To retain the air sealed in the mixture, do not stir.

4 Line a baking tray with baking paper. Place meringue mixture in a piping bag. Hold bag upright and pipe mixture into individual portions on the tray.

5 Place baking tray in preheated oven. Immediately close the oven door. After 2–3 minutes, turn off oven; do not open for 8 hours.

6 For meringues that are to be filled with cream, use your thumb to carefully make an indent in the base of the still slightly moist meringues 1 hour before the end of the drying time.

Try this, too…

Try piping the meringue mixture into different shapes: rosettes, rings or stars, or as wavy lines on a fruit tart. The mixture can also be tinted with 1–2 drops of food colouring. The mixture turns an attractive pale brown if 1–2 tbsp of instant coffee or cocoa powder are dissolved in 1 tbsp water and folded into egg white mixture with icing sugar and cornflour.

Try downsizing. Using the basic recipe, make 40 small meringues. Pipe dots onto prepared baking tray and dry slowly for 1–2 hours.

303

Gingerbread Basics

Festive Cookies

500 g (4 cups/1 lb 2 oz) plain (all-purpose) flour

150 g (1 cup/5½ oz) finely chopped or ground almonds

¼ teaspoon salt

½ teaspoon each of ground cardamom and ground cloves

1 teaspoon ground cinnamon

½ teaspoon each of baking powder and bicarbonate of soda (baking soda)

250 ml (1 cup/9 fl oz) honey

175 g (¾ cup/6 oz) brown or white sugar

MAKES 120

PREPARATION TIME 50 minutes plus 2 hours standing time

COOKING TIME See Cooking Times

● The distinctive gingerbread taste comes from the mix of honey and spices. Ready-mixed gingerbread spices may be used instead of the individual spices given here.

● Remove cookies from baking tray as soon as they are cooked. Because of the high sugar content, gingerbread will continue to darken if left on a hot tray, giving it a bitter taste.

● Candied fruit or almond halves can be pressed into the cookies after they have been brushed with water or milk. Cookies gleam like lacquer if they're brushed with a mixture of water and cornflour just before the end of the cooking time. Add 1 tbsp cornflour (cornstarch) to a scant 125 ml (½ cup/4 fl oz) water and bring to the boil.

Cooking Times

Flat Gingerbread Biscuits
Oven temperature: 160–180°C (315–350°F, gas mark 2–4); middle rack; cooking time 15–25 minutes

1 Moisten baking tray and cover with baking (parchment) paper. Place dry ingredients in a bowl.

2 Heat honey and sugar, stirring, until honey is liquid and sugar has melted. Remove from heat and leave to cool; add to flour mixture.

3 Mix everything with the dough hooks of an electric mixer or food processor, or with a wooden spoon. Then knead vigorously on a floured work surface with the balls of your hands.

4 Using a floured rolling pin, roll out portions of dough between two layers of baking paper. Cut out cookie shapes as desired.

5 Place cookies on the baking trays about 2 cm (¾ in) apart. If possible, leave for 2 hours before baking so that the sugar combines evenly with the flour.

6 Brush cookies with water. Make sure they are not darkening too much during baking or they will taste bitter. Transfer to a wire rack to cool. Decorate as desired.

Try this, too...

For Ginger Honey Cookies, add 1 tsp finely chopped fresh ginger to the flour with the spices.

For Crunchy Nut Cookies, heat 250g (1 cup/9 oz) butter, 200g (1 cup/ 7 oz) brown sugar and 125 ml (½ cup/4 fl oz) honey until sugar has dissolved. Allow to cool. Add 80 g (½ cup/3 oz) finely chopped almonds, 100 g (½ cup/3½ oz) chopped candied lemon zest and spices to the melted mixture. Add 500 g (4 cups/1 lb 2 oz) plain (all-purpose) flour and ½ tsp each of baking powder and bicarbonate of soda (baking soda); knead well to combine. Shape into cylinders 2.5 cm (1 in) in diameter. Wrap in cling wrap and chill for 6 hours. Preheat oven to 200°C (400°F, gas mark 6). Cut dough into 5 mm (¼ in) thick slices. Bake for about 10 minutes. Remove from trays immediately and place on a wire rack to cool.

Baking Q & A

There's always something to learn that will help improve the skills of even the most skilled baker. Here is some expert advice on ingredients and techniques plus troubleshooting tips for those times when things don't turn out quite the way they should.

Can white sugars be substituted for brown sugars?

Brown sugars are distinguished by a delicate caramel aroma. If a recipe calls for 1 or 2 tablespoons of brown sugar, there will not be a problem if white sugar is used instead; it is the sweetness, not the aroma, that is of importance here. While white sugar can still be used in place of brown from 2 tablespoons on, the finished item will lack the intended caramel taste and the mixture will be paler than it should be.

What cookies are suitable for a crumb crust for a cheesecake?

Plain sweet wholemeal (whole wheat) cookies are the best choice. If the recipe you are using requires a chocolate crumb, use chocolate-flavoured cookies, not chocolate-coated ones.

Does it make any difference if you use fresh yeast or dry (powdered) yeast in breadmaking?

There is little difference between the results achieved. The dry type is almost twice as concentrated as fresh. Dry yeast comes in two types: active dry yeast (which is used in the recipes in this book) and quick-rise, also called rapid rise. Active dry yeast is a granular dehydrated yeast that must be rehydrated in lukewarm water before use. Quick-rise is also granular and dehydrated but does not need to be rehydrated before it is used. It raises the dough 50 percent faster than active dry yeast. Some bakers, however, think this does not allow sufficient time for flavours to develop. Whatever type of yeast you choose to use, it's important to remember that yeast is a living organism and it is very sensitive to temperature. It thrives between 32°C and 46°C (90°F and 115°F) and will die in temperatures above 60°C (140°F). Fresh yeast has a short shelf life. It is preferred by many professional bakers. Available in compressed cubes or blocks, it must be stored in the refrigerator.

What is meant by the term 'knock back'?

This term is used for punching the yeast dough with your fist when it has risen to twice its original size. Punching helps to disperse the air bubbles that the yeast produces throughout the dough.

Why should pastry be rested in the refrigerator?

Gluten, the protein present in flour, begins to react when it comes into contact with water during mixing; during resting it becomes firm and elastic. This makes the dough much easier to roll out. Resting pastry in the refrigerator is most important during the folding and rolling stage of making rich layered pastries such as puff and flaky, because it firms up the fat in the pastry, making it easier to roll. It also helps to ensure that the layers rise evenly during cooking.

What do you do if you don't have a rolling pin?

An empty bottle (without the label) is a perfect substitute for a rolling pin. If the pastry has to be kept cool during preparation, fill the bottle with cold water and place it in the refrigerator for about 2 hours. If you are rolling out yeast dough with a bottle, fill it with lukewarm water, as yeast dough needs warmth.

Top Tip

If you're in a hurry, it's easy to line rectangular and round cake tins with baking (parchment) paper without doing any fiddly tracing and cutting. Firmly crush a piece of baking paper of the right size and then unfold it and smooth it out. This makes the paper much more pliable and a lot easier to fit around curves and into corners.

What types of uncooked dough or pastry can be frozen?

Puff pastry and sour cream puff pastry, yeast dough, shortcrust (tart) pastry and strudel pastry can be frozen uncooked. The pastry or dough must be thawed before it is baked. If possible, only thaw the amount you need. Do not refreeze.

How do you peel nuts?

Place shelled almonds or pistachio nuts in a pan of water; cover the pan and bring the water to a boil. Leave the nuts for a few minutes, then drain. Squeeze each nut between your fingers to force it out of its skin. To skin peanuts, walnuts or hazelnuts (filberts), toast them first in a dry pan, then allow them to cool briefly. While they are still warm, place the nuts in a kitchen towel and rub to remove as much of the skin as possible. Peel off any that remains with your fingers.

Must you preheat the oven?

Although preheating is almost always necessary, be guided by the instructions in the recipe. Some mixtures such as cake batter form greasy crumbs on the top if they are placed in an oven that has not reached the required temperature. However, some doughs, such as certain bread doughs, should be placed in a cold oven so that they rise while the oven is heating up.

Why is buttermilk an essential ingredient of soda bread?

Buttermilk is high in lactic acid and when mixed with bicarbonate of soda (baking soda), which is an alkali, the chemical reaction that results produces the gas carbon dioxide. This has the effect of aerating the dough and making it very light. Sour cream can be used instead of buttermilk as it is also acidic.

Why do cakes sometimes have airholes, or crack and peak?

Holes are caused by overmixing or by uneven or insufficient folding in of the flour. The mixture should be soft and dropping after folding; if it's too dry, pockets of air are likely to be trapped. This also happens if the flour and raising (rising) agent are not sifted together thoroughly. To prevent cracking, be sure to use a tin of the right size and check that the oven is not too hot. Place cakes in the centre of the oven, not too high up where it will be hotter and the cake will peak and crack.

How can you tell when a cake is cooked?

Insert a wooden or metal skewer deep into the highest part of the cake and take it out immediately. If small residues of mixture stick to the skewer, the cake is not yet done. If there is nothing on the skewer or only individual crumbs, the cake may be taken out of the oven. Be careful if there are pieces of chocolate in the cake. Chocolate always sticks to the skewer; it does not set until it has cooled down.

What is the best way to remove a baked cake from the tin?

First leave the cake you have just taken out of the oven to rest in the tin for a short time. When cooling, the cake shrinks and a small space forms between cake and tin. Use a small knife to separate the cake from the sides of the tin. Place a wire rack over the tin and invert it and the tin; lift tin from the cake.

What can you do if a cake won't come out of the tin?

Place a warm, damp towel around the tin and invert it again. Do not let the cake cool down too much as this could prevent it from coming out at all. If this happens, return the cake briefly to a warm oven and then try again.

When should you dust cakes with icing (confectioners') sugar?

Directly before serving. If the cakes or pastries are still warm, the icing sugar will melt and discolour.

How does cream become stiff?

The higher the fat content, the quicker cream will thicken. It is easiest to stiffly whip cream if it, the mixing bowl and the beaters are very well chilled. Whip cream until it starts to thicken. Continue to whip more slowly until it stands in soft peaks. Whip slowly until firmer peaks form. Do not over-whip or the cream will go grainy and buttery flakes will appear.

What can you do if cookies have become too hard?

Place them in a plastic container or a tin with an airtight lid. Add an apple, an orange or a piece of fresh bread. Leave for a few days.

What temperature is best for storing eggs?

Store eggs in the refrigerator. They should be brought out about 1 hour before being used. Eggs at room temperature can be whisked to greater volumes than cold ones.

Top Tip

Egg whites that are a few days old whisk better than those that are very fresh because some of the water in the white will have evaporated. The drying makes the albumen stronger. Whites that have been frozen are also more likely to whisk well.

307

Should you grease a tin or line it with baking (parchment) paper?
In general, it doesn't matter which you choose to do. In practice, lining with baking paper has proven to be good because it cuts down on time needed to clean the tins after use, and also makes it easier to remove the baked item from the tin.

How reliable are the baking times given in cookbooks?
The temperatures and baking times given are only guidelines. You need to know how your oven performs and make adjustments accordingly. If you are not sure, it is best to first select a slightly shorter baking time than that given, test for doneness and then extend the baking time if it seems necessary.

How do you use vanilla pods?
Vanilla is the pod of a climbing orchid and is widely grown in the tropics, especially Madagascar and the West Indies. The bean pods are cured and turn black. The strongest flavour is in the tiny seeds and the pulp surrounding them, so the pod should be split open and the seeds and pulp scraped out for adding to custards or ice creams. Infusing a pod in hot liquid is an economical way to extract the flavour; the pod can then be rinsed, dried and used two or three more times. A good way to store used pods, particularly when they have been recycled a couple of times, is in a jar of caster (superfine) or white (granulated) sugar. The sugar will absorb the flavour of the pods and they will keep for a long time. Top up the sugar as you use it, for example in desserts and sprinkled over fruit toppings. You can also use vanilla pods to flavour a bottle of brandy or dark rum. The longer they're left there, the more intense the vanilla flavour will become. Fresh vanilla pods are best kept wrapped in foil or cellophane bags.

What do you need to know when making and using icing?
For a standard portion of icing, stir together 200 g (1⅔ cups/7 oz) well-sifted icing (confectioners') sugar with 4–5 tablespoons liquid: water, lemon or orange juice or rum for white icing; fresh currant or cherry juice for pink icing. Icing will not soak too deeply into the cake if you first spread a thin layer of warmed and strained apricot jam over the cake. Make icing just before use so that it does not form a hard crust.

What can you do if you don't have a piping bag?
If you often decorate baked goods, a piping bag is an indispensable item. If you need one only rarely, there is a simple tool for you. Fill a small freezer bag a third full with cream or icing and twist the bag securely at the top. At the bottom of the bag, make a diagonal cut in one corner. It is best if you first cut off a small corner and do a test run to see how the icing flows. Then make the hole a little larger, if necessary.

Can baking powder go off, and why does it make dough light?
If baking powder has been stored in a damp place and lumps have formed, it will have lost its potency. Baking powder consists of sodium bicarbonate and carbonic acid; they form carbon dioxide when affected by humidity and heat. This chemical reaction occurs inside the mixture during baking. It is actually 'blown up', which raises the mixture and makes it light. If this process is disturbed by the oven door being opened during the first half of the baking time, the cake will collapse. This is because the mixture is not yet stable enough to surround the air bubbles firmly.

How can you stop cookies burning at the edges?
Oven temperatures do vary. If you think your oven may be slightly too hot, check the heat using an oven thermometer. An extra minute or two can be crucial when you are baking thin cookies; you may find you need to use a slightly lower setting than the one indicated in the recipe. Avoid the temptation to overcook. Baked cookies may seem soft when they have just come out of the oven, but they will be firm and crisp when cool.

Top Tip

If brown sugar has turned rock hard in the cupboard, wrap the pack in a damp kitchen towel and microwave it on medium for a minute or two or until the sugar begins to soften. You can then use it as normal.

How do you prevent a cake mixture from curdling and can you save it if it does?
Curdling occurs when the butter and sugar have not been creamed sufficiently (until light and fluffy) to form a strong emulsion to absorb the eggs. Also, if cold eggs straight from the refrigerator are added to the mixture too quickly, separation

will occur. A curdled mixture holds far less air, so the cake will be flat. Have the eggs at room temperature and add them gradually. Adding a teaspoon of flour with each of the additions can also help to prevent curdling. If the mixture does start to curdle, briefly dip the base of the bowl into warm water and whisk to restore the light consistency.

Why does a cake sink?

Cakes will sink if they have not been baked long enough, so follow the time stated in the recipe and use a timer. Don't be tempted to open the oven door during cooking. Using too cool an oven, or opening and shutting the oven door during baking will cause sinking, as will too much raising (rising) agent in the cake mixture. Cakes are ready when they are firm in the centre and have shrunk away a little from the sides of the tin; sponges should spring back when pressed lightly with your finger.

Is there any way to rescue a cake that has turned out badly?

Disguise the damage as follows:
• If the cake breaks up, it's easy to stick the pieces back together with jam. Then cover with icing or jam sprinkled with shredded coconut.
• If the cake sinks in the middle, cut it out and turn the cake into a ring cake. Cover with whipped cream and fill the cavity with fruit.
• If a sponge comes out flat, cut it into fancy shapes, sandwich them together with cream and dust with icing (confectioners') sugar.
• For a slightly burnt cake, slice off the top and shave the sides with a potato peeler. Coat with warm, sieved jam and cover with icing.

Top Tip

If your shortbread tends to break when it's removed from the oven, make sure the next time you make it that you don't work the dough too much; excessive handling will make it tough and brittle. It's also likely to become brittle when it has been cooked for too long.

What makes a good chocolate?

The key things are cocoa solids and cocoa butter. The more cocoa solids a chocolate contains, the more intense the chocolate flavour will be. The wrapping must list the quantity of cocoa solids. Anything containing less than 50 percent has little depth of chocolate taste. One with 70 percent or more will have a much stronger, finer flavour. The more cocoa butter the chocolate contains, the softer it is; it will also melt more easily. As a general rule, the thinner and smaller the pieces of chocolate, the finer the quality. You can also identify the quality of the chocolate by how smooth it feels on the tongue. High-quality chocolate undergoes a long period of conching, or stirring, while it is being made, which contributes to its texture. Very fine chocolate with a superior flavour is expensive, but you do not have to use as much to get an intense taste, so it is worth paying a little more for the best.

What is white chocolate and how do you use it?

Some types of white chocolate have had some or all of the cocoa butter replaced with vegetable oil and these are extremely difficult to melt. Technically, white chocolate is not chocolate at all because it

does not contain any cocoa solids. If a recipe includes white chocolate that has to be melted, check that the type you buy contains a high level of cocoa butter and always chill and then finely grate before very gently melting it. If it seizes, white chocolate cannot be rescued.

How can you prevent homemade pizza bases turning out soft and not crisp?

The most likely reason for a soggy base is that the baking surface was not hot enough. The oven and the cooking surface must be preheated to the highest temperature. Ideally, the dough should then be placed straight onto a preheated pizza stone or tile (available from many kitchenware shops) or onto a large, preheated unglazed tile. This is the closest that home cooks can get to a traditional pizza oven.

Which makes the better pastry: butter, margarine or low-fat spread?

Butter gives pastry a fine flavour, golden colour and a crisp texture. For the richer pastries such as puff and sweet shortcrust (pâté sucrée), where flavour is important, it's best to use butter. Firm margarine can be used to make the plainer types of pastry but it does not add much to the flavour. Low-fat spreads can be used to make a crisp, light choux pastry. Melt the spread with the amount of water given in the recipe over a low heat, then add it to the other ingredients for the dough. To make a cheesecake base (normally done by mixing butter with cookie crumbs), melt the low-fat spread carefully over a low heat and then stir in the crumbs.

Index

Concept code: GR1269/IC
Book code: 400-496 UP0000-1
ISBN: 978 0 276 44640 5
Oracle Code: 250015104S.00.24